D1162089

MUSEUM REGISTRATION METHODS

Dorothy H. Dudley *registrar, The Museum of Modern Art, New York*

Irma Bezold Wilkinson, *formerly registrar, The Metropolitan Museum of Art, New York*

and others.

A Joint Publication of
The American Association of Museums
and the
Smithsonian Institution

Washington, D. C. 1958 *Revised 1968*

Library of Congress Catalog Card
68-20274
Printed and bound in the
United States of America

Guthrie Lithograph Company, Inc.
Washington, D. C.

Foreword

The American Association of Museums has a prime concern for the excellence of the professions serving all the museums of America, and certainly one of the most important of these professions is concerned with the registration of objects constituting our museums' collections. This book, on one hand, is an index to the concern of the Association for this profession, and on the other to the concern of the Registrar for the standards he would maintain.

The techniques of the Registrar apply to all museums and it is most significant that this book, which is one of the principal technical publications of the Association, signalizes the breadth of the common ground in which we work regardless of the disciplines of our individual museums.

The Association is grateful to the authors who produced the original manuscript, and to Dorothy H. Dudley who pursued the revision with care in order to produce this revised edition.

CHARLES PARKHURST
Director, The Baltimore Museum of Art
President, American Association of Museums

Introduction

The first edition of this manual, published in 1958 and now out of print, served to provide much-needed information about registration procedures and has helped to establish professional standards for all museums—large and small. The continued need for this information is made clear by the many requests that have been received for a revised edition from both old and new museums.

At the request of the American Association of Museums we agreed to prepare revisions for this second edition. While the basic procedures for the registration of objects remain the same, the use of certain new methods and equipment, changes in the U. S. Tariff laws and the need for further information on subjects such as insurance made a revision of the first edition desirable. We have expanded chapters in part one, where necessary, and arranged with several authors of articles in part two to bring information up to date. A new chapter on insurance and a chapter on importing and exporting (formerly article 12) describing the changes in the customs laws and the new U. S. Tariff Schedules have been added to part one. Four new articles have been added to part two, one on a procedure for acquiring objects for permanent collections, one on the preparation of an insulated packing box, one on the registrar's role in a building program, and one on computers and registration. New illustrations have been added throughout the book and bibliographic information has been expanded.

In preparing this revised edition we greatly appreciated and wish to acknowledge again the help and encouragement of the many people who made the first edition possible. We should particularly like to mention Murray Pease, Virginia Pearson, and Charles M. Richards whose untimely deaths are a loss to the museum profession. Their good counsel is sadly missed. Special acknowledgment is also due to the authors of articles in part two; to Geraldine Bruckner, Margaret F. Bush, Katherine Coffey, Marianne Gannon, Marcia C. Harty, Lillian M. Kern, David B. Little, Chester H. Newkirk, and Paul Mills, for helping us assemble and check information for the basic procedures discussed in part one; and to Monawee Allen Richards, Pauline H. Swayze, and Ruth Osgood Trovato, for their valuable contributions to chapters 3, 4 and 6.

We wish to express our appreciation to Charles Parkhurst, AAM President, for helping to make this edition possible; Robert T. Hatt and Warren L. Wittry, former Director and Assistant Director of the Cranbrook Institute of Science for checking and approving information in the manuel from the standpoint of science museums and for recommending bibliographic additions; Gertrude Toomey, Registrar of the Philadelphia Museum of Art and David B. Little, Director of the Essex Institute, Salem, Massachusetts, for contributing illustrations and information for chapters 2 and 3; and to Nathan Stolow and Louis Santini for their advice on revisions for the chapter on packing and shipping. Grateful acknowledgment is also made to the authors who prepared new articles 1, 13, 16, and 17 and revised and expanded articles 2, 3, 4, and 5 for part two.

We should also like to add our appreciation to René d'Harnoncourt, Director, Richard H. Koch, Director of Administration and Counsel, and to many members of the staff of the Museum of Modern Art for their encouragement and advice. We are especially indebted to the following: Caroline K. Keck, Consultant in Conservation; Jean Volkmer, Conservator; Helen M. Franc, Senior Editor; and, in the Department of Painting and Sculpture, to Alicia Legg, Associate Curator; Sara Mazo, Assistant Curator; Sarah Weiner, Curatorial Assistant; and, in the Registration Department, to David Vance, Associate Registrar; Elizabeth Burnham and Eric Rowlison, Assistant Registrars; and Caroline Birenbaum and Emily Stark, Cataloguers.

We also wish to thank N. Carl Barefoot, Jr., Editor and Director of Publications of the American Association of Museums, and his Assistant Editor, Elizabeth Heck, for the final editing of the original text as well as the additions and revisions in the second edition.

Photographs for new illustrations in the second edition were made by the following: James Delihas, figure 4 (bottom); Rolf Petersen, figures 5, 9, 27, 28, 32, 39, 40, 42, and 43; Col. Osmund L. Varela, figure 33; George Brauer, figure 41; Alan Solomon, figure 44; George Montgomery, figures 60 and 63. The drawings for figures 64, 65, and 67 in articles 13 and 16 were made by the authors. Photographs of illustrations that appear in both editions were made by the following: Soichi Sunami, figure 4 (top), figures 55-59, 61-62; Ship News Photo, John Rogers and Associates, figure 47. Drawings for figures 34 and 38 were made by Hugh G. O'Neill and A. G. Heim, of the Metropolitan Museum of Art.

IRMA BEZOLD WILKINSON
DOROTHY H. DUDLEY

Contents

Part Two: SPECIAL INFORMATION

Part One

BASIC PROCEDURES

Chapter 1

THE REGISTRATION DEPARTMENT

Whenever any work of art, or scientific specimen, or historical object enters a museum, it is obvious that it must be identified immediately by some clear and ready means, and that its entry and subsequent disposition must be accurately and permanently recorded. By whom and how this record is to be maintained is determined by the administrative head of the museum. He may appoint a registrar to be responsible for the records of all the collections in the museum, or he may make each curator responsible for those of his own department. In either case, a sound basic registration system must be established.

In general, the registration and the physical handling of objects as they move in and out of art and historical museums are responsibilities assigned to a registrar. In science museums, however, particularly in the large museums of natural history, where the handling of different types of specimens requires specialized knowledge and techniques that vary from field to field, this work is frequently a curatorial responsibility, although there may be a central office of records where a registrar maintains a file of accessions, donors, lenders, and other sources of acquisition from information supplied by curators. In the small museums of art, science, and history, on the other hand, the director or curator must often include the registration of objects among his other duties.

The procedures outlined in this manual presume the existence of a central registration department where, in addition to the making and keeping of records, the registrar has other duties closely related to the entry, exit, and safekeeping of museum material, such as arranging for packing, shipping, insurance, and storage. These procedures are the result of the experience of many museums, and are methods which have been found most efficient and least burdensome to all members of the museum staff. For the most part, they are presented with all the detail necessary to a large museum, and each museum must decide how much of this detail should be retained for its own needs. The amount will be determined by the number of people involved and the consequent need for maintaining communication among them. It is important, however, to realize that the fundamental records in the museum and the procedures employed in outside transactions are the same for all institutions, regardless of their size.

FUNCTION

The basic responsibility of a registration department is the recording of all objects that enter or leave the museum. From this follows the responsibility for their safe handling and storage while they are being recorded, for their unpacking, packing, and transportation, and for keeping track of their movement at all times.

Since the first records made should identify an object and serve as a basis for later documentation or cataloguing, it is most important that the entry records be accurate and clear. These entry records are later expanded in various ways and filed under whatever categories will make the information they contain most accessible; for instance, by donors, by cultures, by materials, or by any other breakdown that may be important to the museum.

STAFF

Although the work done in the registration department does not necessarily require the registrar and his staff to have expert knowledge of the subjects covered by the museum, he must have sufficent general background in these subjects, and familiarity with the vocabulary, literature, and documentary sources relating to them, to be responsive to the needs of the respective curatorial departments. A sound formal education, including a degree from an accredited college or university, and specialized study or experience (in-service training) leading to a knowledge of museum methods and techniques are essential. Some familiarity with business procedures is also necessary.

In addition to administrative ability, the registrar must have a real appreciation of the objects that are handled by his department, and a sense of responsibility for their safety. He must also be able to provide complete, clear, and accurate records; he should, however, understand that such records are not an end in themselves but rather a useful tool essential to the functioning of the respective departments of the museum. Finally, the registrar must keep himself informed of new techniques in museum registration and record-keeping in general, in order to realize when established procedures should best be changed or modified. (See "Computers and Registration" part 2, article 17.)

Figure 1.—Receiving, shipping, unpacking and packing rooms, Metropolitan Museum of Art. The receiving and shipping area, which may be seen through the door at the right, is near the loading platform and service entrance. The packing and unpacking room shown here opens into the locked area provided for the registration and temporary storage of incoming and outgoing material.

Whether the registrar works alone or requires assistants depends not so much on the size of the museum as on the extent of its activities. If a large amount of loan material is normally received for current exhibitions, or if the yearly acquisitions are great in number, one person could not possibly handle all the work that would result. Under such conditions, and with the responsibilities mentioned above, for a registration department to function efficiently, the staff required might well comprise a registrar as supervisor, assistants for secretarial work and record keeping, cataloguers, and workmen trained to handle, pack and unpack the objects.

WORK SPACE AND EQUIPMENT

In planning a registration department it is essential to provide space and equipment that will assure the safe handling and safekeeping of all objects handled by it and will enable all necessary records to be made and maintained. The succession of steps necessary in processing objects should be kept in mind in planning work space. When plans are being made for remodelling or building a new museum or a new wing, the architects should be advised of the needs of the Registration Department as well as those of other departments concerned with security and the

Figure 2.—Registrar's examination, recording and temporary storage room, Metropolitan Museum of Art. On the right are shelves for small objects and the door to the vault. The space between the storage screens (on the left) and the vault can be enclosed by curtains and used for photographing new acquisitions or loans as they are received. This room is locked at all times.

Figure 3.—Material being brought from unpacking and packing room to registrar's locked room for registration and temporary storage.

Figure 4.—Dollies with racks for moving paintings. Left, Museum of Modern Art. Right, Metropolitan Museum of Art.

safety of museum collections. In addition to the registration office, where the final records are made and kept, space should be provided for receiving and unpacking, examining and recording, photographing, storing, and packing and shipping. To insure minimum handling, the areas provided for each of these activities should be near to each other and accessible to the service entrance. The registration office with its files may be located either near these working areas or near curatorial departments, depending on the needs of the museum and the physical limitations of the building. (See part 2, article 16 and figures 1, 2, 3 and 67 for description and illustrations of work and safety areas.)

In order to make and maintain his records, the registrar will need cards and forms for receipts which are issued to lenders, donors, or vendors. Other forms may also be useful, depending on the amount of detailed information required by various departments and the extent of the museum's activities. It is recommended that for all permanent records a low acid paper stock or stock of 100 percent rag content be used.

In addition to the usual office equipment, the registration department should be provided with racks and shelves in an area which can be locked (for temporary storage of objects awaiting examination), a safe or vault (for very valuable objects); a large work table with an overhead light, pads for tables used in examining fragile objects, a magnifying glass, a measuring stand, calipers, etc.; tags, stickers, oil paint and other marking equipment; supplies such as polyethylene sheeting, glassine and tissue paper, and Japanese mending tissue for protecting paintings, textiles, unframed prints and drawings, and other objects when necessary; hygrothermographs or sling psychrometers to record temperature and humidity in storerooms; and, if the budget permits, some kind of duplicating machine for making multiple copies of cards or other records. Good lighting for all working surfaces is of the utmost importance, and portable and focusing lights should be provided as well. For the registrar's use in moving objects within the building, there should be available trucks or dollies with racks and padded trays, platform trucks for large or heavy objects, and padded trays for small fragile objects to be carried by hand. (See figures 4 and 5.)

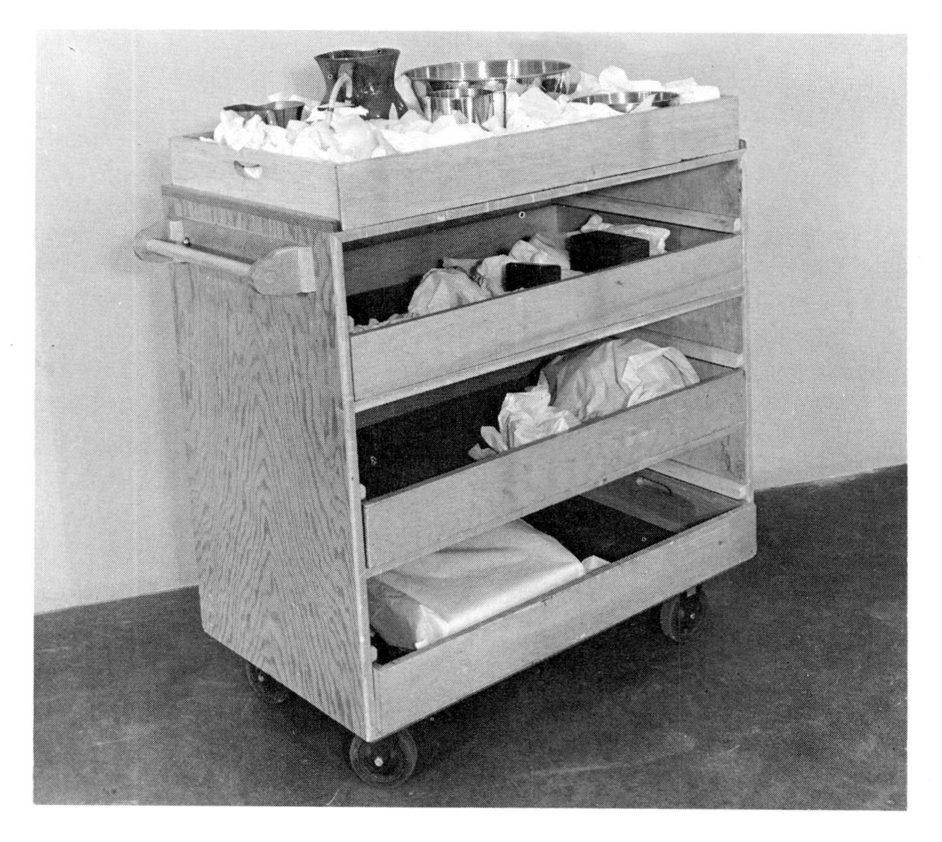

Figure 5.—Truck with removable trays for moving small objects, Museum of Modern Art.

Chapter 2

INCOMING & OUTGOING MATERIAL

In all museums where a registrar is responsible for checking and recording the movement of material into and out of the museum, it is essential (1) that he be advised in writing as far in advance as possible of anticipated arrivals and departures and (2) that objects be routed through his office or recording room. If it is sometimes necessary to have objects brought directly to curatorial departments or placed in a gallery or some other location, the registrar should go to them for the examination and recording as soon as they arrive. If the receiving and shipping room is not directly under the registrar's control, a close cooperation between the two offices should be maintained to assure the immediate reporting of all arrivals.

In some museums, forms are used by the director or curators to notify the registrar to expect, collect, or deliver material, and to explain the purpose for which it is being received or released (see figure 6). Other

THE METROPOLITAN MUSEUM OF ART

TO THE REGISTRAR — DATE

Expect ☐ From
Collect ☐
Deliver To ☐

Delivery or (Date
Collection (Time

The following objects
Valuation $

For — Gift ☐ — Loan ☐ — Special Loan ☐ — Purchase ☐ — Examination ☐

Via — Express ☐ / Parcel Post ☐ — Messenger (Theirs ☐ / (Ours ☐ — Truck ☐ / Station Wagon ☐ (Theirs ☐ / (Ours ☐ — Foreign Shipment ☐

Charges — Collect ☐ — Prepaid ☐

Department ________ Signed ________

Figure 6.—Printed form for notifying the registrar of incoming and outgoing material (size 5½ x 8½ inches).

forms are sometimes used by the shipping custodian or building superintendent to report incoming and outgoing material.

INCOMING MATERIAL

In general, objects are received in a museum for study or examination, as gifts or purchases offered to the permanent collection, as loans for extended periods, or as loans to special exhibitions.

Collecting

For incoming domestic material, the registrar may be concerned only with arranging local collections by van or station wagon. If his museum owns a van he can send men carefully trained in handling museum objects to make these collections; otherwise, he must employ commercial movers, and it becomes his responsibility to see that they are trained in the careful handling of all material they collect. The museum's trained handlers are often sent with commercial van drivers to assist in moving art objects. As Robert P. Sugden wrote in *Safeguarding Works of Art,* published in 1948 by the Metropolitan Museum of Art, "It is best to employ one truckman regularly and, if possible, have the same driver and helpers on the truck each time. If they are not already experienced in art moving, they will become so through proper supervision and tactful suggestion." Domestic shipments arriving from out of town are usually packed and forwarded by lenders, vendors, or donors, or their agents, as arranged by the museum director or curator requesting or authorizing them.

When material is to be shipped from foreign countries, the museum's forwarding agents are instructed by the registrar to collect, pack, and forward unless packing and forwarding arrangements are made by the vendors, lenders, or donors. When these shipments arrive in the United States, brokers are usually employed to clear them through customs and deliver them to the museum for examination by customs (see Chapter 8).

Receiving and Unpacking

Depending on the size and staff or the policy of the museum, the unpacking and packing of shipments is supervised by the director, curator, registrar, or building superintendent. In museums with a registrar on the staff, this is usually his responsibility, and, in any case, he should be well informed about the techniques of safe packing and handling of museum material.

Consideration for efficiency and the safety of the objects being unpacked requires that only one box at a time be opened and that each object be inspected as the wrappings are removed. Unless the objects are permanent acquisitions, packing and wrapping material is preserved for re-use and replaced in the boxes, which are closed and stored after being marked or numbered to identify them with the objects. Complex packing requires that careful diagrams be made to assure repacking in the same manner as received. Only when objects are received in damaged condition resulting from faulty packing, or when it is obvious that it is unsafe to repack them in the same fashion, is any radical departure from the original packing procedure justified. (See chapter 7, and part 2, article 12.)

Records of Entry

It is important that the registrar be allowed enough time not only to unpack objects but also to examine them for condition, place identification marks on them, and make the necessary records. All too often pride of acquisition leads to such a feverish effort to place a new object on public exhibition that the standard routine falls by the way and the registrar is left to complete his records as best he can.

THE NEWARK MUSEUM	Temporary Receipt____
From	Date
The Following:	
Submitted for Gift ☐	
Purchase ☐	
Loan ☐	
Identification ☐	
Copy sent to	Received by
	Received at

Figure 7.—Mimeographed form for temporary receipt. used at the Newark Museum, Newark, New Jersey (size 5½ x 8½ inches).

As a first step in the recording process, an identification tag or label should be attached to each object (see chapter 4).

The first records for all incoming material must include the following information:

Identifying number if assigned on entry
Source (name and address of owner or his representative)

Please preserve this receipt for surrender when withdrawing specimens

THE UNIVERSITY MUSEUM

Philadelphia ....

Received from ....

....

the objects listed below, offered to the

Museum { as a loan / as a gift / for purchase / for examination } subject to the conditions printed on the back of this receipt.

....

....

....

....

....

....

....

CONDITIONS

1. The Museum will give to objects deposited with it the same care they would receive if they were its own property, but it assumes no responsibility in case of loss or damage by theft, fire, or otherwise.

2. It rests with the discretion of the Museum as to whether, or for how long, objects lent to it shall be exhibited to the public.

3. In receiving or surrendering deposits of imported objects the Museum requires that the depositor comply with all government customs regulations.

4. Upon surrender of this receipt, or upon the written order of the depositor or his duly authorized and accredited agent or successor in interest, any object deposited with the Museum may be withdrawn upon reasonable notice.

5. In case of the death of a depositor, the legal representative of the deceased is requested to notify the Museum, giving his full name and address in writing and enclosing a certified copy of his authority.

Figure 8.—Temporary receipt, obverse and reverse, University Museum, University of Pennsylvania (size 4½ x 6½ inches).

Date of entry
Description
Record of condition
Purpose for which received (*i.e.,* for study or examination, as gift, as purchase, as loan)
Value or price, if known
Location in the museum
Disposition

These records are frequently made in the form of a temporary receipt issued when material is received (figure 7). In some museums, a copy of this receipt is attached to the object or, if the receipt is numbered, its number is written on the identification tag or label. (Another receipt form is shown in figure 8.)

Many objects are brought in on approval and are not accepted, or are brought in for examination and opinion, when this service is offered to the public by the museum. Consequently, the complete documentation or formal registration of incoming objects does not, as a rule, take place until they have been officially accepted as part of the museum's permanent collection or as loans for extended or specific periods. In the case of loan exhibitions, the registrar is usually advised in advance of all objects being borrowed, so that registration of the objects can be completed at the time of entry and they will be ready for installation in the galleries. (In chapter 3 is discussed the formal registration of museum accessions and loans for special exhibitions. See also part 2, article 1 for discussion of a procedure for acquiring objects for the permanent collection.)

Examining for Condition

The examination of objects for condition is an important function of the registrar in many museums. In others, this examination is made by the director, curator, or conservator. Ideally, every important piece should be photographed when first received, and when it is in first-class condition, this entry photograph may then be used as the descriptive or catalog photograph. But if the object shows any damage, distortion, or disintegration, a record photograph should be made to bring out graphically every detail of this condition, both as a guide to the conservator and as a record. Such record photographs, of course, are not suitable for reproduction or for sale to the public. In any case, the date of the photograph is an important part of the record and should appear on the negative. (See figure 9.)

When damage has occurred in transit it must be reported at once to the carrier and to the insurance company covering the shipment. In such cases a photographic record of condition must be made for the protection of the museum. A polaroid camera is useful for this purpose, particularly in museums without a photographer on the staff. The damaged object and the packing materials should be preserved for inspection by the representatives of these agencies. No repairs are made until per-

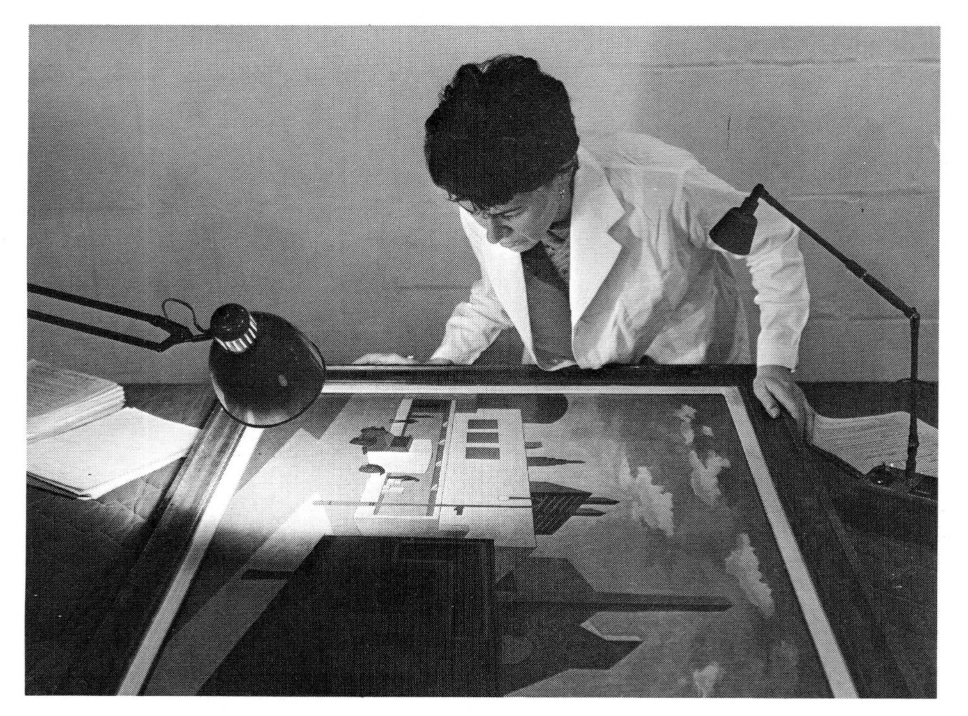

Figure 9.—Examining a painting for condition, Museum of Modern Art.

mission has been obtained from the owner. Damage to museum objects being returned from a loan must be handled in the same way, the director or curator authorizing repairs. If the registrar handles insurance on shipments, he must make the claim for damage when the cost of repairs and the degree of depreciation have been determined.

Storing

Objects in the custody of the registrar must be safely stored, and the space assigned to the registrar for such temporary storage during unpacking, packing, inspection and processing, should be controlled by him. Separate areas should be provided for the storage of packing cases and packing materials if they are to be used for future shipments. The registrar's records must show the disposition of all objects, as well as of the packing cases in which they were shipped. (See chapter 5 for a general discussion of the storage and care of collections.)

OUTGOING MATERIAL

UNIVERSITY MUSEUM
OUTGOING

Make in Duplicate
Both Copies to Service Door

Date ....
Dep't ....
By ....

Ship to ....
....
....

Express .... Collect .... Prepaid ....
Parcel Post .... Insure .... No. Cases ....
Truck ....
Date Shipped .... Time .... Cost ....

Contents ....
....
....

Figure 10.—Shipping order, University Museum, University of Pennsylvania (size 5 x 8 inches).

Records of Exit

Complete records of all outgoing shipments of museum material must be kept by the registrar. Before such shipments are permitted to leave the building, they should be covered by an order or "release" signed by the registrar or other responsible staff member. (Examples of the forms used for these orders are shown in figures 10–12.) When these shipments consist of objects from the permanent collections or of objects brought in on approval or for examination, they must first be approved by the director or curator, who notifies the registrar and supplies him with the necessary information for his records and receipts. Loans received for special exhibitions, however, are usually automatically returned to the lenders by the registrar unless he receives other instructions from the directors of exhibitions or from lenders.

Before releasing any objects, the registrar should check his records to see that none of the conditions of gift or loan and none of the regulations of the museum are violated by shipping them. He must also see that insurance is in effect or being arranged to cover them when they leave the museum. Above all, it is his duty to make certain that the objects are released only into the hands of the legal owner or a properly authorized and properly identified recipient.

The following excerpts from a paper by David B. Little, Director of Essex Institute, Salem, Massachusetts and formerly Secretary-Registrar

The Museum of Modern Art
11 West 53 Street, New York 19, N.Y.

2

PASS

Memorandum to the Department of Security:
Please pass ______________________________ ,
on ____________________ , with the material itemized below only:
(date)

Museum number | Artist or maker | Description

Remarks:

The Department of ______________________________ has been notified.

This pass is valid only when presented at the proper exit by the bearer named above on the date(s) shown above, signed by the Registrar and countersigned by the Security Agent on duty.

(date signed) ____________ Registrar ____________

To the Registrar:
The bearer named above left the Museum with the items listed
at ____________ o'clock ____________ (date)

Security Agent

Received of
The Museum of Modern Art
11 West 53 Street, New York 19, N.Y.

2

RECEIPT

in good condition unless otherwise noted
by ______________________________ ,
on ____________________ , the material itemized below:

Museum number | Artist or maker | Description

Remarks:

The Department of ______________________________ has been notified.

(date signed) ____________ Registrar ____________

(date signed) ____________ Recipient (The person named above or his authorized agent.)

The Museum of Modern Art
11 West 53 Street, New York 19, N.Y.

2

RELEASE

Memorandum To The Shipping Room:
Please have the following material ready for release
to ______________________________ ,
on ____________________ NOTE: MESSENGERS MUST IDENTIFY THEMSELVES.

Museum number | Artist or maker | Description

Remarks:

The Department of ______________________________ has been notified.

(date signed) ____________ Registrar ____________

If the above material is not collected on the date(s) shown, all copies of this release must be marked "VOID" and returned to the Registrar.

The Museum of Modern Art
11 West 53 Street, New York 19, N.Y.

2

REGISTRAR'S RECORD

I have authorized release
to ______________________________ ,
on ____________________ , of the material itemized below:

Museum number | Artist or maker | Description

Remarks:

The Department of ______________________________ has been notified of this release and must be informed at once if it is voided.

(date signed) ____________ Registrar ____________

Figure 11.—Registrar's five-page release, receipt and pass form for outgoing material made up with snap-out carbons. The top page (*pass* bearing Registrar's original signature), second page (*receipt* to be signed by whoever is authorized to remove material) and third page (*release*, authorization for material to be released) are sent to the shipping custodian, who obtains a signature on the *receipt*, gives the *pass* to the carrier or messenger collecting the material and returns the signed *receipt* to the Registrar. The *pass* is countersigned by the security guard at the exit and returned to the Registrar. The fourth page is the Registrar's record kept in the office until the signed *receipt* and the *pass* are returned and the fifth (identical with the fourth) is used by the Registrar to inform the department concerned that material has been released. The same serial number appears on all five pages. (Size 5⅛ x 8¼ inches.)

of the Museum of Fine Arts, Boston, emphasize the importance of this:

"The Museum, having received an article on loan, must never return it to anyone other than the person (or the legal representative of his estate) from whom it was received unless it has written authorization to do so. It is not permitted to the Museum, as bailee, to deny the bailor's rights to the article.

"In the event that a third person claims an article on loan to the Museum as his, the Museum should not deliver it to either party. There is available a court procedure by which the Museum, as stake holder, may request that the court determine which of the two is entitled to the article. This procedure is the only safe one for the Museum, since, if it delivers to the wrong person, it will be liable for so doing.

"It cannot be too strongly stated that an authorization from the bailor

No. 15283 **ORDER FOR SHIPMENT**

19—

To The Registrar:

Please arrange to ship the following:

To ______

Insurance $______ Express Valuation $______ Carrier______

Charges: *Director*

To the Superintendent: ______ 19___

______

______ *Registrar*

To the Registrar: ______ 19___

Date of Shipment ______ Time ______

Carrier______ Paid $______ Collect $______

Remarks ______

______ *Superintendent*

______ 19______

______ *Registrar*

Figure 12.—Shipping order used at the Cleveland Museum of Art (size 8 x 11 inches).

to deliver to another should always be in writing for the purpose of proving the Museum's right to deliver." (*The Registrar, Taxes and the Burden of Proof,* presented at the 1958 meeting of the American Association of Museums in Charleston, South Carolina.)

If the owner has died, the executor or administrator of his estate must ordinarily provide, as a minimum, a court certificate of recent date showing his appointment and, in states where applicable, a waiver by the state inheritance tax authorities. These papers must be in the hands of the institution before it surrenders any property of an owner who has died during the period of the loan. Local law may also impose additional restrictions or requirements, and it is advisable in every case for each museum to consult with its attorneys regarding these. Finally, the museum should require written authorization from the duly certified executor or administrator before making delivery to any other person, and it goes without saying that a receipt signed by the recipient should be secured in every case.

Examining, Packing, and Shipping

Before outgoing material leaves the museum its condition should be checked by the registrar or curator or conservator, as policy may dictate. In museums without conservation departments the inspection is frequently made by the registration department. If condition photographs exist, this inspection should include comparison of object and photograph.

The registrar should call to the attention of the curator any condition which may in his opinion prejudice the safety of the object in transit. The decision whether shipment should be made is the duty of the curator.

Arrangements must be made for safe packing and transportation of all objects leaving the museum. Instructions should be issued to packers for rebuilding old boxes or making new ones for special shipments. After objects are packed, the boxes should be inspected to see that they are properly marked and labeled with the addresses of the shipper and consignee and instructions given to the carrier selected. For foreign shipments, special papers are required by U. S. Customs and by transportation companies, and by customs offices in the countries of destination. Arrangements are usually made for these shipments to be handled by customs brokers, who are freight forwarding agents (see Chapter 8).

INSURANCE, REPORTS, INVENTORY

Arrangements for adequate insurance coverage of incoming and outgoing material in transit and during its stay in the museum or in a borrowing institution are sometimes the responsibility of the registrar and sometimes that of the treasurer or business office. Valuations are those established by the curatorial department or, in the case of a loan, by the owner. Additional nominal insurance may be placed with R E A Express or another carrier as a careful-handling precaution.

Many museums carry no insurance on the permanent collection or else a type of insurance virtually inactive except when objects are in transit or away from the museum, but loans to special exhibitions are usually covered by the borrowing museum under an all risk, wall-to-wall policy.

If values must be reported to insurance companies, arrangements should be made to report periodically, rather than on the date of each arrival or departure, the total amount added or canceled.

The director may require from his registrar periodic reports of material received and released during the calendar or fiscal year. The information in these reports varies according to the requirements of each museum, but it usually includes the following statistics:

- Number of objects acquired for the permanent collection
- Number of objects lent from the permanent collection to other institutions
- Number of objects acquired as extended loans
- Number of objects borrowed for special exhibitions
- Lists of donors, lenders, and borrowers

Periodic checks or inventories of collections as to location and physical presence in the museum are the duty of the registration department in many museums. In some museums "spot inventories" only are taken.

Chapter 3

THE REGISTRATION OF OBJECTS

A register, by definition, is an official written record, and "to accession" is to record an increase or augmentation. The registration of objects as they are accepted for museum collections and the maintenance of an accessions file or cumulative inventory are the responsibility of the registrar. Registration has the primary purpose of providing an immediate, brief, and permanent means of identifying each object in the collection. It differs from cataloguing, the function of which is to classify objects methodically and usually with descriptive detail. Cataloguing objects in a museum, or arranging them in their proper classifications or periods, requires special knowledge and is the responsibility of the curator. In many museums, however, catalogue information is recorded by the registrar after consultation with curators, and a card catalogue is maintained in his office.

As the procedures for registering permanent accessions and loans are basically the same, both are discussed in this chapter. Cataloguing is considered only to the extent that it influences registration. (In part 2, article 1, a procedure for acquiring objects for the permanent collection is discussed, and in articles 5, 6, 7, and 10, cataloguing is discussed in detail.)

THE NUMBERING SYSTEM

Since each object in a museum is identified by its number, the first step in planning registration is the determination of the numbering system. The registration or accession number should be one that can be assigned and attached to an object by the registrar as soon as it is officially accepted as a permanent accession or loan. The most satisfactory number shows when, and whether, an object enters the museum collection as a permanent accession, extended loan, or loan for temporary exhibition.

A sequence of simple numbers (1, 2, 3, 4) may be satisfactory for a small, homogeneous collection under the care of one person, but it is inadequate for dealing simultaneously with accessions of single objects and large groups of objects. For example, when a large group is acquired from an archaeological expedition, it is almost impossible to estimate accurately how many numbers need be assigned if it includes objects such as sherds which will eventually be reconstructed into vessels. Pending this determination, the registration of other objects that enter the collection subsequently must be delayed.

The use of letters preceding the numbers to designate material or function (P, painting; C, ceramics; F, furniture) or geographical area (NA, North America; A, Asia; AF, Africa) makes it possible for each group to be numbered independently. However, such a system requires that an object be identified before it is given a number, and this, again, may cause registration to be delayed in cases where the material, use, or provenance is not easily determined. Another disadvantage is that a later change in the original attribution (a rare but not impossible occurrence) would necessitate changing the accession number of the object in accordance with the new attribution.

The difficulties encountered when using a sequence of simple numbers, or numbers preceded by designating letters, are obviated by the use of compound numbers consisting of two or three parts separated by a decimal point or a hyphen, each part following its own sequence. This system is both more uniform and more flexible than those discussed above. Of several variations, the simplest and the one in most general use today for registration is composed of the year of acquisition and the number assigned to the object in the year in which it is officially accepted as a permanent accession or as a loan. For permanent accessions, the first part of the number is usually the year, and changes annually; the second part of the number begins with "1" each year and runs consecutively through the number given to the final accession for that year.

In museums where accessions are for the most part single items, a number composed of two parts (the year and the number assigned to the object within the year of its acceptance; i.e., 55.1, 55.2, etc.) is generally satisfactory. The advantage of the compound system is, however, that the accession number may be extended as required by additional decimal points followed by further numbers or letters. In museums where large collections are received at one time from a single source, it is not always possible to determine immediately the exact number of objects to be accessioned; but delay in registration can be avoided by using a number composed of three parts: the year of acquisition; the number assigned within that year to a collection accepted at one time from a single source such as an expedition, bequest, or gift; and the serial number of the individual item within that collection.

For example, in the year 1955, the numbers 55.1 through 55.5 inclusive would be assigned to the first through the fifth accession, each consisting of a single object. The sixth accession, consisting of a group of objects, would receive the number 55.6, and the twenty-second object in that group would be assigned the number 55.6.22. The first two parts (i.e., 55.6) can be assigned and placed on all objects in the group immediately upon its acceptance; the third part may either be assigned and attached at the same time, or after the collection has been catalogued and the exact number of objects determined, but in any event without delaying the registration of other acquisitions. Similarly, when an accession consists of a group of objects which belong together as a set or series, or when a single object is composed of several parts, the accession number may be extended by adding a decimal point followed by numbers or letters. Thus, for a portfolio of six prints, the two- or three-part number would be followed by a decimal point and a number for each print. The number for a teapot with a cover would be followed by "a" for the teapot and "b" for the lid.

Numbers used for loans should indicate that the objects to which they are attached are loans and not permanent accessions. Many museums accomplish this by reversing the permanent accession system just described. Loans are numbered consecutively within the year they are received; the loan number assigned to the object or group of objects borrowed at one time from one source is placed first, followed by the year in which the loan is accepted and, lastly, if for a group of objects, the serial number of the individual object within the loan. On rare occasions, with this method, a loan may be confused with a permanent accession number. For example, 55.36.1 may be the first object in permanent accession 36 of the year 1955, or it may be the first object in loan 55 of the year 1936. This confusion can be avoided by writing the year in full or with an apostrophe (55.1936.1 or 55.'36.1) on all loans or by including the letter "L" in the number.

If it seems desirable to distinguish between extended loans and temporary loans for special exhibitions, the letters "EL" and "TL" may be used. Instead of reversing the system used for permanent accessions, some museums prefer to retain for loans the same order of year, accession number and serial number, but to begin another separate series preceded by "L," "TL," or "EL," as appropriate. Thus, the first object in the first temporary loan in 1956 would be numbered TL 56.1.1. If desired, three separate series of numbers may be used, one for permanent accessions (56.1.1.), one for extended loans (EL 56.1.1.), and one for temporary loans (TL 56.1.1.).

In many museums the two- or three-part numbers assigned by the registrar and written on the objects are also called catalogue numbers. Since all recorded information may be traced through them, other numbers are not considered necessary. However, in some museums, particularly in the science field, special numbers are assigned by each curator to the objects in his collections. In such cases, when a registrar keeps a central file of accessions, these "curatorial" numbers should be recorded in his records (see part 2, articles 7 and 8).

All objects should be marked with permanent accession or loan numbers as soon as possible after they have been officially accepted. Numbers for permanent accessions and extended loans should be applied as permanently as possible, and any preliminary tags or stickers attached at the time of entry should be removed. The numbers for temporary loans to special exhibitions are never painted on, but are usually typed on stickers, tape, or tags and applied where they can be easily removed before objects are returned to lenders. (See chapter 4 for details on the marking of museum objects.)

PERMANENT ACCESSIONS AND EXTENDED LOANS

The Register or Accessions File

The first formal records made for permanent accessions should include the following information (records made at time of entry are described in chapter 2):

Accession number
Date received
Date accepted
Source of acquisition
Artist, maker, cultural group, species (if known)
Title and/or description
Date or period, if known
Exact measurements (in inches or centimeters or both)
Condition
Price paid, if purchased by the museum[1]
Insurance value[1]
Date recorded and initials of recorder

These records are listed or filed in the order of their acquisition as shown by their accession numbers. When a compound numbering system showing the year of acquisition is used, the accessions file becomes a cumulative record showing the objects acquired for the permanent collection each year.

[1] These records are sometimes kept by other departments and do not appear in the registration files.

THE SOLOMON R. GUGGENHEIM MUSEUM
MUSEUM COLLECTION AND LOANS

MUSEUM NUMBER:
DATE AND PLACE RECEIVED:
DATE ACCEPTED OR RETURNED:

SOURCE:

CREDIT LINE:

ARTIST: DATES AND COUNTRY:

TITLE:

PLACE AND DATE:

MEDIUM:
SURFACE:
GROUND:
SUPPORT: DIMENSIONS:

MOUNT: DIMENSIONS:
MAT: DIMENSIONS:
FRAME: DIMENSIONS:
BASE: DIMENSIONS:

CASE: DIMENSIONS:

LOCATION OF SIGNATURE:

MARKS, REFERENCES:

PRICE: DATE AND VOUCHER:

INSURANCE VALUATION: DATE INSURED:

PHOTOGRAPH NEGATIVE:

HISTORY:

REMARKS:

RECORDED BY ____________ DATE ____________

INFORMATION APPROVED BY ____________ DATE ____________

Figure 13.—Mimeographed form for assembling catalogue data (size 8½ x 11 inches).

Accession records may be kept in a ledger or on cards. The early records in most of the older museums were kept in ledgers. As the leaves of a bound book cannot be removed, entries must be written by hand. This is a laborious process and lacks uniformity, as different people may make entries in the book. If a loose-leaf accessions book is used, sheets may be removed and put in the typewriter. There may be some risk of losing a sheet or replacing it incorrectly, but this does not seem very great if the sheets are numbered and if entries are made only by the registrar or the staff member responsible for registration. The disadvantage of the accessions book, whether bound or unbound, is that it becomes more and more cumbersome and inflexible as new accessions are listed or as more space is needed for changes or additional information concerning previous entries.

Many registrars consider it much simpler to keep accession records on cards, and, if early records have been kept in books, to have them retyped for the new file. Cards have uniformity, space for additional information, maneuverability, and may be duplicated to form other files. Records on accession cards can be kept in numerical or chronological order, as they would in an accessions book. The possibility that a card may be mislaid or lost is minimized if the cards are held in drawers by rods or if drawers are locked. In some museums both accession cards and books are kept, but this does not seem necessary.

It is suggested that accession records be microfilmed so that they can be easily removed from the museum in case of an emergency. Better protection, of course, is provided if the microfilmed records are stored outside the museum.

The Catalogue and other Registration Files

As mentioned before, cataloguing is a curatorial function, but catalogue cards are frequently made in the registration department on the basis of information supplied or approved by curators. In this event, the following and possibly other information pertinent to the particular collection being registered and catalogued may be recorded:

Accession number
Catalogue number, if different from accession number
Artist, maker, cultural group, species
Provenance
Marks (labels, seals, etc.)
Date or period
Title or description
Medium or material
Source of acquisition—purchase, gift, bequest, expedition (including field number), etc.

Object:

Country: Material:

Date: Artist:

Description:

Dimensions:

Remarks:

Source:

Room:
Case:
Shelf:
Box:

02- REMINGTON RAND INC -13 310-63513 10M 3-54 (533)

LOCALITY
CULTURE OR PEOPLE
DESCRIPTION

DIMENSIONS
COLLECTED
PURCHASED
CATALOGUED

ARTIST TITLE MUSEUM NUMBER

REMARKS LOCATION

TAKEN BY OR SENT TO	DATE OUT	DATE RET'D

Figure 14.—Card forms. Top: Catalogue card used at the Cooper Union Museum for the Arts of Decoration, New York (size 5 x 8 inches). Center: Catalogue card used at the University Museum, University of Pennsylvania; the accession number and the name of the object are typed at the top of the card (size 4 x 6 inches). Bottom: Storeroom location card used at the Museum of Modern Art (size 4 x 6 inches).

Date received
Date accepted
Insurance value
Purchase price
Photograph and/or negative number or sketch of object
Location and description of signature (copyright mark if it occurs)
Exact measurements (in inches or centimeters or both)
Condition
Publications or references
History (ex collections, exhibitions, etc.)
Date catalogued and initials of cataloguer

In assembling information for records it is helpful to use a work sheet, a mimeographed, multilithed, or printed form with headings indicating the data to be filled in (see figure 13). Terminology used in recording this information should be uniform and clear. When the information is transferred from the work sheet to the accession or catalogue card, a definite arrangement should be established and followed. Accession number, title or description, measurements, and other data should appear in the same location on each card.

The assembled information may be typed on one card and exact duplicates made to form the files in the registrar's office, or one master card may be prepared with complete information and other cards with skeletal information filed under whatever headings are necessary. In some museums duplicate cards are made by the registrar for curatorial offices. Sample card forms are shown in figures 14 to 17, and in part 2, articles 5, 6, and 8.

If it is possible to duplicate records by mechanical methods, a great deal of time can be saved and the possibility of typographical errors reduced to a minimum. Several duplicating methods are used in American museums. In some, the original record is made on a master sheet and duplicates made by an offset lithography process; in others carbon copies are made of the original record, or it is duplicated by a photographic, electrostatic or other process (see part 2, article 4 and figures 15, 16 and 17). It is desirable to record only basic information on the master sheet or card so that the duplicate cards will be suitable for use by the general public as well as by the museum staff. Confidential information such as names of anonymous donors, and records of condition can then be recorded on additional cards and kept with the basic records in a file that is not used by the public. See figure 17 for example of a master card which is duplicated for use by both public and staff in a study storeroom.

Duplicate cards are filed under such headings as:

Accession number (showing date of acquisition)

Source of acquisition
Medium or material
Country, culture, or species
Location
Artist or maker
Subject

Location records of all objects in a museum's collection should be kept by curators or the registrar. If this is the responsibility of the registrar, he must keep for each object a file showing its location in the museum exhibition galleries and storerooms, and he must be advised of changes in this location so that his records can be kept up to date. This information may be entered on the accession or catalogue cards (for this purpose a second card may be filed behind the first) and the cards flagged with colored signals indicating whether the object is on exhibi-

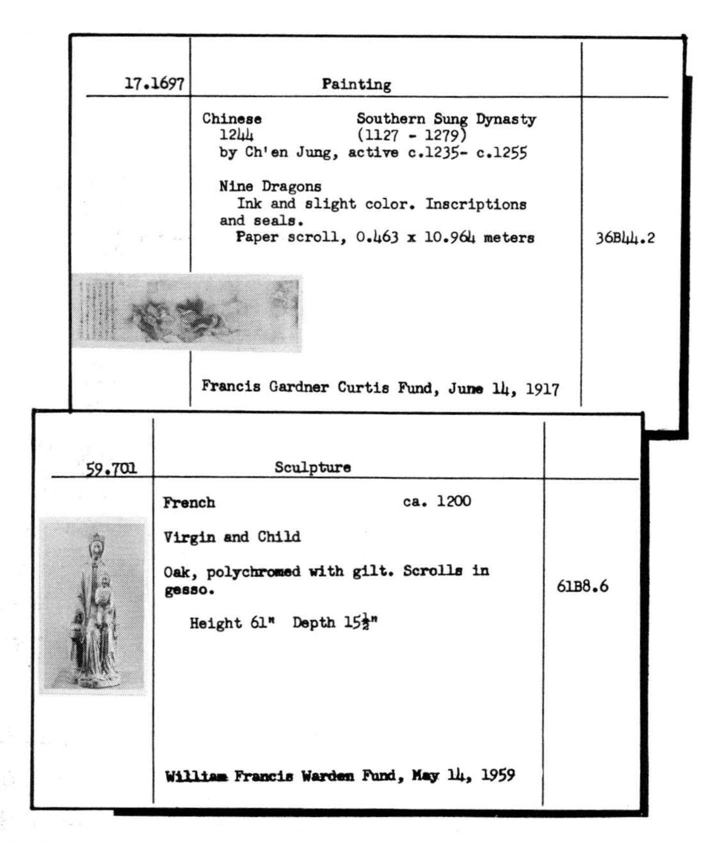

17.1697 Painting

Chinese Southern Sung Dynasty
1244 (1127 - 1279)
by Ch'en Jung, active c.1235- c.1255

Nine Dragons
Ink and slight color. Inscriptions and seals.
Paper scroll, 0.463 x 10.964 meters

36B44.2

Francis Gardner Curtis Fund, June 14, 1917

59.701 Sculpture

French ca. 1200

Virgin and Child

Oak, polychromed with gilt. Scrolls in gesso.

Height 61" Depth 15½"

61B8.6

William Francis Warden Fund, May 14, 1959

Figure 15.—Catalogue cards, Museum of Fine Arts, Boston. Four copies of each card are printed from a multilith master. A registration photograph of the object described is fastened on each with casein glue. One copy is retained by the registrar and filed in accession number order. Three copies go to the curatorial department holding the object. There they are filed by accession number, by category and by location. (Size 4 x 6 inches.)

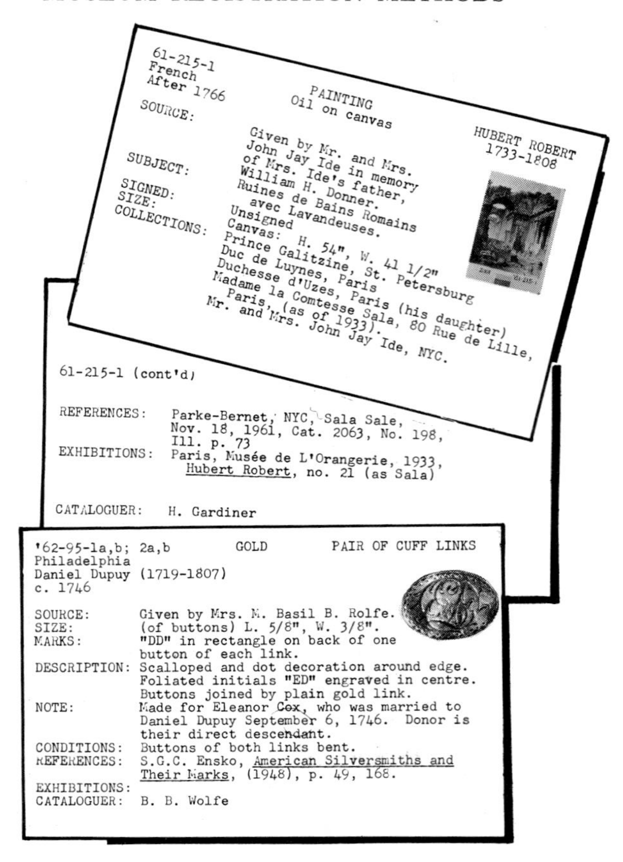

61-215-1
French
After 1766
PAINTING
Oil on canvas
HUBERT ROBERT
1733-1808

SOURCE: Given by Mr. and Mrs. John Jay Ide in memory of Mrs. Ide's father, William H. Donner.
SUBJECT: Ruines de Bains Romains avec Lavandeuses.
SIGNED: Unsigned
SIZE: Canvas: H. 54", W. 41 1/2"
COLLECTIONS: Prince Galitzine, St. Petersburg
Duc de Luynes, Paris
Duchesse d'Uzes, Paris (his daughter)
Madame la Comtesse Sala, 80 Rue de Lille, Paris, (as of 1933).
Mr. and Mrs. John Jay Ide, NYC.

61-215-1 (cont'd)

REFERENCES: Parke-Bernet, NYC, Sala Sale, Nov. 18, 1961, Cat. 2063, No. 198, Ill. p. 73
EXHIBITIONS: Paris, Musée de L'Orangerie, 1933, Hubert Robert, no. 21 (as Sala)

CATALOGUER: H. Gardiner

'62-95-1a,b; 2a,b GOLD PAIR OF CUFF LINKS
Philadelphia
Daniel Dupuy (1719-1807)
c. 1746

SOURCE: Given by Mrs. M. Basil B. Rolfe.
SIZE: (of buttons) L. 5/8", W. 3/8".
MARKS: "DD" in rectangle on back of one button of each link.
DESCRIPTION: Scalloped and dot decoration around edge. Foliated initials "ED" engraved in centre. Buttons joined by plain gold link.
NOTE: Made for Eleanor Cox, who was married to Daniel Dupuy September 6, 1746. Donor is their direct descendant.
CONDITIONS: Buttons of both links bent.
REFERENCES: S.G.C. Ensko, American Silversmiths and Their Marks, (1948), p. 49, 168.
EXHIBITIONS:
CATALOGUER: B. B. Wolfe

Figure 16.—Catalogue cards, Philadelphia Museum of Art. Five copies are printed from a carbon master on a fluid process duplicating machine. A registration photograph is dry mounted on each. Three copies are retained by the registrar and filed by accession number, by location and by style. One copy goes to the curatorial department concerned, and one copy to the photographic department where it is filed by subject. (Size 4 x 6 inches.)

tion in the museum, on loan, or in storage; or separate files of duplicate cards may be maintained for specific galleries or other locations, and the cards shifted as objects are moved. If the storage of permanent collections is one of the duties of the registrar, a file can be kept (see figure 14, bottom) showing storage location, date removed, where sent, and date returned. The registrar at the Art Institute of Chicago, for example, has developed a separate easy-reference visual file (see figure 18) showing the location of all paintings and sculpture in the permanent collection.

Source-of-acquisition records are of great importance in every museum. The accession or catalogue cards for each object may be duplicated for this purpose and filed under the names of each donor, bequest, expedition, vendor, purchase fund, or lender. Duplicate filing cabinets, plus space in which to house them, must be provided if the source file is made by this method. To save space, a card may be made for each donor, vendor, or other source of acquisition; gifts, purchases, or loans can then be listed chronologically, with accession or loan numbers, on the appropriate card.

Photographic records of museum accessions should, if possible, be included on the registrar's cards. In some museums 35-millimeter photographs are made from existing 8 x 10-inch photographs or directly from the objects and mounted on the cards. In other museums, the objects are photographed and prints are made on sensitized paper cut to the size of catalogue cards. In some instances photographs made to the scale of objects are prepared. It is especially important that the negative number of record photographs be included on the cards.

Records of condition which appear on the registrar's cards should be supplemented with condition photographs made at the time of entry whenever possible. If the museum budget permits, condition photographs should be made for a valuable work of art each time it leaves the museum, and again when it returns, if any change has taken place.

A separate registration file is sometimes kept for gifts in which a museum has only a remainder (future) interest or fractional interest. Cards in this file include as much of the information mentioned above as possible and also show what the museum's equity is at the date of acquisition. It is customary to assign accession numbers to these gifts even though a museum's interest in them may be small. (See part 2, article 1 for a discussion of remainder and fractional interest gifts.)

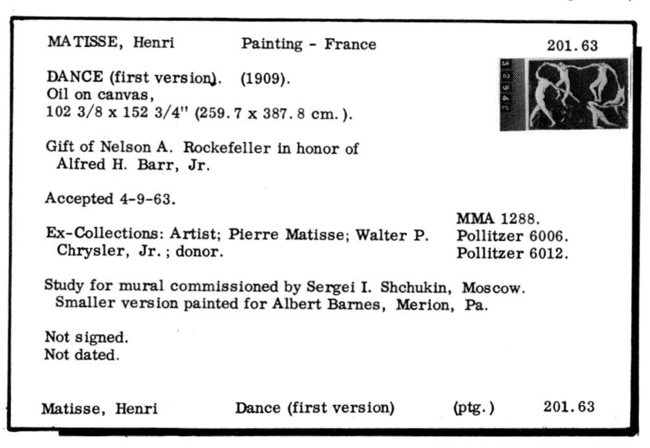
MATISSE, Henri Painting - France 201.63

DANCE (first version). (1909).
Oil on canvas,
102 3/8 x 152 3/4" (259.7 x 387.8 cm.).

Gift of Nelson A. Rockefeller in honor of
Alfred H. Barr, Jr.

Accepted 4-9-63.

Ex-Collections: Artist; Pierre Matisse; Walter P. Chrysler, Jr.; donor.

MMA 1288.
Pollitzer 6006.
Pollitzer 6012.

Study for mural commissioned by Sergei I. Shchukin, Moscow.
Smaller version painted for Albert Barnes, Merion, Pa.

Not signed.
Not dated.

Matisse, Henri Dance (first version) (ptg.) 201.63

Figure 17.—Catalogue card, The Museum of Modern Art, New York. Note filing data both top and bottom for either "visible" or vertical files. Original cards, followed by separate cards for inscriptions and references, exhibition history, and condition, form the registrar's alphabetical catalog. The first card only is reproduced electrostatically on all rag card stock for the accession file, duplicate accession file, subject file, donor file, vendor file, study storeroom file, and various files kept in curatorial departments. The photograph, bearing its own negative number, is mounted with library paste after reproduction of the card. Duplicate photographs are supplied to the curators for their cards. (Size 4 x 6 inches.)

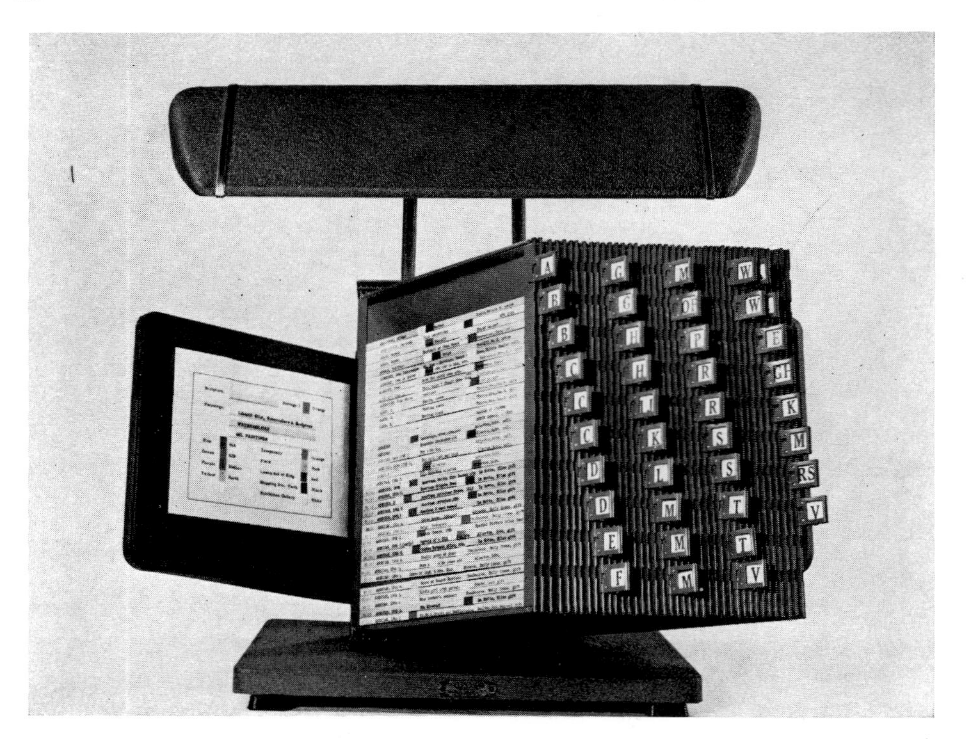

Figure 18.—Location record for paintings and sculpture, Art Institute of Chicago. In this file each strip represents one painting or piece of sculpture in the collection. Typed on each strip are the accession number, artist's name, title, and collection. The color of the strip represents the media: buff for oil, salmon for watercolor, and blue for sculpture.

Each strip holds a white tab, slipped on over one end, on which is written the number of the gallery in which the painting or sculpture is exhibited. Colored tabs represent a particular storage location other than a gallery, or a loan out of the building. On the white tab next to the colored tab is written the number of the bin or screen where the object may be found.

The flexoline (strips) comes in sheets which fit a standard typewriter. Strips are separated after the typing is done.

Registrars should plan for the future growth and use of museum records and keep informed about new methods of handling information such as the new electronic data processing systems that are constantly being improved. Readers are referred to "Computers and Registration," part 2, article 17, and to the bibliography at the end of this chapter.

Extended Loans

Loans which are accepted by the museum for use with a permanent collection, or for extended periods rather than for special exhibitions, belong in the category of extended loans. The identifying loan numbers may be preceded by the letters "EL" (extended loan), as discussed under the numbering system earlier in this chapter. These loans are often treated as an adjunct of the permanent collection. Records for these objects may be made on cards and filed with the permanent collection cards or separately according to whatever method is most useful.

When the museum returns a loan, a notation must be made on all records, and a receipt of delivery obtained from the lender and filed by the registrar. If an extended loan eventually becomes part of the permanent collection, all records are, of course, changed accordingly, but the record of the former status must be retained in the appropriate file.

Acknowledgments, Receipts, Statements from Donors

A receipt should be issued to donors, vendors, and lenders for objects offered as gifts, purchases, or extended loans. One copy is filed by the registrar and others are sent as required to curatorial and other offices.

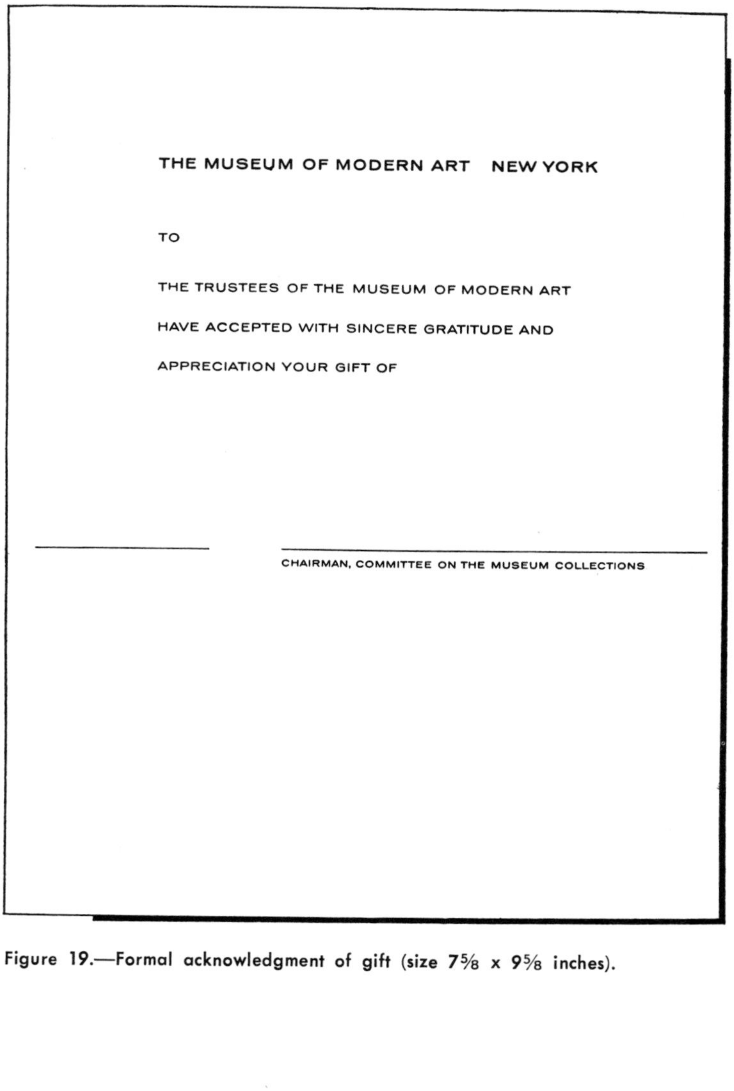

THE MUSEUM OF MODERN ART NEW YORK

TO

THE TRUSTEES OF THE MUSEUM OF MODERN ART

HAVE ACCEPTED WITH SINCERE GRATITUDE AND

APPRECIATION YOUR GIFT OF

CHAIRMAN, COMMITTEE ON THE MUSEUM COLLECTIONS

Figure 19.—Formal acknowledgment of gift (size 7⅝ x 9⅝ inches).

Boston, Massachusetts

On behalf of the Museum of Fine Arts the undersigned begs to acknowledge receipt, subject to the conditions printed on the back hereof, of the objects listed below which you have kindly offered as a gift to the Museum. This offer will be submitted to the proper authorities and you will be informed of their decision.

Registrar of the Museum

NOTICE

Possession of the objects listed on the face of this receipt is accepted by the Museum subject to the conditions following:

1. The Museum may require a written order of the owner or of his or her duly authorized agent or legal representative before it delivers or returns said objects.

In case of the death of the owner, his or her legal representative is requested to notify the Director of the Museum forthwith, giving full name and address in writing.

2. The Museum will not, and shall not be required to, carry any insurance against loss or destruction of or damage to such objects, or in other respects to exercise greater precautions for the care and safety of such objects than it exercises with respect to its own property of the same or similar nature.

3. The Museum will not grant permission to copy or photograph such objects without first securing the consent of the owner or of his or her duly authorized agent or legal representative.

4. The Museum will give the owner or his or her duly authorized agent or legal representative notice of not less than one month if it desires to return any such object to the owner and at the expiration of said period of one month such object, if not accepted by the owner or his or her duly authorized agent or legal representative, may be placed in storage at the owner's risk and expense.

5. In no event shall the Museum be liable for the destruction of, or damage or injury to, such objects caused by act of war, invasion, foreign enemies, civil commotions, riots, or any military or usurped power whatsoever.

The Museum is a Massachusetts corporation and its legal name is *Museum of Fine Arts.*

Please read the notice on the back hereof

The following has been donated by me as a gift to

THE BALTIMORE MUSEUM OF ART
Wyman Park
Baltimore 18, Maryland

in agreement with the conditions printed on the back of this form:

ACCESSIONS NUMBER	OBJECT	DESCRIPTION

NOTICE

Acceptance of gifts by the Board of Trustees of the Baltimore Museum of Art is subject to the following conditions:

1. Because of limited gallery space and the policy of changing exhibitions, the Museum cannot promise the permanent exhibition of any object.

2. The objects accepted become the PERMANENT PROPERTY of The Baltimore Museum of Art.

GIFTS TO THE BALTIMORE MUSEUM OF ART ARE DEDUCTIBLE FROM TAXABLE INCOME IN ACCORDANCE WITH THE PROVISIONS OF THE FEDERAL INCOME TAX LAW.

The museum is a Maryland corporation and its legal name is The Baltimore Museum of Art.

Signature of Donor________________

Address________________

Witness________________

Date________________

PLEASE SIGN AND RETURN AT YOUR EARLIEST CONVENIENCE TO THE REGISTRAR, THE BALTIMORE MUSEUM OF ART.

Figure 20.—Left: Receipt sent to donors, showing conditions printed on back (size 8½ x 11 inches). Right: Gift agreement, showing conditions printed on back (size 8½ x 11 inches).

THE SOLOMON R. GUGGENHEIM MUSEUM 1071 Fifth Avenue, New York 28

Date ....

LOAN RECEIPT

The objects described below have been received by The Solomon R. Guggenheim Museum as loans under the conditions noted on the back of this receipt.

from ....

for ....

....
Registrar

Museum Number	*Description*

Conditions governing the receipt of loans

Objects lent to The Solomon R. Guggenheim Museum for exhibition shall remain in its possession for the time specified on the face of this receipt, but may be withdrawn from exhibition at any time by the Director or by the Trustees. Loans will be returned only to the owner or lender or his or her duly authorized agent or representative.

Under the terms of this agreement, The Solomon R. Guggenheim Museum will exercise the same care in respect to loans as it will in the safekeeping of its own property.

Objects lent to The Solomon R. Guggenheim Museum at its request will be insured by the Museum under a fine arts policy against all ordinary risks in transit and while in its possession. The Museum will insure invited loans at the valuation requested by the lender, which request must be in writing; when written notice of valuation is not given, the Museum will insure invited loans at its own estimated valuation. The insurance referred to excludes loss or damage caused by war, invasion, hostilities, rebellion, insurrection, confiscation by order of any Government or public authority, risks of contraband or illegal transportation and, or trade.

Otherwise the lender may continue his own insurance for the period of the loan. The Museum, however, will not accept responsibility for any errors or deficiencies in information furnished to the lender's insurers, or for lapses in insurance coverage, arising from this practice.

Unless The Solomon R. Guggenheim Museum is notified in writing to the contrary it is understood that objects lent to it may be photographed, sketched or reproduced.

THE SOLOMON R. GUGGENHEIM MUSEUM 1071 Fifth Avenue, New York 28.

Date ....

RECEIPT OF DELIVERY

The following objects which were lent to The Solomon R. Guggenheim Museum

by ....

for ....

have been returned. Will you please sign and return this statement which is our receipt of delivery.

....
Registrar

Museum Number	*Description*

Received by .... *Date* ....

Figure 21.—Left: Receipt sent to lenders, showing conditions printed on back (size 8½ x 11 inches). Right: Receipt of delivery, which may be typed as a carbon copy of the form on left.

THE BROOKLYN MUSEUM REGISTRAR'S COPY

THE BROOKLYN MUSEUM LENDER'S COPY
Eastern Parkway,
Brooklyn 38, N. Y.

Date..........

LOAN RECEIPT

Lender: .... Dates of Loan ....

Address: ....

Purpose of loan: ....

The objects described below have been received by the Brooklyn Museum as loans for the purpose specified and under the conditions specified on the back of this receipt.

The Brooklyn Museum,

By ....
Registrar

Loan No.	Description	Insurance Value

CONDITIONS GOVERNING OBJECTS

OFFERED AS LOANS

1. Any object accepted by the Museum as a loan for exhibition shall remain in its possession for not less than six months unless otherwise indicated on the face of this receipt, or otherwise stipulated in writing at the time of the loan, but it is understood that such object may be withdrawn from exhibition at any time by the Trustees or by the Director.

2. Any object accepted by the Museum as a loan shall be returned only upon presentation of this receipt, or upon the written order of the lender, or his duly authorized agent, or legal representative. Such agent or legal representative shall submit proof of his authority, any necessary tax waivers and such other documents and instruments as the Museum may require.

3. The Museum will exercise such precautions as are now in force, or may hereafter be put in force for the safekeeping and preservation of property of the same general kind or character owned by the Museum, and shall not otherwise be responsible for said property.

4. The right of the Museum to return any property shall accrue absolutely on the date of and by mailing the notice to the owner to withdraw said property either because it is declined by the Museum, the loan period has terminated or the Museum no longer desires the loan thereof. If the owner shall not withdraw such property within thirty (30) days from the date of such notice, then the Museum shall have the absolute right to dispose of such property in any manner it may elect, and if it stores such property to charge regular storage fees therefor and to have and enforce a lien for such fees.

5. In case of the death of the lender, the legal representative of the deceased should notify the Director of the Museum forthwith giving his full name and address in writing. Such legal representative shall submit proof of his authority, any necessary tax waivers and such other documents and instruments as the Museum may require.

6. All notices required to be sent by this Receipt shall be considered sufficient if sent by registered mail to the lender at the address given in this Receipt.

7. The aforesaid conditions shall apply to all objects sent to the Museum on loan and cannot be altered, changed, waived or otherwise affected except by written consent of the Museum.

Keep this receipt. It must be presented for the return of the objects listed above.

THE BROOKLYN MUSEUM
Eastern Parkway,
Brooklyn 38, N. Y

Date..........

RECEIPT OF DELIVERY

Lender: .... Dates of Loan ....

Address: ....

Purpose of loan: ....

The following objects which were lent to the Brooklyn Museum have been returned in good condition. Will you please sign and return this statement which is our receipt of delivery.

Received by.......... Date ....

Loan No.	Description	Insurance Value

KEEP THIS COPY FOR YOUR FILES

Figure 22.—Combined loan receipt sent to lenders, receipt for return of loan, and pick-up order, Brooklyn Museum (size 8½ x 11 inches). Left: Loan receipt (white), showing conditions printed on back; registrar's copy (blue), is shown beneath it. Right: Receipt for return of loan (green); the file copy

Loan Agreement The Museum of Modern Art 11 West 53 Street, New York, N.Y. 10019 Tel. (212) 245-3200

White copy to be retained by lender

EXHIBITION:

LENDER: ____

ADDRESS: ____

Exact form of lender's name for exhibition label and catalog: ____

NAME OF ARTIST: ____

TITLE OF WORK: ____

MEDIUM OR MATERIALS: ____

DATE OF WORK: ____ Does date appear on work? ____ Where? ____

SIGNATURE: Is the work signed? ____ Where? ____

SIZE: Painting, drawing, etc. (without frame or mat): Height ____ Width ____
Sculpture (without pedestal): Height ____ Length ____ Approximate weight ____

FRAMING: Is the work framed? ____ If necessary for the exhibition, may we reframe or remat your work? ____
May we substitute plexiglas for glass? ____
(All works will of course be returned to the lenders in their original frames and mats unless other arrangements are made with the Museum in writing.)

CATALOG AND PUBLICITY: Where can the Museum obtain photographs of this work for catalog reproduction and publicity? (If known, please indicate photograph and negative number) ____
May the Museum reproduce this work in its publications and for publicity purposes in connection with this exhibition? ____
May this work be used for telecasts for publicity or educational purposes? ____ May slides of it be made and distributed by the Museum and its designees for educational use? ____

INSURANCE (See conditions on reverse of this loan agreement): Insurance value of work (U.S. currency): $ ____
(Insurance value cannot exceed selling price, if any).
Do you elect to maintain your own insurance? ____ If so, what is estimated cost of insurance premium? ____

SELLING PRICE (U.S. currency): $ ____ (See conditions regarding handling charges on reverse of this loan agreement.)

SHIPPING: Recommended procedure: ____

(Unless the Museum is notified to the contrary in writing before the close of the exhibition, the work will be returned to the lender's address given above.)

SIGNED: ____ Date: ____
(Name of lender or authorized agent)

CONDITIONS GOVERNING LOANS

1. The Museum of Modern Art will exercise the same care in respect to loans as it does in the safekeeping of comparable property of its own.

2. Loans shall remain in the possession of The Museum of Modern Art and/or other museums participating in the exhibition in question for the time specified on the face of this loan agreement, but may be withdrawn from exhibition at any time by the director or trustees of any such museum.

3. Unless the lender expressly elects to maintain his own insurance coverage, the Museum will insure this loan wall-to-wall under its fine-arts policy, for the amount indicated on the face of this loan agreement, against all risks of physical loss or damage from any external cause while in transit and on location during the period of the loan. The policy referred to contains the usual exclusions of loss or damage due to such causes as gradual deterioration, inherent vice, war, invasion, hostilities, insurrection, confiscation by order of any government or public authority, risks of contraband or illegal transportation and/or trade.
If the lender elects to maintain his own insurance, the Museum must be supplied with a certificate of insurance naming The Museum of Modern Art as additional assured or waiving subrogation against The Museum of Modern Art. Otherwise, this loan agreement shall constitute a release of the Museum from any liability in connection with the loaned property. The Museum can accept no responsibility for any error or deficiency in information furnished to the lender's insurers or for lapses in coverage.

4. If the loan listed on the face of this loan agreement is for sale, it is understood that the selling price shall include a handling charge as follows:

On sales up to $10,000.	10%
On the next $15,000.	7-1/2%
On everything over $25,000.	5%

Printed 7/67

Figure 23.—Loan Agreement, Museum of Modern Art (size 8½ x 11 inches). The conditions printed on the back (right) are based on some of the recommendations for a standard loan form for museums made in 1967 by the Association of Art Museum Directors and proposed for adoption with certain modifications.

Formal acknowledgments of gifts and extended loans and also letters declining objects not accepted are usually issued by curatorial or administrative offices after official action has been taken by the trustees of the museum.

In many museums, donors are asked as a matter of form to sign a

ARTIST	EX'N. & CAT. NUMBERS	TITLE	MUSEUM NO.	DATE REC'D	DATE RET'D

NAME ADDRESS

10 20 30 40 50 60 70

TYPIST PLEASE NOTE – THIS SCALE CORRESPONDS TO ELITE SCALE – SET PAPER GUIDES SO THAT CARD SCALE WILL REGISTER WITH MACHINE SCALE WHEN CARD IS TURNED INTO WRITING POSITION. START INDEX (3) POINTS FROM LEFT EDGE OF CARD. USE OTHER POINTS OF SCALE FOR OTHER DIVISIONS OF VISIBLE TITLE. SET TABULATORS TO INSURE PERFECT ALIGNMENT OF EACH DIVISION OF INFORMATION. FOLD BACK OR REMOVE STUB AFTER TYPING. USE NEW TYPEWRITER RIBBON.

KARDEX VISIBLE DIVISION 886—200-75272—38 REMINGTON RAND INC.—13 Printed in U.S.A.

Artist Title Museum No.

Lent by

Cat. Acknowledgment

Date Exhibition No. Catalog No.

Medium

Size ☐ Frame ☐ Mat ☐ Inner Fr. ☐ Glass

Ins. Value S.P. Signed

Remarks

Photo No.

Reproduced

Condition (see over)

02—REMINGTON RAND—13 5M 6-56 (58)

Figure 24.—Top: Lender's card used in visible index file, Museum of Modern Art (size 4¾ x 6 inches). Bottom: Loan card used at Museum of Modern Art (size 5 x 8 inches).

statement to the effect that objects are offered as gifts to the permanent collection. These statements complete the museum's records and although they may be filed in the office of the treasurer, secretary or director, the registrar should have access to them. The registrar should be informed in writing of any special conditions pertaining to gifts, loans, or bequests. In some instances it is advisable for photostatic copies of original documents to be filed in the registrar's office. Purchases are, of course, recorded in the treasurer's office by the usual accounting procedures.

Examples of forms used for these purposes are shown in figures 19 and 20.

De-Accessioning

When an object is removed permanently from the collection it is de-accessioned or canceled. The object may be retired or withdrawn for a variety of reasons such as deterioration or loss, or transferral as a gift, sale, or exchange.

The disposition of the object is noted in red on the accession record which, if a card, can either be refiled in its original place or placed with other de-accessioned cards. If it is removed from the accessions file, a substitute card bearing the accession number and a reference to the original card is filed in its place. A record of disposition must also be noted on source-of-acquisition cards. All other cards should be removed from the active files and destroyed if not needed, or the disposition of the object noted on them and the cards placed in a special file for de-accessioned objects. Photographs should also be removed to an inactive file.

Insurance

If the permanent collection is insured under a scheduled policy based on the individual values of each object, a record of valuations is kept in the curatorial, business, or registration departments and changes in value are reported to the insurers as required. The procedure for handling insurance depends on the kind of coverage arranged by each museum. (See chapter 9.)

LOANS FOR SPECIAL EXHIBITIONS

The registration of loans for special exhibitions is, in some ways, more complex than the accessioning of objects acquired for permanent collections or as loans for extended periods. Although the numbering system and the records made are basically the same, the work is complicated by the number of objects involved and by the fact that they must be collected from and returned to lenders. This involves making arrangements for packing, transportation, and insurance; issuing receipts when objects are received; and sending receipts of delivery for lenders to sign and return to the museum when objects are returned. In addition, the registration of all loans must frequently be expedited in order to allow sufficient time for the objects to be installed in the galleries.

Information to be Recorded

A convenient way of notifying the registrar of incoming domestic and foreign shipments or of any loans which are to be collected by truck or station wagon is for the director of an exhibition to send him copies of his letters requesting loans and copies of subsequent correspondence. In any case, the director should furnish him with lists showing the names and addresses of lenders, description of the objects to be borrowed, insurance valuations, and any other information he needs for his receipts and records. The loan numbers given the objects as they are registered should be noted on these lists. When a separate numbering system is used for loans, a file showing numbers previously assigned should be kept in the registration department so that these numbers will not be reused.

In some museums, loan agreement forms are sent to lenders to be filled in with information and returned. These forms take the place of a list. They are checked by the director of the exhibition for catalogue information and subsequently given to the registrar for use as work sheets in checking, numbering, and recording loans as they arrive.

The following information should be recorded on loan agreement forms or work sheets for exhibitions of works of art (see figure 23):

- Name of exhibition and dates
- Name and address of lender
- Form of acknowledgment (*i.e.*, way in which lender wishes acknowledgment to appear in catalogue and on label)
- Name of artist
- Exact title of work
- Medium
- Date executed
- Signature
- Exact measurements (if sculpture, also weight) in inches or centimeters, pounds or kilograms, or both
- Insurance value (if museum is to insure)

Selling price
Shipping instructions
Photograph source
Condition
Date and method of arrival
Registration number
Lender's permission, if granted, to photograph and reproduce his loan in catalogue, or for publicity, to remove frames and glass if necessary and to reframe or remat if desirable

Some of this information is supplied by the director of the exhibition and by the lenders; the rest is obtained as each loan is checked by the registration department. Special forms following this general outline may be devised for other types of exhibition material. In some cases it is advisable to provide space for listing several items on one sheet. The condition of the loan should be recorded as soon as it is received, and if it is damaged, a condition photograph should be made (for some works of art it may be advisable to ask lenders to supply borrowing museums with condition photographs made before shipment). If the condition record is made by curatorial or conservation departments, a copy should be sent to the registrar for his files. After all necessary information has been recorded on the work sheets, these are used by the registrar in preparing receipts to send to lenders and in making whatever other records are needed in his office.

Receipts to Lenders

Receipts should be issued to lenders as soon as possible after loans have been registered. Copies are filed by the registrar and sent as needed to directors of exhibitions and other departments. Some museums have found it time-saving to make an additional copy to be signed by the lender as a receipt of delivery when the loan is returned. The following information should appear on the receipt:

Lender's name and address
Title and dates of exhibition
Loan number and description of loan
Date received by museum
Insurance value or statement to the effect that the lender is insuring
Condition (optional)
Legal conditions governing the receipt of loans

Reports on the condition of loans are omitted from receipts in many museums unless parts appear to be missing or there are obvious new damages. All condition records should, however, be filed carefully. Legal conditions governing the receipt of loans in each museum are usually printed on the reverse of the receipts. (See figures 21, 22, and 23.)

The registrar's copy may be filed under the title of the special exhibition or, if receipts are numbered, it may be filed numerically and reference to the receipt number made on the lender's card. After receipts for several exhibitions have accumulated, they are usually bound and become part of the permanent records kept in the registration department.

Receipts for Loan Returned

It is important that receipts signed by lenders acknowledging the return of their loans be filed in the registrar's office. In some museums lenders are asked to surrender the museum's original receipts issued when their loans were received. In others, separate receipts of delivery or copies of the original receipts are sent to lenders to sign and return to the museum (see figures 21 and 22).

Lenders' File and Loan File

A record of lenders with reference to the objects borrowed from them is usually made on cards for a source or lenders' file (see figure 24, top). Each loan may be recorded on these cards with dates received and returned, or reference made to the loan receipt where this information appears.

A permanent card record is sometimes made for each loan (see figure 24, bottom). However, copies of receipts and a file of lenders are frequently the only permanent records kept in the registration department for loans to special exhibitions.

Insurance

Since loans to special exhibitions are usually insured by the borrowing museum under an all risk, wall-to-wall policy, values must be recorded and reported to the insurers as required. These reports, as well as any claims for damages, are frequently made by the registrar, although in some museums they are handled by the treasurer or business manager. If insurance claims are handled by another department, the registrar must report damages to that department as soon as they have been noted. (See chapter 9 for discussion of insurance.)

Summary

In broad outline the records made for the permanent collection and for special loan exhibitions are similar, though they may vary in detail. The parallels are shown in the following summary of the records discussed in this chapter:

Permanent Collection and Extended Loans	Loans for Special Exhibitions
Preliminary record: work sheet	Preliminary record; loan agreement, work sheet, or checklist
Accession record	Numerical record of loan numbers assigned
Receipt: to donor to vendor to lender for extended loan	Receipt: to lender
Insurance: as museum system applies	Insurance: as lender specifies
Photographic condition file	Photographic condition file
Gift acknowledgment [1] when gift accepted	Receipt for loan returned
Source-of-acquisition card	Lender's card
Final record: catalogue card	Final record: loan card (optional)

[1] Purchase records are kept in the treasurer's office.

References:

ANONYMOUS (1963) Procedure manual. Curatorial Department, San Diego Museum of Man, 39 pp. Spiral bound.

ANONYMOUS (1961) Registrars manual. Detroit Historical Museum, 11 pp. plus samples of appropriate office forms.

BOARDMAN, EDWARD T. Simplified records for small science and history museums, The Museum News, Vol. 25, March 1, 1948, pp. 6–8.

BORHEGYI, STEPHAN F. DE. Curatorial neglect of collections, Museum News, Vol. 43, no. 5, January, 1965, pp. 34–40. (Includes illustration of an accession sheet and a field manual or cataloguing guide for science museums.)

BORHEGYI, STEPHAN F. DE and MARRIOTT, ALICE. Proposals for a standardized museum accessioning and classification system, Curator, Vol. I, no. 2, spring 1958, pp. 77–86.(1) (Discusses cross-reference card system using abbreviations and code numbers for an anthropological museum.)

BURNS, NED J. Field manual for museums. U. S. Dept. of the Interior, National Park Service, Washington, D. C., Government Printing Office, 1941.

CHOUDHURY, AMIL ROY. Art museum documentation and practical handling. Hyderabad, India, Choudhury & Choudhury, 1963. (Describes procedures and illustrates forms used by leading art museums in various countries.)

COLEMAN, LAURENCE V. Manual for small museums. New York, G. P. Putnam's Sons, 1927.

DUDLEY, DOROTHY H. Methods of handling loan exhibitions in The Museum of Modern Art, The Museum News, Vol. 24, February 15, 1947, pp. 6–8.

FREUNDLICH, A. L. Museum registration by computer, Museum News, Vol. 44, no. 6, February, 1966, pp. 18–20.

GIFFORD, PHILIP C., JR. The elephant and the tortoise, Curator, Vol. IX, no. 2, June, 1966, pp. 125–133. (Contains information on numbering, cataloguing, repairing, preserving and storing ethnological collections.)

GRAHAM, JOHN M. II. A method of museum registration, Museum News, Vol. 42, no. 8, April, 1964. Technical Supplement, no. 2, pp. i–viii.

GUTHE, CARL E. Documenting collections: registration and records. American Association for State and Local History, Technical Leaflet no. 11. History News, Vol. 18, no. 9, July, 1963.

———. So you want a good museum. American Association of Museums, Publications, new series, No. 17, Washington, D. C., 1957. Reprinted 1964 (Contains chapters on collections, their records, and care.)

HUMPHREY, JAMES III. The computer as art cataloguer, Computers and the Humanities, a Newsletter. Flushing, New York, Queens College of the City University of New York, Vol. 1, no. 5, May, 1967, pp. 164–169.

LITTLE, DAVID. Safeguarding works of art: transportation, records, and insurance. American Association for State and Local History, Technical Leaflet no. 9. History News, Vol. 18, no. 7, May, 1963.

LYTLE, DOROTHY L. Where to learn about new data processing systems, Museum News, Vol. 46, no. 3, November, 1967, pp. 32–34. (Includes bibliography compiled for museum registrars who have little or no experience with automatic or electronic data processing and who wish some background information on its operation and application.)

MACDONALD, ROBERT D. The application of electronic data processing methods to botanical garden and arboretum records, The Garden Journal, The New York Botanical Garden, Vol. 16, pp. 246–247; 257–258.

MCINTYRE, DAVID. Knowing when to change, Museum News, Vol. 46, no. 3, 1967, pp. 28–29. (Suggests that registrars keep fully abreast of new methods of storing and retrieving information.)

NEUSTUPNY, JIRI. The prehistoric collection of the National Museum in Prague. Museums Journal, Vol. 64, no. 3, December, 1964, p. 203.[2] (Discusses registration, indexing and recording of collections.)

RIEFSTAHL, RUDOLF M. Museum photography, Museum News, Vol. 44, no. 2, October, 1965, pp. 21–23.

SHINE, CAROLYN R. The registrar: curator-without-portfolio, Museum News, Vol. 42, no. 6, February, 1964, pp. 33–35. (Discusses how a registrar can assist with documentation in museums without full curatorial coverage.)

STURTEVANT, WILLIAM C. Ethnological collections and curatorial records, Museum News, Vol. 44, no. 7, March, 1966, pp. 16–19. (Emphasizes curator's responsibility for providing answers to the following questions: Where is the object from? How old is it? What do we have from this culture? Where is it kept within the museum?)

SQUIRES, DONALD F. Data processing and museum collections: a problem for the present, Curator, Vol. IX, no. 3, September, 1966, pp. 216–227. (Describes the experiences of the Museum of Natural History, Smithsonian Institution in developing a data processing program from punched cards to the use of computers.)

TOOMEY, GERTRUDE. Essential records at the Philadelphia Museum of Art, The Museum News, Vol. 28, December 1, 1951, p. 8.

VAN GELDER, RICHARD G. and SYDNEY ANDERSON. An information retrieval system for collections of mammals, Curator, Vol. X, no. 1, March 1967, pp. 32–42.

VANCE, DAVID. New ways of keeping and finding information, Museum News, Vol. 46, no. 3, November, 1967, pp. 29–32. (Compares and contrasts filing methods and equipment from ledgers and manual cards to computers.)

WHITING, ALFRED F. Catalogues: dam'em, Curator, Vol. IX, no. 1, March, 1966, pp. 85–87.

Note: for further references, for the registration, and documentation of museum objects, readers are referred to *Selective Reference Guide to Historic Preservations,* edited and compiled by Frederick L. Rath, Jr. and Merrilyn Rogers respectively, Cooperstown, New York Historical Association, 1966, and to future editions of this book.

(1) Quarterly publication of the American Museum of National History, New York.

(2) Quarterly publication of the Museums Association in England, London.

Figure 25.—Recording measurements of a painting, Museum of Modern Art.

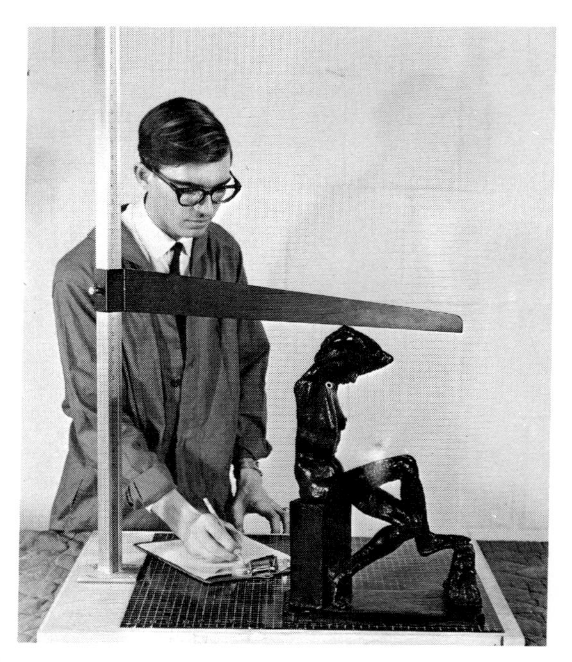

Figure 26.—Recording measurements of sculpture with measuring stand, Museum of Modern Art.

Chapter 4

MEASURING AND MARKING OBJECTS

MEASURING

Measuring is important both for identification and for calculating storage or exhibition space requirements. The equipment should include a folding rule, steel and cloth tapes (one with metric measurements), a measuring stand (a stand with an upright measuring rod and a movable arm at right angles), and calipers. In general, the dimensions (height, length, width, depth, diameter) are all taken at the greatest point. If this is not done, a note should state the point of measurement. (Fig. 25, 26.)

It is convenient to give the dimensions always in the same order, for

Figure 27.—Marking objects, Metropolitan Museum of Art.

example, height, width, depth; length, width, thickness; height, diameter; or any other combination of these. Height usually precedes width in recording the measurement of paintings, drawings, and prints. Over-all measurements are given for objects with separable parts, such as a teapot with a cover. Whether separate measurements will be recorded for component parts depends on the type of work.

In general, the English system of feet and inches is used, but in some museums the metric system is preferred, or both are used. In some American museums paintings and classical objects are measured in both inches and centimeters to facilitate their identification in European catalogues. Paintings are measured at the reverse left (or right) and lower edges of the stretcher or panel. If the frame prevents this, sight measurements are taken from the front until the painting can be unframed.

Measurements of watercolors, gouaches, drawings, and prints are taken at the right and lower edges of the composition, or of the sheet if the whole sheet is included in the composition. If it is impossible to remove the mat, the opening is measured and "sight" noted on the card. If the composition is very irregular, it is squared off by enclosing the outermost points within imaginary lines by means of transparent triangles or strips of transparent material, and the dimensions of the resulting rectangle taken.

For sculpture, measurements are taken of the greatest height (or length) and width (or depth), or both. If the base is an integral part of the sculpture, it should be included in the height. If not, its height and width may be noted separately. For example, H.8″ (base H.2″, W.4″, D.4″).

In general, for three-dimensional materials, the principal dimensions are taken with notes indicating whether handles, bases, etc., are included. If a sherd must be measured, dimensions are taken as it touches a flat surface. The more delicate calculations of curvatures and indentations are left to the archaeologist.

In many science museums detailed measurements of natural history specimens are made and kept only by curators. The average size of a bird, animal, or plant is known to a scientist and if a registrar is making a preliminary record it may only be necessary to note whether a specimen is immature or adult to indicate its normal size. However, if there is something unusual about the size it should be noted on the registrar's record.

If a registrar is responsible for recording detailed measurements of natural history specimens, he must receive instructions from the scientific staff of his museum. To measure an animal, for example, he may be required to record the length of the body and of the tail, length of the hind leg, width of the skull, etc. (See part 2, article 8.)

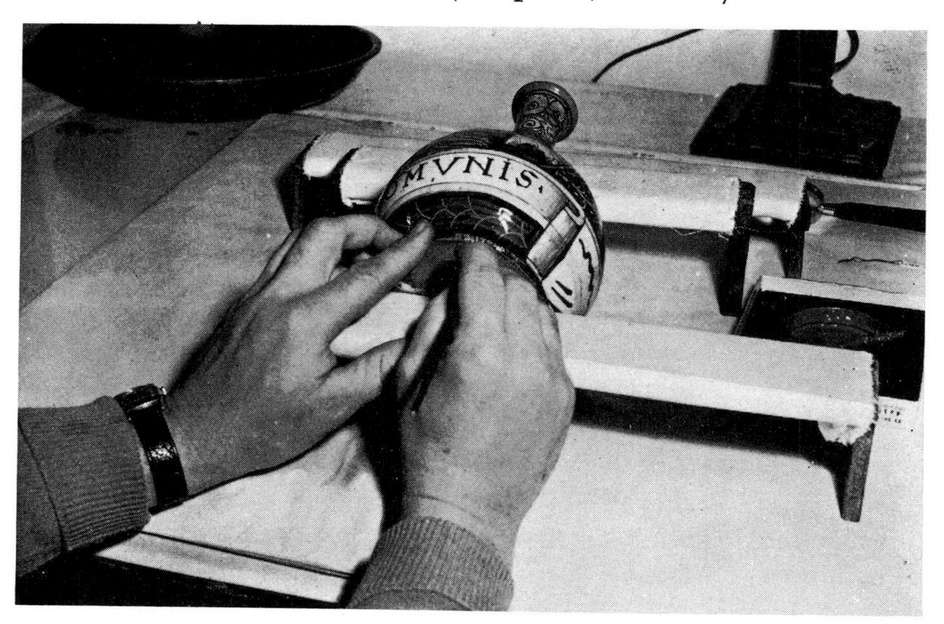

Figure 28.—Painting accession number on vase, Metropolitan Museum of Art.

Rules for Measuring Collections

It is convenient for the registrar to have a set of measuring rules applicable to the collections in his museum. Examples of measurements recorded for paintings, watercolors and drawings, and sculpture taken from rules used in an art museum are listed below.

1. Measure in both English and the metric systems. English measurements are expressed in inches (not feet), and metric measurements in centimeters. The metric measurements include one digit to the right of the decimal point, even if it is zero.
2. Take measurements to the next larger unit, not the nearest unit. Paintings, watercolors, drawings and sculpture are measured to the next larger eighth of an inch and to the next larger millimeter. Prints are measured to the next larger sixteenth of an inch and to the next larger millimeter.
3. Record height first, then width, then depth if needed, or diameter. If more than one dimension is given for sculpture, record height first, then greater horizontal dimension, then lesser horizontal dimension. If a work is circular or irregular in shape the abbreviations "(diam.)" and "(irreg.)" follow the inch measure-

ments in parentheses. (See examples below under *Paintings, Watercolors and Drawings,* and *Sculpture.*)

Paintings—Measure the rigid support, on the reverse if possible.

Examples:

Rectangular painting	reverse left and lower edges 14 x 20″ (35.5 x 50.8 cm.)
Circular painting	Diameter 63 7/8″ (diam.) (162.3 cm.)
Oval painting	Major and minor axes 42 1/2 x 28″ (oval) (108.0 x 71.1 cm.)
Lozenge-shaped painting	Major and minor axes 27 3/4 x 27 3/4″ (diagonal) (70.5 x 70.5 cm.)
Irregular painting	Maximum height and width, and whatever else is necessary (describe shape)

Watercolors and Drawings—works, other than prints, on paper or similar nonrigid material, including oil on paper if it is not mounted on a rigid support.

a. Always give sheet measurements first preceded by the word "sheet."

b. If it is impossible to measure the sheet, measure the mat opening and record this measurement first preceded by the word, "sight."

c. If the artist has made an outline, give the measurement also, preceded by the abbreviation, "Comp."

d. In some cases where there is no outline, measure the composition or decorated area in addition to sheet measurements.

Examples:

Watercolor	Sheet 21 3/4 x 36″ (55.2 x 91.5 cm.) Comp. 20 x 34 1/2″ (irreg.) (50.8 x 87.7 cm.)
Drawing	Sight 9 x 12 1/2″ (22.9 x 31.8 cm.)

Sculpture—Include base in height measurement if it is an integral part of the sculpture. Otherwise record height and width of base separately. If the greater horizontal dimension of a sculpture is larger than the height, measurements should be recorded as height, length, and depth, rather than height, width and depth. The weight of sculpture should also be recorded in pounds of the whole and each separate piece.

Examples:

(Bronze sculpture) 29 1/8″ h. (74.0 cm.) including bronze base

6″ h. x 5″ l. x 4 1/2″ w. (15.3 x 12.7 x 11.4 cm.) Wt. 56 lbs. including base.

(Wood sculpture with separate stone base by the artist) 73″ h. (185.3 cm.) Stone base 8″ h. x 14 1/4″ diam. (20.3 x 36.2 cm.) Wt. 124 lbs. (a. 56 lbs., b. 68 lbs.)

(Stone sculpture without base) 22″ h. (55.8 cm.) At base 6 x 5 3/4″ (15.2 x 14.6 cm.) Wt. 24 lbs.

(Plaster relief) 34″ h. x 23 1/4″ w. x 2 1/2″ d. (86.4 x 59.0 x 6.3 cm.) Wt. 17 lbs.

(Mobile) 23″ h. x 52″ (approx.) max. diam. (58.4 x 132.1 cm.) Wt. 10 1/2 lbs.

NOTE: It is often impossible to measure a mobile as precisely as other sculpture. It should be measured in its most extended natural position.

MARKING

Marking museum objects is obviously an important task in all museums for it is by the number that an accessioned object is easily identified in the records. However, before an object is accessioned a preliminary identification must be established.

Temporary Marks for Incoming Material

When objects are first received, it is not always known that they will be accepted as permanent accessions or as loans. In many museums material is brought in for examination only, and is released after a brief period. Identification marks on these objects show the source, date received, purpose for which they entered the museum, or a number corresponding to that on temporary receipts issued when objects are received, copies of which are filed in the registration department. The marks may be made on paper stickers, tags, or adhesive tape, although the last must be used with care, as it will cause permanent harm to the surface of such materials as silver, lacquer, or enamel.

Temporary Marks for Loans

The marks on loans for special exhibitions do not need to be permanent but should be clear and readily accessible. Loan numbers are usually typed on stickers or tags and placed on the objects as soon as they are received. In many museums the lender's name appears with the loan number. In others, a label with lender's name and address, title or description of loan, artist's name, and other information is attached to each loan. The stickers are frequently left on the stretchers or the cardboard or other backings of paintings as a record of their exhibition history; but borrower's marks on all other objects must be removed before they are returned to the lenders.

Permanent Marks for Accessions

Marks on objects in the permanent collection should be permanent, clear, and readily accessible, but so placed that they will not detract from the appearance of the object. Marking materials vary somewhat according to the objects. In general, museums have found that artists' oil colors for glass, metal, ceramics, wood; linen tape for textiles; and medium lead pencil (not indelible) for paper objects are satisfactory. Stamps are also sometimes used on the backs of prints. Other marks such as metal tags with hand-stamped numbers for armor, labels typed or handwritten for bottles containing natural history specimens, and tags to be placed under insect pins are used when paint, tape, and pencil marks are not satisfactory. It may be necessary for some very small objects to be marked with jeweler's tags or kept in boxes marked with the identifying numbers.

The oil paint generally used is vermilion or cadmium red, slightly thinned with turpentine, white and black paint being applied where red would not be discernible. On some objects such as mineral specimens a small band of paint is applied in one color and the number painted on it in a contrasting color. A drop of dryer may be added if quick drying is necessary; otherwise two or three days are required before drying is complete. If lacquer thinner is used instead of turpentine, the addition of a few drops of clear lacquer to the paint makes it adhere better to smooth surfaces and makes it harder when dry. If the material to which the number is to be applied is porous (for example, old wood), a thin layer of shellac is first applied to the surface to keep it from absorbing the paint.

The numbers are painted on with a water-color brush (sable or camel's hair are used) flattened for heavy numbers and made into a fine point for small ones. For very small numbers, such as those painted inside rings, the brush is reduced to three or four hairs. After numbers have dried it may be advisable to protect them with a coat of shellac. New paints manufactured for use on plastics are satisfactory for objects made of the new synthetic materials. These paints adhere well and do not need shellac to make them permanent. Sometimes it is necessary to remove the number when an object is being cleaned, but at other times the number can be covered with Scotch tape. (See figures 27, 28.)

Linen tape is sewed on textiles. On some fragile material such as laces, the tape is attached by a small loop of thread. The numbers may be typed on the tape (using ordinary red or black typewriter ribbon) or written in indelible ink.

Medium lead pencils are used in marking paper objects, since a hard pencil might scratch or dent the paper; ink, which has a tendency to spread, and indelible pencils, should not be used. In addition to marking numbers on prints in pencil, it is common practice to stamp them on the reverse to indicate the museum's ownership. Great care must be taken, however, to keep the mark from showing through the paper, and in some cases it may be advisable not to stamp them at all. To mark prints in this manner, a small rubber stamp carrying the museum's monogram or name is tinted with dark brown printer's ink which has been rolled out on glass to the desired tone, according to the thickness or opacity of the paper. Writing ink, India ink, or an ordinary stamping pad should never be used. The stamp should be applied behind a worked part of the composition to insure its being invisible from the front. Prints bound in books usually have a bookplate pasted inside the cover. A selected page further on may be stamped with the museum's monogram and the identifying number repeated in pencil.

For all objects in the same class, the number should be placed in the same location so that it can be readily found. All separable parts of the same object should be numbered, for example, a snuff box and its cover or a knife and its sheath, 41.120a and 41.120b. Several museums have found the following general rules satisfactory: heavy objects should never be numbered on the bottom; small objects should be numbered near the base; coins, if possible, on the rim; rugs and large textiles which will be rolled, on the reverse of the lower right and upper left corners; scroll paintings, on the knob of the scroll; paintings on the reverse of the lower right corners of stretcher and frame. Some museums have found it most useful to have numbers painted on the reverse upper left corners of stretcher and frame as well, so that when the painting is hanging in the gallery the lower number can be seen without removing the painting from the wall, and when it is stacked in the storeroom the upper number can be seen.

Marking Methods

The marking methods most suitable for the various types of objects in the permanent collection must be determined by each museum. Some of the methods used in art, history, and science museums are tabulated on pages 52–62 (further information on marking natural history specimens is to be found in part 2, article 8). The information on which this tabulation is based was supplied by the following museums, whose initials appearing in the tabulation will identify them as the source of that particular information:

A.I.	Art Institute of Chicago
A.M.N.H.	American Museum of Natural History, New York
A.S.H.M.	American Swedish Historical Museum, Philadelphia
B.M. of S.	Buffalo Museum of Science
C.A. of S.	California Academy of Sciences, San Francisco
C.H.S.	Chicago Historical Society
C.I. of S.	Cranbrook Institute of Science, Bloomfield Hills, Michigan
C.M. of G.	Corning Museum of Glass, Corning, New York
C.N.H.M.	Chicago Natural History Museum
C.P.L.H.	California Palace of the Legion of Honor, San Francisco
C.U.M.	Cooper Union Museum for the Arts of Decoration, New York
F.H.	Fenimore House, Farmers' Museum, Cooperstown, New York
M.F.A.	Museum of Fine Arts, Boston
M.M.A.	Metropolitan Museum of Art, New York
M.MO.A.	Museum of Modern Art, New York
N.G.A.	National Gallery of Art, Washington, D. C.
N.J.H.S.	New Jersey Historical Society, Newark
N.M.	Newark Museum, New Jersey
O.A.M.	Oakland Art Museum, California
P.M.	Peabody Museum of Anthropology and Ethnology, Cambridge, Massachusetts
S.F.M.A.	San Francisco Museum of Art
T.M.	Textile Museum, Washington, D. C.
U.M.	University Museum, University of Pennsylvania, Philadelphia
U.S.N.M.	United States National Museum, Smithsonian Institution, Washington, D. C.

In the table, it is understood that numbers in artist's oil colors are applied with a camel's hair or sable brush. A steel nib pen is used to apply numbers in ink. Brown's Resistal paper or Parson's linen ledger paper is suggested for labeling specimens preserved in alcohol. And Higgins' Eternal Black ink is mentioned as having special uses in science museums.

Numbers may be typed on linen tape by fastening it with scotch tape to a piece of paper for insertion into the typewriter.

References:

ANDERSON, R. M. Methods of collecting and preserving vertebrate animals. Ottawa, National Museum of Canada Bull. 69, 1948.

COLEMAN, LAWRENCE VAIL. Manual for small museums. New York, G. P. Putnam's Sons, 1927.

NEWKIRK, CHESTER H. Procedure for marking objects, The Clearing House for Western Museums Newsletter 178, December 1954.

RICHARDS, CHARLES M. Formulae for museum measurements, The Museum News, Vol. 25, April 1, 1948, pp. 7–8.

MARKING METHODS IN ART, HISTORY, AND SCIENCE MUSEUMS

Type of object	*Marking material*	*Position*	*Special instructions*	*Source of information*
ARMS AND ARMOR	Metal tags stamped with number and attached to piece with wire.	Most inconspicuous place.	Mark in same position on each type of piece.	M.M.A.
BASKETRY	India ink, or cadmium or vermilion oil color on object or on tag.	Most inconspicuous place.		C.I. of S. P.M. U.M.
BIRDS				
EGGS	Number and set mark on eggs in pencil. Data on egg cards with Higgins Eternal ink or other indelible ink.	Numbers written above and below opening in egg.		C.A. of S. C.N.H.M. N.M.
MOUNTED	Waterproof ink on heavy paper labels, or paint directly on bill.	Label tied to feet of specimen. Ink underside of base of mount.	Tied with good linen or nylon thread. Label removed or pasted underneath when on display.	A.M.N.H. B.M. of S. N.M.
NESTS	Label with data attached to each specimen in the field. Number subsequently added in indelible ink or typed on linen tape.	Tied to inside edge of nest.		C.N.H.M. N.M.
SKELETONS	Indelible ink on each of larger bones.	Numbers written in center or largest part of bone.	Often desirable to apply shellac over inked numbers.	A.M.N.H. C.A. of S.
SKINS	Heavy paper label or linen tag with data attached to each specimen in the field. Number subsequently added in indelible ink.	Label tied to feet of specimen.	Tied with good linen or nylon thread.	A.M.N.H. B.M. of S. C.A. of S. C.N.H.M.
SPECIMENS IN ALCOHOL	Ink or crayon on resistant paper.	In jar or crock with specimen.	Second label can be placed on outside of jar.	A.M.N.H.

Object	Material	Location of number	Remarks	Source
BOOKS	Book plate. Lead pencil and/or stamp.	Inside front or back cover; number stamped or written on plate.	Loose pages marked in pencil.	C.U.M. M.M.A.
MANUSCRIPT ALBUMS	Pencil, no. 3 or 2⅔.	Reverse lower right or left of each leaf.		C.U.M. M.M.A.
PORTFOLIOS	Pencil, no. 3 or 2⅔.	Reverse lower right or left of each sheet.		M.M.A.
SCRAPBOOKS, SKETCHBOOKS	Pencil, no. 3 or 2⅔.	Where drawings or water colors are pasted to a page of a book, number is pencilled on page immediately to lower right of drawing.		M.M.A. C.U.M.
BOTANICAL SPECIMENS				
ECONOMIC SPECIMENS	Typed labels.			C.N.H.M.
HERBARIUM SPECIMENS	India ink or typed labels.	Lower right corner of sheet on which specimen is mounted.		B.M. of S. C.N.H.M. C.I. of S. N.M.
SEEDS AND FRUITS	Typed labels or painted numbers.	On top of box or in glass vial or bottle, or on specimen.		C.N.H.M.
TYPE PHOTOS	Typed labels.		At the time the photo is made a small scale with the number of the print is fastened to the herbarium sheet. The herbarium labels of the institution to which the original specimen belongs are also photographed.	C.N.H.M.
WOOD SAMPLES	Typed labels.	Upper left corner.		C.N.H.M.

BRONZES
See METAL OBJECTS

MARKING METHODS IN ART, HISTORY, AND SCIENCE MUSEUMS

Type of object	*Marking material*	*Position*	*Special instructions*	*Source of information*
CERAMICS *See also* POTSHERDS	Artists' oil colors (vermilion or cadmium red; black or white if red not discernible).	On base or underside or in an inconspicuous place not likely to be worn by handling.	Protect with lacquer or shellac after numbers are dry.	A.I. C.P.L.H. C.H.S. C.U.M. M.M.A. M.MO.A. N.J.H.S. N.M. U.M.
CLOTHING	Written in India ink or typed on narrow linen tape or small jeweler's tag.	Where possible, sewn on inside of hem, or on neckband at middle of back, waistband at one end, button holes or lapels, depending on type of clothing.	For accessories, number may be written directly inside of hats, shoes, moccasins, gloves, etc.	A.M.N.H. M.M.A. N.J.H.S. N.M. U.M.
CYLINDER SEALS	India ink.	On end.	Never on carving.	U.M.
DRAWINGS	Pencil, no. 3, 2⅔, or 2.	Reverse lower left or right, or if impracticable, on the reverse side of a dark area in the drawing. Reverse lower left or right of mat or mount.	Property stamp can be placed on back.	A.I. C.U.M. M.M.A. M.MO.A. N.G.A.
EMBROIDERIES *See* TEXTILES				
ENAMELS	Artists' oil color (vermilion or cadmium red).	On the base or underside, or in an inconspicuous place not likely to be worn by handling.		M.M.A.
FANS	Artists' oil color (vermilion or cadmium red).	On back of end stick.		C.U.M.
FEATHERS	Typed or written on white tape.	Sewn on in most inconspicuous place.		P.M.

FISHES				
SPECIMENS IN ALCOHOL	Typed on resistant paper label, or written or stamped on parchment tag.	Label put into jar with specimen; tag tied through mouth or gill opening or around caudal peduncle.		C.A. of S. C.N.H.M.
SKELETAL MATERIAL	Typed on label or number written on each bone with Higgins Eternal Black ink.	On top of cardboard box.		C.A. of S. C.N.H.M.
FOSSILS				
VERTEBRATES	White ink or India ink, according to color of specimen, coated with shellac; or India-inked number on dried dab of white paint.	On the specimen, placed so as not to obscure any important character; on interior or flat surface where it will not rub off.	Steel nib pen used; in the case of specimens consisting of several pieces, such as disarticulated fossil vertebrates, the catalogue number is marked on each fragment. Thin solution of clear Duco cement can be used to harden surface before numbering.	A.M.N.H. B.M. of S. C.A. of S. C.N.H.M.
INVERTEBRATES, MEGASCOPIC (visible to the naked eye)	Numbered paper labels with glue backing.	Label pasted on specimen on any surface smooth and flat enough to hold, but not interfere with study; or placed on or in corked vial in which specimen is stored.	Labels are prepared in Museum's print shop, in sheets of 50 consecutive numbers, with 100 duplicate sheets for large suites of specimens.	A.M.N.H. B.M. of S. C.A. of S. C.N.H.M.
INVERTEBRATES, MICROSCOPIC (including thin sections of megascopic invertebrates)	India ink.	On the cardboard or glass mount of these specimens.		A.M.N.H.
FURNITURE	Artists' oil color (vermilion or cadmium red; black or white if red not discernible).	Commodes, chests, etc.: on bottom left corner of the back. Chairs, etc.: at the base of the back left leg. Tables, etc.: underneath a leaf, on the apron, or at the base of a leg.	Camels' hair brush or red-sable watercolor brush. Protect with lacquer or shellac. Heavy or fragile pieces marked so that numbers are visible without moving object.	A.I. C.P.L.H. C.H.S. C.U.M. M.M.A. M.MO.A. N.G.A. N.M.

MARKING METHODS IN ART, HISTORY, AND SCIENCE MUSEUMS

Type of object	*Marking material*	*Position*	*Special instructions*	*Source of information*
GEMS *See* MINERALS				
GEOLOGICAL SPECIMENS *See also* FOSSILS, MINERALS	India ink on small rectangle of enamel (red for holotype, orange for paratype, blue for hypotype).	On interior or flat surface where it will not be rubbed off.		C.A. of S.
GLASS	Artists' oil color (vermilion or Venetian red) or India ink, protected by clear lacquer or colorless nail polish.		The number should be as small and legible as possible. It should not be seen when piece is on exhibition.	C.P.L.H. C.H.S. C.M. of G. C.U.M. M.F.A. M.M.A. M.MO.A. P.M.
GOLD *See* METAL OBJECTS				
GOURDS	India ink if possible, otherwise cadmium red.	Most inconspicuous place for exhibition purposes.	Pen or watercolor brush.	P.M.
HERBARIUM SPECIMENS *See* BOTANICAL SPECIMENS				
INSECTS				
SPECIMENS PINNED DRY	Pin labels of 100-percent rag content. Mostly printed from zinc cuts. Handwritten data, such as dates, are in Higgins black waterproof ink. Tiny linen tags can be used.	Labels, directly below specimen, on the pin; position on pin kept uniform by using pinning block.	Parallel to insect's longitudinal axis, readable from left side. Parallel to point in case of point-mounted insect. Number specimens with catalogue or accession numbers.	A.M.N.H. B.M. of S. C.A. of S. C.N.H.M. N.M.
SPECIMENS PRESERVED IN ALCOHOL	Labels of 100-percent rag paper. Machine printing in alcohol-proof printer's ink.	Lengthwise in vial, printed face outward.		C.N.H.M.

	Most data hand printed in Higgins drawing ink.			
SPECIMENS PRESERVED ON MICROSCOPIC SLIDES	Standard-type square microscopic slide labels printed by hand with Higgins Eternal black ink; occasionally machine printed. Paper a high quality semigloss finish with fish glue backing.	On left side of slide; if second label is needed, it is placed on right side of slide.	Commercially available slide labels are usually made of poor quality paper and have a poor quality glue.	C.N.H.M.
IVORIES AND BONE *See* CERAMICS				
JEWELRY	India ink on jeweler's tag; or artists' oil color (vermilion or cadmium red; black or white if red not discernible).	On the base, back, or underside; or in an inconspicuous place not likely to be worn by handling.	Attach tag with linen thread the same color as piece; protect very small painted numbers with lacquer or shellac.	C.U.M. M.M.A. N.G.A. N.M.
LACES	White linen tape, ⅛″ or ⅜″ wide, typed or India ink.	Tape sewed on lower right corner or near end of piece at edge.	Attach tape by a small loop of thread, or one or two stitches on reverse.	C.U.M. M.M.A. N.M.
LEATHER	India ink, except that if surface is rough a numbered name tape is sewn on.			C.I. of S.
LOWER INVERTEBRATES				
DRIED CRUSTACEANS, etc.	Typed label with data and India ink number on specimen.			C.N.H.M.
CRUSTACEANS IN ALCOHOL	Typed on resistant paper label.	In container.		C.N.H.M.
MAMMALS				
SKELETONS	India ink on each bone. Small bones kept in numbered boxes.	Numbers written in center of largest part of bone; or near proximal end of long bones, at lower back center of skull, or on right ramus of jaw.	Often desirable to apply shellac over inked numbers.	A.M.N.H. C.A. of S. U.M.

MARKING METHODS IN ART, HISTORY, AND SCIENCE MUSEUMS

Type of object	*Marking material*	*Position*	*Special instructions*	*Source of information*
SKINS, SMALL	India ink on label.	Tied to a hind foot.	Fine steel nib pen used.	A.M.N.H. B.M. of S. C.A. of S. C.N.H.M.
SKINS, LARGE FLAT	Perforated with three-cornered awl, or written on attached label.	Perforations in middle of lower back; label attached to head.		A.M.N.H. C.A. of S. C.N.H.M.
SKULLS	India ink number plus data label.	On cranium and mandible, plus label in vial or on box.		A.M.N.H. C.N.H.M.
SPECIMENS IN ALCOHOL	India ink or soft pencil on label.	Label attached to a hind foot.	A sized label should not be used.	A.M.N.H.
MANUSCRIPTS *See* BOOKS				
MASKS	India ink.	Lower right edge, or inside.		U.M.
METAL OBJECTS	Artists' oil color (American vermilion) or white enamel; number is sometimes also etched on with a diamond point marker.	On the base or underside, or in an inconspicuous place.	Use camels' hair brush; protect by clear lacquer or shellac.	A.I. A.S.H.M. C.P.L.H. C.U.M. M.F.A. M.M.A. M.MO.A. N.J.H.S. P.M. U.S.N.M.
MINERALS, ROCKS	White ink or India ink, according to color of specimen; or India ink on white enamel.	On the specimen, placed so as not to obscure any important character; or on small rectangle in lower right hand corner.	Protect with lacquer or shellac. Surface can be prepared by brushing on clear Duco cement. If a specimen is too small to number directly,	B.M. of S. C.A. of S. C.N.H.M. C.I. of S. N.M.

			place in vial and number the vial.	
PAINTINGS	Artists' oil color (American vermilion or cadmium red; black or white if red not discernible).	Reverse lower right corner of stretcher and frame (and reverse upper left corner of stretcher and frame if desired).	Apply with camels' hair brush or sable watercolor brush. Protect with lacquer or shellac. On loans, use gummed sticker bearing label information and name of owner.	A.I. C.H.S. C.P.L.H. F.H. M.M.A. M.MO.A. N.M. O.A.M. P.M. N.G.A. S.F.M.A.
PHOTOGRAPHS	Pencil, No. 3, 2⅔, or 2.	Reverse lower right or left of photograph; reverse lower right or left of mat or mount.	Museum label pasted on cardboard backing; artists' oil paint accession number on lower right corner of frame.	C.H.S. M.MO.A.
PORCELAIN *See* CERAMICS				
PORTFOLIOS *See* BOOKS				
POTSHERDS	Artists' oil color (alizarin crimson in turpentine) or India ink.	Side of sherd without decoration.		U.S.N.M.
POTTERY *See* CERAMICS				
PRINTS	Pencil, no. 3, 2⅔, or 2, and a small museum stamp of brown oil color.	On the reverse side of a particularly dark area in the print, if stamped. Vertical prints, hinged along right side, are marked on reverse lower right corner; horizontal prints, hinged at top, are marked on reverse of each free corner.	The accession number and the stamp are placed together. Mat label pasted with library paste on lower right corner of inner matboard below print (write lightly so as not to damage).	A.I. C.H.S. M.M.A. M.F.A. M.MO.A. N.G.A. N.M. S.F.M.A.

MARKING METHODS IN ART, HISTORY, AND SCIENCE MUSEUMS

Type of object	*Marking material*	*Position*	*Special instructions*	*Source of information*
REPTILES AND AMPHIBIANS				
EGGS (BLOWN)	Higgins Eternal ink.	Above and below hole drilled in egg.		C.A. of s.
SPECIMENS PRESERVED IN ALCOHOL	Metal or resistant paper or fiber tag.	Tags are tied with carpet thread to a leg of a limbed specimen and to the neck region of legless forms.	Data stamped on pure sheet tin with steel type.	A.M.N.H. C.A. of s. C.N.H.M.
SKELETAL SPECIMENS	Metal and fiber tags or Higgins Eternal ink.	Tags are attached to the larger parts; markings on each bone.		A.M.N.H. C.A. of s. C.N.H.M.
SKINS AND SKULLS	Each specimen has heavy cardboard identification tag.			
ROCKS *See* MINERALS				
RUGS *See also* TAPESTRIES, TEXTILES	Typed on linen tape or written with ink on cloth or paper tags.	Attach to lower right or left corner of reverse of rug, or on diagonal corners so number is easily found when rug is rolled.	Tape with Museum's name woven in with room for number below sewn on piece. Number can be typed on linen tape by fastening tape to piece of paper with scotch tape for insertion into typewriter.	C.P.L.H. N.G.A. N.M. T.M.
SCIENTIFIC INSTRUMENTS	India ink. Metallic objects are usually engraved.	In an inconspicuous place.	Where necessary, surface is prepared by brushing on a stripe of clear Duco cement.	C.I. of s.
SCRAPBOOKS, SKETCHBOOKS *See* BOOKS				

SCROLL PAINTINGS	Ink number on jeweler's tag, or artist's oil colors.	Tag attached to cord at opening end of scroll; number painted on knob of scroll.		M.F.A. M.M.A.
SCULPTURE	Artists' oil color (vermilion or cadmium red; black or white if red not discernible).	Lower rear of base (on large pieces—where it can be seen without moving object) or, if no base, inconspicuous place not likely to be worn by handling.	Protect with lacquer or shellac. Large linen tags with needed information tied to objects for quick identification when in storage.	A.I. C.P.L.H. M.F.A. M.M.A. M.MO.A. N.G.A. N.M.
SILVER *See* METAL OBJECTS				
SHELLS	India ink.	Inconspicuous place not likely to be worn by handling.	Protect with lacquer or shellac.	B.M. of S. C.A. of S. N.M. P.M.
TAPESTRIES *See also* RUGS, TEXTILES	Typed on linen tape, or written with ink on cloth or paper tag.	Attached to lower right or left corner of reverse of tapestry, or on diagonal corners so number is easily found when tapestry is rolled.	Tape with Museum's name woven in, and with room for number below, sewn on piece.	C.P.L.H. M.M.A. N.G.A.
TERRA COTTAS	Artist's oil colors (American vermilion or cadmium red; black or white if red not discernible).	Where it will not be rubbed off.	Protect by undercoating of shellac.	M.M.A.
TEXTILE SAMPLE BOOKS *See* BOOKS				

MARKING METHODS IN ART, HISTORY, AND SCIENCE MUSEUMS

Type of object	*Marking material*	*Position*	*Special instructions*	*Source of information*
TEXTILES. *See also,* RUGS, TAPESTRIES	Linen tape, typed or India ink. Jeweler's tags sometimes used for textiles too fragile for sewn tape.	Lower right corner on reverse side (or lower left corner). If jewelers' tag is used, in a position that does not obscure design and is strong enough to hold tag; should not have to be removed when piece on exhibition.	Tape with Museum's name woven in, and with room for number below, sewn on piece.	A.I. B.M. of S. C.P.L.H. C.N.H.M. C.U.M. M.M.A. M.MO.A. N.M. T.M.
WATER COLORS	Pencil, no. 3, 2⅔, or 2.	Reverse lower right or left of water color. Reverse lower right or left of mat or mount.	If framed, mark with oil paint on lower right corner. A museum label can be pasted on backing, on stretcher, or on frame.	U.S.N.M. M.F.A. M.M.A. M.MO.A. N.M.
WEAPONS (arrows, clubs, harpoons, knives, etc.)	India ink.	Near butt end, writing from the end toward the point.		U.M.
WOOD	Artist's oil colors (vermilion or cadmium red; black or white if red not discernible).	Most inconspicuous place.	If wood is old, porous, or absorbent, paint number over shellac or varnish undercoating.	F.H. M.M.A. N.J.H.S. P.M.
ZOOLOGICAL MATERIAL	Follow standard accepted practices for each category of animal. Refer to published manuals of several big museums.			C.I. of S.

Chapter 5

STORAGE AND CARE OF OBJECTS

The storage and care of museum collections is essentially the province of curators and conservators. However, since the registrar is responsible for the temporary storage of objects while they are unpacked, packed, examined, and recorded, and since in some museums he may handle the storage of permanent collections for the curators, he must be well informed about safe handling techniques and must have a basic knowledge of approved storage methods. This chapter is intended to guide the registrar in the physical handling and temporary storage of incoming and outgoing material, and to help him to work intelligently with curators.

The material presented here is based partly on pamphlets by Robert P. Sugden, published by the Metropolitan Museum of Art (see references) and on answers to a request for information about storage and marking methods circulated among 24 museums of art, science, and history in various sections of the country. These museums are listed on p. 68. Information received on the storage of natural history specimens has also been included as an aid to registrars in small museums, who are sometimes called upon to handle mounted birds and animals, shells, minerals, and other specimens which in the larger museums are handled only by specialists, with special equipment, in the scientific departments.

In their replies to this inquiry, several curators contributed information on the care and preservation of collections as well as on storage methods, and this information has likewise been included here to give registrars a better understanding of this phase of curatorial activities.

CONTROL OF STOREROOMS

A safe or vault either in the registrar's office or in a storeroom should be available for the safekeeping of small valuable objects which are being processed. Ideally, a separate area should be assigned to the registrar for the processing and temporary storage of objects moving in and out of the museum, and this area should be controlled by him (see figures 1–3, chapter 1). However, in many museums this is not possible, and objects may be processed and stored in the registrar's office, in the storerooms for the permanent collections or, in the case of loans to special exhibitions, in the galleries in which they are to be exhibited. In some museums all collections may be stored in one room. In any case, access to storage areas must be controlled by the departments responsible for the objects stored within them and records kept of storage locations. The circulation of pass keys should be restricted not only because of the possibility of loss or damage, but also because material may be disarranged by people not familiar with the storage system.

PROTECTION WITHIN STOREROOMS

As far as possible, storage areas and equipment should be fireproof, proper conditions of temperature and relative humidity should be maintained, and dirt should be prevented from entering. Hygrothermographs should be provided for all storage areas to register the temperature and relative humidity. Otherwise a frequent check should be made with a sling psychrometer, not at the same time each day, but at various hours and during all kinds of weather. Adequate lighting should be provided, and both storage and work areas should be kept clean and uncluttered, to avoid accidents and damage. Unnecessary cotton, tissue paper, cardboard containers, or other packing materials, alcohol, benzine, or any of the allied paint-thinning or cleaning agents used in repairing objects constitute a fire hazard and should not be kept in storerooms. Textiles used as dust covers should be periodically cleaned and fireproofed. Dollies, picture trucks, tray trucks, and ladders should be provided for safety in moving objects from one location to another, and should be kept near the storerooms. (See figures 4 and 5, chapter 1.)

It is equally important that objects be moved only by personnel trained in the physical handling of works of art or other museum objects. For instance, handlers should know that ceramic and glass vessels and sculpture should never be picked up by the handle or the rim or an arm but should be held in the hand and, if large, be supported by the other hand; that furniture should be lifted, never pushed, as the legs are frequently fragile; that the faces of paintings should never be touched and that paintings are best held by placing one's hands against opposite edges, or, if two men are handling a large painting, by each placing one hand beneath and the other on the side; that in handling silver, gloves or a soft cloth should be used to prevent contact with the skin and consequent tarnishing.

Constant Relative Humidity

The importance of maintaining a constant relative humidity in storerooms cannot be over-emphasized, but it is extremely difficult to maintain, particularly in old buildings in those sections of the country with variable climatic conditions. The effect of humidity and temperature on museum material is ably explained by the late Murray Pease,[1] who was Conservator of the Metropolitan Museum of Art:

Relative Humidity. Definition: *Relative humidity is the proportion of actual moisture to the maximum possible amount of moisture in the air at a specified temperature.* It is expressed in percentages.

All air contains some water vapor, mixed with the air gases. The amount varies, but at a given temperature there is a maximum limit to the amount the air will hold. This limit is low at low temperatures, high at high temperatures.

When air holds its limit of moisture, it is at 100% relative humidity. If the temperature of that air is then raised, its capacity for moisture will increase but its moisture will be the same, therefore its relative humidity will go down. If the temperature is reduced instead of raised, its capacity will be unequal to the amount of moisture present, and condensation will occur.

Measurement. The simplest and one of the most accurate instruments for measuring relative humidity is the sling psychrometer. It consists of two ordinary thermometers, one having a sleeve of wet cloth over its bulb. When a rapid current of air is passed over it, evaporation from this sleeve cools the bulb, and the wet-bulb thermometer registers lower than the dry. The amount of evaporation, and therefore the wet-bulb temperature, is controlled by the relative humidity of the air. Prepared tables, known as psychrometric tables, give the relative humidity figures for all wet- and dry-bulb thermometer readings.

Significance. Fibrous materials such as paper, wood and cloth absorb moisture from the air at high relative humidities and give it off at low relative humidities. Their fibres expand when moisture is absorbed, contract when it is given off. Therefore all changes in relative humidity of the surrounding air will affect the shape and condition of works of art made from these materials. The forces involved are great, and the effects may be serious.

Ideal Conditions. Paintings on paper, wood, cloth, and other hygroscopic materials are safest in an atmosphere of uniform, moderate temperature and humidity (40-60%). High or low extremes, and repeated fluctuations of humidity are equally to be avoided. The same is true of temperature, not because of the temperature itself, but because of its effect on relative humidity.

Control. Extremes of temperature and humidity vary so widely over the country as a whole that any general recommendations on control could be no more than emergency measures suggested to correct conditions temporarily. In addition to local atmospheric conditions, the physical construction of a given building, the uses to which it is put, and the types of exhibition material to be protected, present special problems. Other factors include proximity of museum premises to industrial hazards such as smoke, chemical exudations, etc.

So complex and variable are the factors involved that a satisfactory long-range solution cannot be achieved without the help of air conditioning engineers thoroughly informed as to local conditions and specific requirements.

[1] *In* Sugden, 1948, p. 32 (see references at the end of the chapter).

Fumigation

Rugs and textiles containing wool or silk, fur garments, ethnological specimens with wool or feather decoration, mounted animals and birds as well as animal and bird skins, pinned insects, and some botanical specimens require constant protection against moths and other pests. In some museums gas chamber storerooms or refrigerated vaults are used for the protection of objects in storage. Gas chamber storerooms are sealed periodically and gas injected into the room from cylinders. This method of fumigating must be done only by experienced personnel. Various insecticides are also used for the protection of collections. Paradichlorobenzene is probably the most effective protective agent which can be used with almost complete safety. As it is the vapor which kills both moths and larvae, the objects to be protected should be stored in a closed room or in an air-tight cabinet. Napthalene and camphor flakes protect in the same way but vaporize less quickly than paradichlorobenzene and are therefore less immediately effective but last longer. Some material for which the closed-area vapor treatment is impractical may be protected with one of the good commercial sprays. The ordinary spray gun is satisfactory for most textiles but is not powerful enough to get through thick fur.

Before a newly acquired object is stored, it should be examined carefully for possible infestation. It should be remembered that the larval stage is the feeding stage in the moth cycle, so there can be danger even though there are no moths flying around; and also that as a soiled object is much more susceptible to insect damage than a clean one, anything which can be cleaned safely should be cleaned. Since this information is quite general, and is not intended as instruction in the use of the materials mentioned, curators, conservators, and other authorities, such as those listed at the end of the chapter, should be consulted for information about the protection of collections.

Storage Units

There is a trend today toward the use of metal rather than wood for cabinets, shelving, and work tables; but the comparative value of each material should be examined in relation to the safety of the objects before deciding which to use. According to Robert P. Sugden (1948, p. 15):

> Selection on fire protective standards alone would seem the most reasonable basis of determination, yet even on that ground decision is difficult. Wood, it is true, can be completely consumed by fire, whereas metal, even at extremely high tempera-

tures, retains some semblance of its outer form. This would indicate that metal is preferable to wood. Actually, however, the welfare of the stored object must be put before that of the container which holds it, and wood, in some cases, affords the better protection. Metal is so positive a heat conductor that unless its heat conduction properties can be retarded by the use of fireproof insulation, wooden equipment must be the choice for storing books, art works on paper, or basic administrative records.

Among the inherent disadvantages of metal containers for books, paper, bronze, and unglazed pottery, is condensation of moisture on metal surfaces. In sections of the country where relative humidity, particularly in summer, rises to points as high as ninety to one hundred percent, condensation on metal equipment is very troublesome. Hence wood is the preferred choice. (Certain textiles, costumes, and costume accessories might also suffer through exposure to such conditions.)

In basement storage areas, the condensation problem assumes even more serious proportions. In some cases it has been necessary to improvise means to reduce the sweating of metal by the use of electric light bulbs set into the bases of storage cabinets. This provides a measure of drying heat to counteract the dampness. Electric heaters and fans are also effective in larger areas of exposure.

Ceramics, and works on paper, would not be damaged if stored in a tightly closed wooden cabinet even though its exterior was scorched in a fire quickly brought under control. In uninsulated metal storage equipment the rapidity of heat conduction endangers this type of material no matter how relatively brief its exposure to fire.

Another important consideration in the use of metal is the lack of surface resilience which creates a certain hazard when pottery, porcelains, and similar objects are placed upon it. The natural resilient quality in wood allows for a margin of error and reduces the possibility of chipping and breakage. This, however, need not eliminate metal base and metal frame storage equipment for ceramics. The heavy-grade linoleum used as the working surface on modern metal office desks can also be used for table tops or shelving surfaces in steel cabinets.

Whatever the material and the type of shelves or cabinets decided upon, the shelves should be adjustable so that objects of various sizes can be stored and removed easily and safely. Storage units which are interchangeable in location are useful in some cases. For example, in the division of archaeology of the United States National Museum, small objects are stored in a series of interchangeable cardboard trays fitting into wooden drawers in standard cabinets (see figure 29).

For protection of objects in storerooms, many museums use bags and boxes with plastic openings through which the contents may be seen. The accession number should be clearly marked on the outside of all containers to avoid unnecessary opening.

STORAGE REQUIREMENTS AND METHODS

The information on storing and caring for specific types of material in museum collections given on pages 68–80 (see also part 2, article 8) was furnished by the following museums, whose initials appear in or at the end of paragraphs containing information contributed by them:

A.I.	Art Institute of Chicago.
A.M.N.H.	American Museum of Natural History, New York
B.M. of S.	Buffalo Museum of Science
C.A. of S.	California Academy of Sciences, San Francisco
C.I. of S.	Cranbrook Institute of Science, Bloomfield Hills, Michigan
C.M.A.	Cleveland Museum of Art
C.M. of G.	Corning Museum of Glass, Corning, New York
C.N.H.M.	Chicago Natural History Museum
C.P.L.H.	California Palace of the Legion of Honor, San Francisco
C.U.M.	Cooper Union Museum for the Arts of Decoration, New York
F.H.	New York State Historical Association, Fenimore House, Cooperstown, New York
M.F.A.	Museum of Fine Arts, Boston
M.M.A.	Metropolitan Museum of Art, New York
M.MO.A.	Museum of Modern Art, New York
N.G.A.	National Gallery of Art, Washington, D. C.
N.J.H.S.	New Jersey Historical Society, Newark
N.M.	Newark Museum, Newark, New Jersey
O.A.M.	Oakland Art Museum, California
P.M.	Peabody Museum of Anthropology and Ethnology, Cambridge, Massachusetts
R.M.A.S.	Rochester Museum of Arts and Sciences, Rochester, New York
S.F.M.A.	San Francisco Museum of Art
T.M.	Textile Museum, Washington, D. C.
U.S.N.M.	United States National Museum, Smithsonian Institution, Washington, D. C.
U.M.	University Museum, University of Pennsylvania, Philadelphia

The relative humidity figures are those recommended by the late Murray Pease; they are necessarily arbitrary figures and need not be adhered to absolutely; but it is essential that fluctuation in relative humidity be reduced to a minimum, as fluctuation is the commonest cause of deterioration.

It should be remembered that there are objects which do not fall neatly into any one of the categories used; a leather belt ornamented with silver discs or a steel knife with ivory grip and painted wooden sheath will always be a problem. Then, too, considerations other than the purely physical enter into the planning of storage, as it is sometimes desirable to store together groups of quite different objects; for example, in an ethnological collection, everything from a particular tribe or village, or in a historical collection, everything associated with one person.

REQUIREMENTS AND METHODS

AMPHIBIANS: See Reptiles and amphibians.

ANATOMY: embalmed material is stored in concrete vats, monel metal tanks, or in glass jars, depending on the size of specimens, and is protected from light. Skeletons, depending on their size, are stored loose or in cardboard boxes in wooden drawers. (C.N.H.M.)

ARCHAEOLOGICAL SPECIMENS: large objects, including whole stone and pottery vessels, are stored on open shelving and in covered cartons on top of storage cases. Small objects (stone, bone, potsherds) are stored in trays, or in cardboard boxes that fit into trays, in a cabinet (see figure 29). Perishable objects (textiles, metals, jewelry) should be given the same care as other materials of the same fragility. See Ceramics, Glass, Metals, Stone, Textiles. (P.M., R.M.A.S., U.M., U.S.N.M.)

ARMS AND ARMOR: metal armor should be stored in a reasonably dry room; wooden accessories and shields in a moisture-controlled room (see Wood); and lacquered Japanese objects in a room with some humidity (see Lacquer). Metal pieces should be waxed (a neutral shoe polish is used by the Metropolitan Museum of Art). Oil is not advisable, as it is sticky, becomes gummy in time, and rubs off too easily. Cotton gloves should be worn when handling these pieces. Ideal storage methods for the various types of armor are: suits of armor in dead storage, in fibreboard cartons; suits of armor used frequently for exhibition, on their mannequins (custom built for each suit) covered with a plastic sheet; large parts of armor (helmets, breast plates, etc.), on open shelves, covered with plastic sheets; objects of great importance or fragility, in specially made plywood boxes with one plastic side to enable examination without handling; shields, in plastic bags, hung on the wall; banners, rolled, in tubes; polearms, standing in racks; swords, in cabinets provided with vertical panels of a large-meshed wire through which blades are passed so that all hilts are visible at a glance; delicate 18th-century court swords and Japanese mounted swords, in cabinets with shallow trays; long firearms, in specially constructed wooden cabinets, one to three pieces to a drawer (metal cabinets are apt not to be sturdy enough for these heavy pieces, nor are metal cabinets in special sizes likely to be available); objects less than 15 inches in length (pistols, daggers, elements and accessories of armor, etc.) in drawers in metal or wood cabinets; Japanese sword fittings, in cabinets with shallow drawers, individual spaces allocated for each piece. (M.M.A.)

BARK CLOTH AND BARK CONTAINERS: including birchbark and elmbark as well as the so-called tapa cloth of the Pacific Islands. A rather high relative humidity, about 55%, is best. Birch bark containers are stored on open shelves (P.M.). If possible, tapa cloth should be stored flat or rolled; large pieces which have been folded can be straightened by pressure in a very damp atmosphere (U.M.).

BASKETS: relative humidity should be at least as high as for wood, that is, about 55%. Baskets which have become brittle can be softened by exposure to a gentle rain, provided of course there is no surface decoration which water will damage (U.M.). They are stored in cartons or loose on open shelves or in cabinets, protected against dust, and may be stacked inside each other—in fact, for flexible baskets this is desirable. If ornamented with feathers or wool, they must be protected against moths. (P.M., U.M.)

BIRDS: mounted specimens are stored on shelves in cabinets with napthalene flakes or in a fumigation vault; nests and skins, in wooden trays or drawers in dust-proof cabinets which are fumigated periodically; skeletons, in boxes in room with fairly constant temperature to prevent cracking; eggs, in cotton-lined drawers or trays and in individual glass-covered boxes in dust-proof cabinets which are fumigated periodically. (B.M. of S., C.A. of S., C.N.H.M., N.M., R.M.A.S.)

BOTANICAL SPECIMENS: wood samples, dry seeds and fruits, fibers, gums, and resins are stored in glass containers of various sizes, in boxes, or in trays in drawers. Pickled specimens are kept in glass bottles. Herbarium specimens are stored flat in standard genus covers. Protection against insect pests is necessary. (B.M. of S., C.I of S., C.N.H.M.)

CERAMICS—SCULPTURE, TILES, VESSELS: both relative humidity and the degree of protection against dust depend on the degree of firing and on the type of surface. Poorly fired pieces and those with a fugitive paint surface should not be exposed to high relative humidity nor should they ever be washed; on the other hand, a Chinese porcelain vase cannot be hurt by a thorough washing; in between these two extremes, there is much ceramic ware which can be sponged quickly or held under running water for a few seconds with perfect safety (U.M.). Ceramics are stored on shelves or in drawers in cabinets, or on open shelves (see figure 35). In some museums they are stored in old exhibition cases. For some pieces, shelves covered with a resilient material may be desirable. Shelves should be narrow enough for objects to be readily accessible. (C.M.A., C.P.L.H., M.F.A., M.M.A., M.MO.A., N.J.H.S., U.M.)

CLOTHING: see Costumes.

COINS: a low relative humidity, under 40%, is desirable. They are stored in individual boxes or in small individual envelopes in a tray or shallow drawer or box. See Metals. (C.M.A., M.F.A., M.M.A., N.J.H.S.)

Figure 30.—Live study storage, an arrangement of racks with protective transparent covers based on the principle of a library, making every article readily available for study, Costume Institute, Metropolitan Museum of Art.

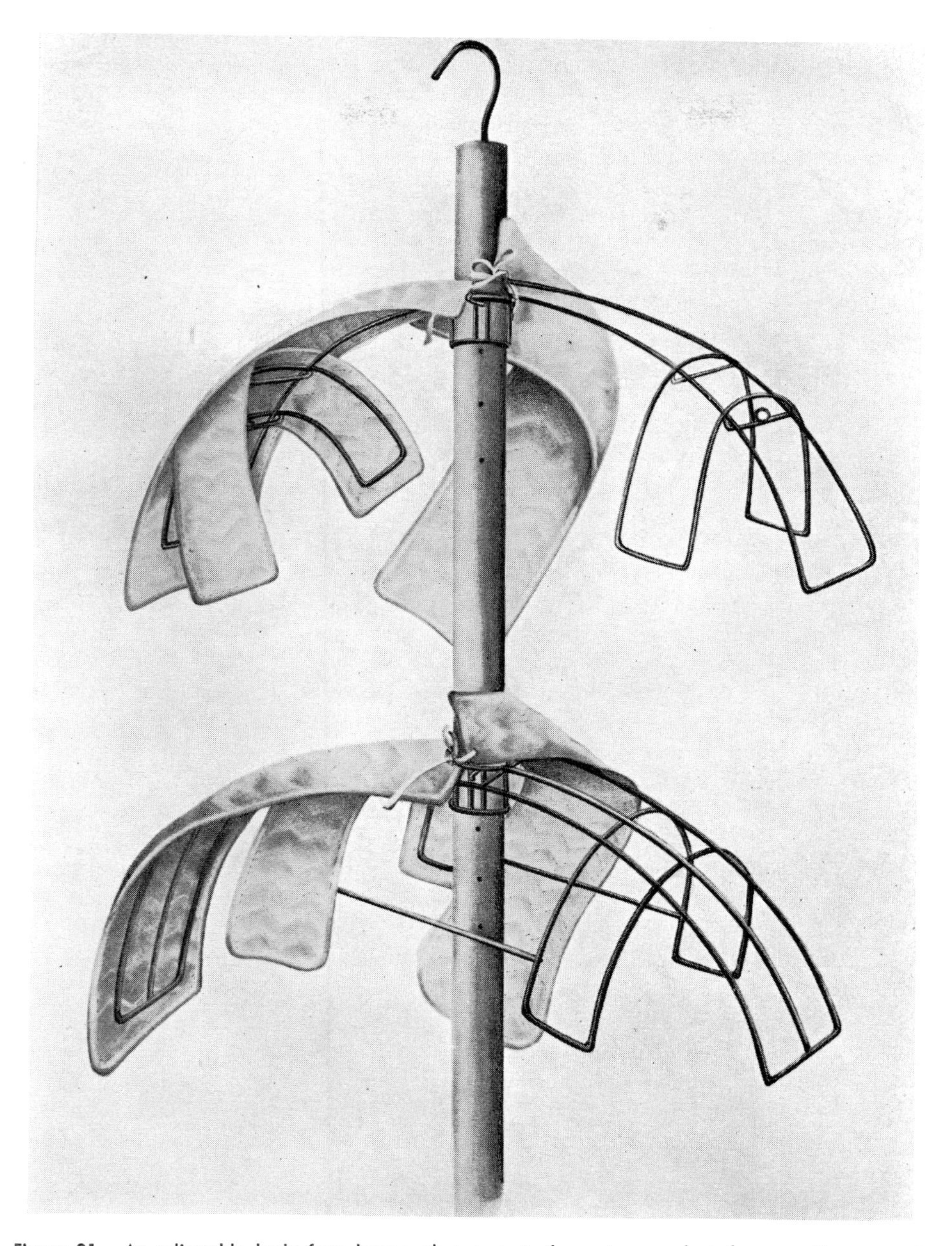

Figure 31.—An adjustable body form hanger that protects the costume and at the same time suggests the silhouette of the period, Costume Institute, Metropolitan Museum of Art.

COSTUMES: a cool, dry atmosphere is best; see Furs, Textiles. Filtered air is desirable and for some materials periodic mothproofing is essential. Light should be used only when the costumes are being worked on or studied. Storing costumes on padded hangers in transparent pliofilm bags is usually preferable to storing them in drawers or boxes. Accessories such as shoes, hats, and gloves, may be kept in cabinets nearby. Robes are sometimes rolled or stored flat in boxes or shallow drawers instead of being hung or folded. Garments with extremely heavy applied ornamentation on fragile material (whether originally so, or because of age) are stored flat or loosely folded; examples are the heavily beaded buckskin dress of the Plains Indian woman and some ecclesiastical vestments. The Costume Institute of the Metropolitan Museum of Art has a live storage system, based on library methods, for which was designed special storage equipment utilizing all the space from floor to ceiling (see figures 30 and 31). (M.M.A., M.MO.A., N.J.H.S., P.M., U.M.)

CRUSTACEANS: see Lower invertebrates.

DRAWINGS: see Paper.

EGGS: see Birds, Reptiles and amphibians.

EMBROIDERIES: see Textiles.

ENAMELS: stored on wooden shelves in closed cabinets; small pieces in padded drawers. Relative humidity should be less than 50%. (C.M.A., M.M.A.)

ETHNOLOGICAL SPECIMENS: nonperishable objects are kept on open shelves or hung on walls or wire screen. Perishable objects are stored in trays or drawers in moth-proof cabinets. Objects with an easily damaged surface should be kept in a dust-proof cabinet, or if that is impossible, should be wrapped in soft paper. For many ethnological specimens, protection against moths and other insect pests is essential. See Baskets, Ceramics, Costumes, Furs, Leather, Masks, Matting, Metal, Shields, Stone, Textiles, Weapons, Wood. (A.M.N.H., B.M. of S., C.I. of S., C.N.H.M., P.M., R.M.A.S., U.M., U.S.N.M.)

FANS: are stored in drawers in standardized storage cases (U.S.N.M.) or in specially designed cases of cloth-covered cardboard, with slots shaped to fit the fans and designed to fit into 16½ x 24½-inch storage boxes (C.U.M.)

FISHES: specimens preserved in alcohol are stored in drums, crocks, tanks, or glass jars depending on the size; skeletal material, in wooden or cardboard boxes in cabinets. All specimens are protected from light. (C.A. of S., C.N.H.M.)

FOSSILS: large fossils are placed on shelves or open racks; small fossils, in steel storage cans or in cardboard or wooden trays in drawers in dust-proof cabinets; tiny fossils, in gelatine capsules or glass vials; microscopic specimens, in cardboard slides with a central depression covered by a glass slide; thin sections are covered by glass cover-slips that protect the specimens. (A.M.N.H., B.M. of S., C.A. of S., C.N.H.M.)

FURNITURE: see Wood; furniture should be stored on platforms in ventilated rooms. It should be covered with muslin, plastic material, or heavy paper, and may require protection against moths. If covered with heavy paper, care should be taken in the fitting so as to avoid sharp creases which might scratch the surface. (C.M.A., C.P.L.H., M.M.A., M.MO.A., N.G.A., N.M.)

FURS: cold storage is best; see Costumes, Textiles. If cold storage is impossible, furs should be kept in a cool dry atmosphere and fumigated periodically. (U.M.)

GEOLOGICAL SPECIMENS: specimens preserved in alcohol are stored in hermetically sealed jars in cabinets; shells, rocks, and minerals, in trays or drawers in dust-proof cabinets or, if large, on open shelves. (B.M. of S., C.A., of S., C.I. of S., C.N.H.M., R.M.A.S.) Deliquescent minerals are coated with vinylseal diluted with acetone and stored in wooden drawers in dust-proof cabinets. Light-sensitive materials are boxed in black containers and stored in cabinets. (C.N.H.M.) See also Fossils.

Glass: a constant relative humidity of about 40% is best. Glass is stored on wooden or metal shelves, preferably felt-covered so as to be shock-proof and narrow enough for all pieces to be seen. The shelves should have sliding doors with screens or glass windows. Glass objects should not touch each other and should be protected from dust and moisture. (C.M. of G.) Closed cabinets, old exhibition cases, and open shelves are also used for storage. (C.P.L.H., M.F.A., N.M.)

Herbarium Specimens: see Botanical specimens.

Illuminations: see Paper.

Insects: dry pinned specimens are stored in cork-lined trays in glass-topped drawers in insect-proof cabinets; unmounted specimens, on sheets of cellucotton in covered, shallow, cardboard boxes in insect-proof cabinets. Low humidity is desidable; light should be excluded as far as possible, and there should be periodic fumigation. (A.M.N.H., B.M. of S., C.A. of S., C.N.H.M.) Depending on the size, specimens preserved in alcohol are stored in glass screw-cap jars or spring-top mason jars; homeopathic vials (with long-fibre cotton plugs) kept in spring-top mason jars with rubber ring gaskets; and in 9 x 33-mm. shell vials (with long-fire cotton stoppers) kept in larger homeopathic vials (C.N.H.M.). Specimens preserved on microscopic slides are stored in standard slide boxes or in cardboard trays on open shelves (C.A. of S.), and in "Lab-Aid" flat filing units with removable slide trays (C.N.H.M.).

Ivory: a rather high humidity, at least 55%, is best and it is important that it be constant. Old ivory is particularly susceptible to sudden changes in temperature. Ivories are protected from dirt with cloth covers and stand on open shelves or on padded shelves or trays in a cabinet. (C.M.A., M.M.A.)

Jewelry: a relative humidity of 40% is best for fine metal jewelry, as a high humidity fosters tarnish. It is stored in shallow drawers lined with tarnish-resistant cloth in tightly closed cabinets (C.M.A.). Decorative jewelry is mounted on silk- or velvet-lined trays which fit in drawers in cabinets (C.U.M.). Ornaments of shell, teeth, feathers, which constitute the jewelry of some areas, may be stored with costumes (U.M.).

Laces: the same rules should be followed as for textiles.

Lacquer: if dry and in good condition, lacquer should be kept in about 55% relative humidity. Fluctuation of heat or humidity is fatal, as is low humidity. Lacquer pieces should be wrapped in fine cloth (silk) and enclosed in soft wood (Japanese Paulownia for example) and then in a second outer container of hardwood. If lacquer is wet, and much ancient Chinese lacquer is, then a qualified technician should be consulted. Pending this, such objects are usually kept in water-tight containers with a dampened cotton lining. (C.M.A.)

Leather: a relative humidity of 55% with moderate light air and no draft is best (M.M.A.).

Lower Invertebrates: dried crustaceans are stored in individual trays in drawers in steel cabinets (paradichlorobenzene is kept in the cabinets and checked periodically); alcoholic crustaceans, in individual vials or jars on shelves in steel cabinets. (C.N.H.M.)

Mammals: mounted specimens are stored on shelves in cabinets with insect repellent or on open shelves in fumigation vaults; skins, hanging from racks or bars or in boxes or trays in cabinets; all should be fumigated periodically. Skeletons are stored in boxes or trays (temperature should be fairly constant to prevent cracking); large skulls, with antlers, are hung from metal racks or kept in boxes; small skulls are stored in vials or in trays with skins or in special skull boxes. Specimens preserved in alcohol are kept in jars on shelves or in cabinets. (A.M.N.H., B.M. of S., C.A. of S., C.N.H.M., N.M., R.M.A.S.)

MASKS: relative humidity and the degree of protection required against dust and insects depend on the material of which they are made. They are stored in cases on shelves, on wire racks, or hung on a heavy wire mesh screen by means of hooks inserted in screw eyes in the backs. (C.N.H.M., P.M., U.M.)

MATTING: the same high relative humidity as for baskets (about 55%) is best. Mats should be stored flat or loosely rolled, never folded. (U.M.)

METALS: BRONZE, COPPER, GOLD, IRON, SILVER, STEEL: a low relative humidity, below 40%, is best. Metals are stored on open shelves or in a closed cabinet with wooden trays or shelves; usually these should be padded to prevent scratching. It may sometimes be desirable to store objects in individual bags. Cabinets in which silver is kept should be lined with some tarnish-resistant cloth; camphor may be used for added protection against tarnishing. Archaeological bronzes should be checked periodically for bronze disease (though this is unlikely to occur in a dry atmosphere) and any affected pieces should be promptly removed and treated by an expert. (C.M.A., C.P.L.H., M.M.A., U.M.)

MINERALS: see Geological specimens.

MINIATURE PAINTINGS: See Paintings.

MOLLUSKS: see Shells.

MUSICAL INSTRUMENTS: the chief characteristic of musical instruments is that they are "live" objects—their vibrating strings, membranes and reeds, their bone plectra and ivory keys are all means of making sound. The storage of instruments must be considered accordingly. Many are composed of several different materials, e.g., wood, metal, and leather; and even instruments of one material, such as wood, may have several varieties, each with individual reactions and problems of care. Thus the basic requirement for storage is that all instruments be kept in an area with controlled humidity and temperature; sharp or sudden changes in either can cause opposite and destructive effects in a single instrument. Instruments constructed of plant fibers (e.g., bamboo) and instruments that have been lacquered or varnished, require a fairly high humidity; keyboard instruments, a moderate humidity; brasses, less susceptible to changes, a dryer air. Instruments can be stored on wooden shelves by kind and size; wood is preferable to metal because it will not buckle with weight and will not scratch. Small instruments, e.g., pottery whistles, clappers, bells, etc., can be stored in partitioned wood boxes or narrow drawers. Accessories are stored with the instruments to which they belong; if there are additional collections, such as mouthpieces, bows, reeds, they can be stored in the same manner as the small instruments. Lacquered and varnished instruments should be wrapped for protection. The problem of dead storage does not arise with musical instruments because they require continuous care to keep them "alive" and so must be within reach. (M.M.A.)

PAINTINGS: a constant relative humidity of about 55% should be maintained and there should be moderate air circulation and light. Paintings are stored in wooden and metal bins, with separation sheets of corrugated cardboard between them, and on fixed or sliding screens (see figure 32). The sliding screen method is preferred: screens of heavy diagonal mesh are supported by overhead tracks; paintings are hung on both sides of the screens with S-hooks of a size to fit the regular installation screw eyes on the frames; care should be taken to use screw eyes that do not penetrate through the frame. Protective coverings of plywood, cardboard, or fibreboard should be attached to the backs of stretchers (see figure 55 in part 2, article 12). Stacking should be avoided if possible; however, if paintings must be stacked, they should be separated by sheets of corrugated cardboard and should rest on pads; composition or fibreboard separation sheets are satisfactory but corrugated cardboard, though not permanent, is best, as it gives under pressure. It is better not to use covering pads and blankets as they become dirty and can do considerable damage if allowed to come into contact with the painted surface. Miniature paintings may be stored in shallow drawers in closed cabinets. See also Panel paintings, Scroll paintings. (A.I., C.M.A., C.P.L.H., F.H., M.F.A., M.M.A., M.MO.A., N.G.A., N.M., O.A.M., S.F.M.A.)

PANEL PAINTINGS: as with all complex pieces of which wood is one of the elements, a constant relative humidity of about 55% is absolutely essential; circulation of air is desirable to provide uniform conditions in the storage area, but direct drafts should be avoided. The surface must be protected against dust and against scuffing. (M.M.A.)

PAPER—DRAWINGS, ILLUMINATIONS, WATER COLORS, PRINTS, PHOTOGRAPHS, ETC.: a constant relative humidity of not more than 50% must be maintained for the preservation of paper objects. They should not be exposed to direct light, should be completely sealed against dust, and are best stored on wooden shelves. Since paper with woodpulp or chemical content is dangerous, only rag-stock paper or mat board should be used in direct contact with such objects. Unframed works of art such as drawings, water colors, and prints should be covered with glassine paper or Japanese mending tissue and placed in hinged mats with window fronts. They are hinged to the mats with Japan paper and a small amount of library

Figure 32.—Painting storeroom with bins and sliding screens, Museum of Modern Art.

paste along one edge only. Two or three standard-size mats should be used and storage boxes (usually solander boxes) made to fit these sizes so the material will not shift around in the box and cause damage by abrasion. Oversize material may be stored in portfolios. Cabinets with shelves designed to accommodate the standard-size solander boxes and portfolios are usually used for storage. Shelves that pull out facilitate the handling of the boxes; in particular, a pull-out shelf on which to rest one box at a time as it is taken out is very helpful. Framed watercolors, drawings, prints, etc., are stored in bins or on screens. (A.I., C.M.A., M.F.A., M.M.A., M.MO.A., N.G.A., N.M., U.M.) A thymol chamber is used for fumigation to prevent fungus growth and foxing stains (A.I.). Photographs are protected with glassine paper or Japanese mending tissue and stored in solander boxes and portfolios. They are dry mounted on the mat board. Handling mats (folders of lighter weight rag content) are useful in protecting valuable material. (M.MO.A.)

PAPYRUS (INSCRIBED): a very slightly higher relative humidity than for paper is desirable. Papyrus documents should be stored flat or mounted between glass. (M.M.A.)

PARCHMENT: see Leather; a slightly lower relative humidity is desirable (M.M.A.).

PHOTOGRAPHS: see Paper.

PLASTER OBJECTS: relative humidity should be less than 50%. They are protected with dust covers and stored on wooden shelves. (M.M.A.)

PORCELAIN: see Ceramics.

POTSHERDS: see Archaeological specimens.

POTTERY: see Ceramics and Archaeological specimens.

PRINTS: see Paper.

RAWHIDE: same as Leather.

REPTILES AND AMPHIBIANS: hard-shell eggs are stored in cardboard trays in moth-proof cabinets; skins, on wooden stacks in a closed, ventilated, dark room with air vent to roof; and skeletal specimens are stored in wooden boxes (C.A. of S.). Skulls are stored unboxed on shelves and specimens preserved in alcohol are stored in tanks or jars, depending on the size, in an open room but protected from light (C.N.H.M.).

ROCKS: see Geological specimens.

RUGS: when exhibited, rugs are almost always hung, and they may also be hung

Figure 33.—Rug storage racks. Catalog numbers are visible, making any rug easy to find. The Textile Museum, Washington, D. C.

(unrolled) when in storage, but it should be remembered that they need a periodic rest period. They should not be folded but may be rolled and wrapped, using moth crystals. A satisfactory method is to roll against the pile with the right side inward on poles, 3 inches or more in diameter, of thoroughly seasoned wood so that there is no danger of sap leakage. The pole should extend beyond the rug on each side and the pole itself should be suspended at its ends. Rolls should not be stacked on shelves, as this exerts undesirable pressures on the lower ones. However, a roll more than 12 feet long will sag in the middle if suspended, and so must be laid on a shelf, but its position should be changed periodically (see figure 33). A relative humidity of 40% is best, and periodic fumigation is required. There should be facilities for examination in the rug storage area. (A.I., M.M.A., M.MO.A., N.G.A., T.M.)

If at all possible, rugs and tapestries should be kept in cold storage. The following method of storing rugs and tapestries is that employed in the cold-storage room of a well-known storage and warehouse company in New York City:

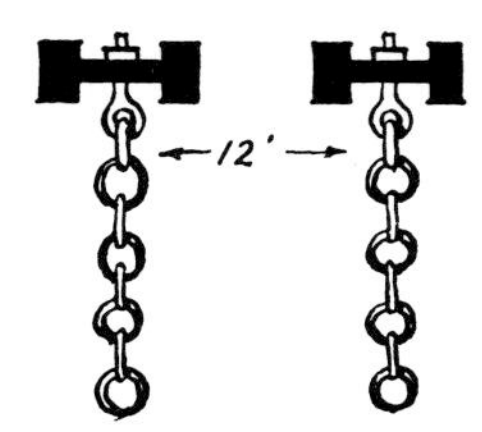

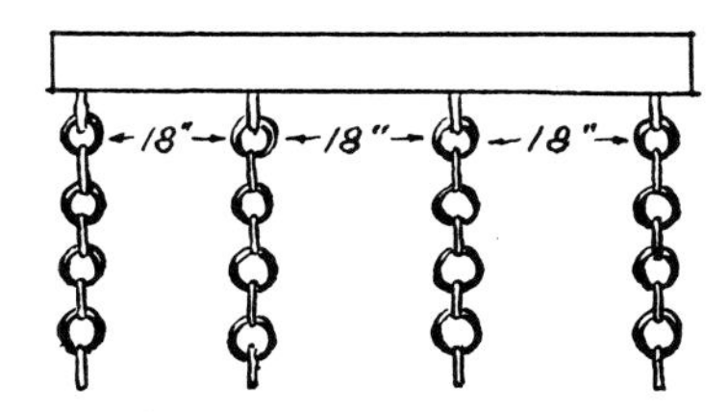

Figure 34.—System of beams, chains and hooks for storing rugs.

Cold dry air is blown through the storage area from a cooling unit located just outside the area. The room is kept at a fairly constant temperature of 35°F. A series of heavy steel chains is suspended by eyebolts from overhead steel beams (see figure 34). The beams are placed parallel in pairs on 12-foot centers. The chains are spaced 18 inches, center to center, along the beams. The tapestries or rugs are rolled on strong, well-seasoned wooden poles, approximately 12½ feet in length and 2½ or 3 inches in diameter. They are then hung on the chains by means of special steel hooks. This allows the free circulation of cold air around each tapestry or rug. If more than one pair of beams is installed, sufficient aisle and work space should be provided along each side of the chains. The same method can be followed, if so desired, for smaller rugs by decreasing the spacing between the overhead beams. It is not advisable to use poles with a greater span than 12½ feet, as the weight may cause the poles to sag or break. Metal poles or pipes should not be used because of the danger of staining. Larger rugs and very small rugs are rolled on poles and placed on shallow shelving around the perimeter of the room. These rugs are placed alongside one another, never stacked and are turned fairly frequently. A system using geared chain hoists was found impractical, as the constant weight strain caused the chains to jam in the gears. Another deciding factor against this system was the additional space required and the high cost of installation.

Screens (Oriental): because of their complicated construction, screens require a higher relative humidity than other paper products; 55% is best. They may be stored as they are in Japan: folded and wrapped separately in cloth covers and placed, usually in pairs, inside wooden storage boxes with removable covers, or in cabinets with padded grooves at the top and bottom to hold them in place. See Paper. (C.M.A., M.F.A., M.M.A.)

Scroll Paintings: in general, the same rules apply to scrolls as to paper items, but the relative humidity should be slightly higher; about 55% is best. They are wrapped in cloth, and stored in individual boxes or tagged with accession numbers and kept in drawers or on shelves. (C.M.A., M.F.A., M.M.A.)

Sculpture: see Metals, Stone, Wood, Plaster objects, Ceramics. Small pieces are stored on open shelves, in bins or in cabinets; large heavy pieces, on platforms with the weight evenly distributed and the object held in place with wedges (see figure 35). Small terra cotta and bronze reliefs may be hung on sliding screens. (A.I., C.M.A., C.P.L.H., M.MO.A., N.G.A., N.M.)

Shells: are stored in trays or drawers in dust-proof cabinets. (B.M. of S., C.A. of S., C.I. of S., C.N.H.M., R.M.A.S.)

Shields: are stored flat on shelves, or hung on walls or on heavy wire mesh screens. If carved or painted, care should be taken to protect the surface; if of skin with the hair on, or if decorated with feathers, they should be protected against insect pests. Metal shields should be given the same care as other metals. (U.M.) See also Arms and armor.

Silver: see Metals.

Skeletons: see Anatomy, Birds, Fishes, Mammals, Reptiles and amphibians.

Statues, Stelae, etc.: see Sculpture.

Figure 35.—Shelves for storing sculpture and small objects, Cleveland Museum of Art.

STONE: for archaeological specimens which may contain salts, and for ancient soft stones generally, like limestone, in which dampness can produce serious de--terioration, the relative humidity should be kept below 50%. For harder stones in good condition relative humidity is not particularly important, but should remain constant. See also Archaeological specimens, Sculpture. (M.M.A., U.M.)

TAPESTRIES: relative humidity of 40% is best. Tapestries are hung, or rolled, folded, or, if small, stored flat. If they are folded the first folds should be parallel to the warp threads, so that when they are later hung these folds will be horizontal and the weight of the tapestry will take them out in a few days; vertical folds will never come out through hanging. Rolled tapestries may be hung or stored on shelves as described and illustrated under Rugs. Small pieces should be stored flat in boxes. Facilities for examination should be installed in the storeroom, and may consist of a bar, long enough to accommodate the widest piece, suspended from the ceiling on pulleys. (A.I., C.P.L.H., M.F.A., M.M.A., N.G.A.)

TERRA COTTA: see Sculpture and Ceramics.

TEXTILES: relative humidity of 40% is best. Textiles should be stored in ventilated rooms and protected from light when not being used, and against insects and dirt (paradichlorobenzene crystals will protect against mildew and mold as well as against insects; blue tissue paper will help to prevent the discoloration of lace and linen). Some textiles are mounted and framed under glass (B.M. of S.) and may be stored in bins or hung on screens or walls. Others are mounted on uniform stretchers which fit in study-room cases where they are placed horizontally (M.F.A.) or mounted between pieces of glass or plastic and stored in shallow drawers (C.U.M.). Unmounted textiles are stored flat whenever possible but may be lightly folded with tissue or rolled on drums or cardboard tubes with tissue or soft plastic material. They may also be hung. Rolling is preferred to folding in some museums. Since folding can endanger the thread structure, it must be done with great care and the textiles refolded periodically with the folds in different places but parallel to the warp threads (C.M.A.). The rolling of textiles must also be done with care since a crease rolled in would cause more damage than a fold (M.F.A.). Unmounted textiles are kept in boxes, drawers, and trays in dustproof cabinets, or in dustproof boxes or packages on open shelves. (Tar-lined paper should never be used in wrapping textiles as high temperature and paradichlorobenzene vapor will melt or dissolve the tar and cause serious damage to fabrics. Kraft-type paper over tissue will serve as dust protection.) (A.I., B.M. of S., C.M.A., C.N.H.M., C.P.L.H., C.U.M., M.MO.A., M.M.A., M.F.A., N.M., P.M., T.M.) Among the types of containers used by museums for storage are trunks for quilts and coverlets and steel lockers fitted with boxes for other textiles (A.I.); solander boxes made to fit storage shelves, cabinets for small textiles, and deep sliding shelves and drawers for larger pieces (M.M.A.); metal blanket chests (M.MO.A.); and metal architectural drawing cabinets (T.M.). See also Costumes.

VESSELS—BOWLS, BOXES, CUPS, ETC.: the type of storage depends on the material. Those with a carved surface should be treated as small sculptures. (U.M.)

WATER COLORS: see Paper.

WEAPONS WITH LONG SHAFTS—ARROWS, HARPOONS, LANCES, SPEARS, ETC.: may be hung vertically, head end up, on a heavy wire mesh screen, by attaching a hook to wire wrapped around the shaft behind the head. If this vertical storage is impractical, they may be stored flat on shelves, preferably in bundles. *Bows* should be unstrung and stored flat or on special holders. (U.M.) See also Arms and armor.

WOOD: a constant relative humidity about 55% is best for all wooden objects; for composite pieces of which one or more elements are wood (furniture or painted panels, for example), it is absolutely essential. Circulation of air is desirable to provide uniform conditions in storage areas, but direct drafts on wooden objects should be avoided. All fine wooden pieces should be protected against dust; this is particularly important for painted pieces which should be provided with dust covers or wrapped in soft paper. Spraying with a fixative will set the chalky paint used on many ethnological specimens, particularly Melanesian (U.M.). Uncoated wood may be left untouched or treated with oil, depending on the nature of the object. Varnished surfaces can be polished with commercial wax polishes. Dry, cracked wood can sometimes be restored by immersion in warm beeswax, but this should be undertaken only by an expert (M.M.A., P.M.). See Furniture.

ZOOLOGICAL SPECIMENS: see Anatomy, Birds, Fishes, Insects, Lower invertebrates, Mammals, etc.

References:

AMDUR, ELIAS J. Humidity control—isolated area plan, Museum News, Vol. 43, no. 4, December, 1964. Technical Supplement, no. 6, Part II, pp. 58–60.

BACK, E. A. Carpet beetles and their control. U. S. Dept. of Agriculture Farmers' Bull. 1346, Washington, D. C., Government Printing Office, 1923.

———. Clothes moths and their control. U. S. Dept. of Agriculture Farmers' Bull. Washington, D. C., Government Printing Office, 1923.

———. The silverfish as a pest of the household. U. S. Dept. of Agriculture Farmers' Bull., Washington, D. C., Government Printing Office, 1931.

BARTLETT, JOHN. Storage and study collections—museums, Museums Journal, Vol. 63, nos. 1 and 2, June—September 1963, pp. 62–63.(2) (Discusses value of study-storage.)

BORHEGYI, STEPHAN F. DE. Organization of archaeological museum storerooms, Museum, Vol. V, no 4, 1952, pp. 251–260.

BUCK, RICHARD D. A specification for museum airconditioning, Museum News, Vol. 43, no. 4, December, 1964. Technical Supplement, no. 6, Part I, pp. 53–57.

BUECHNER, THOMAS S. The open study-storage gallery, Museum News, Vol. 40, no. 9, May, 1962, pp. 34–37.

BURNS, NED J. Field manual for museums. U. S. Dept. of the Interior, National Park Service, Washington, D. C., Government Printing Office, 1941.

COLBERT, EDWIN H. Inexpensive racks for the storage of large specimens, Curator, Vol. IV, no. 4, October 1961, pp. 368–370.(1) (Discusses and illustrates use of perforated structural steel racks at the American Museum of Natural History, New York.)

COLEMAN, LAURENCE V. Manual for small museums. New York, G. P. Putnam's Sons, 1927.

———. Museum buildings. Washington, D. C., The American Association of Museums, 1950.

Conservation Department, The Textile Museum, Washington, D. C. Principles of practical cleaning for old and fragile textiles. Museum News, Vol. 43, no. 6, February, 1965. Technical Supplement, no. 6, Part II, pp. 50–52. (Reprint of

The Textile Museum Workshop Notes Number 14, issued in 1956, with additions by Joseph V. Columbus.)

DAIFUKU, HIROSHI (see below UNESCO Museums and Monuments IX).

FALL, FRIEDA KAY. Art objects: their care and preservation, Washington, D. C., Museum Publications, 1967.

———. Enamelled objects, Museum News, Vol. 45, no. 10, June, 1967. Technical Supplement, pp. 47–50. (A chapter from the book, *Art Objects: Their Care and Preservation.*)

———. General rules for handling art museum objects, Museum News, Vol. 43, no. 1, September, 1964, pp. 33–39.

FELLER, ROBERT L. The deteriorating effect of light on museum objects—principles of photochemistry, the effect on varnishes and paint vehicles and on paper, Museum News, Vol. 42, no. 10, June, 1964. Technical Supplement, no. 3, pp. i–viii.

GESKE, NORMAN. The new art gallery of the University of Nebraska, Lincoln, Museum, Vol. XVII, no. 3, 1964, pp. 127–135.[3] (Showing packing, shipping and storage areas.)

GRAHAM, JOHN M. II. Solving storage problems, Museum News, Vol. 41, no. 4, December, 1962, pp. 24–29.

GREATHOUSE, GLENN A. and WESSEL, CARL J. editors. Deterioration of materials, causes and preventive techniques. New York, Reinhold Publishing Corporation, 1954.

HARVEY, VIRGINIA I. Space and textiles, Museum News, Vol. 42, no. 3, November, 1963, pp. 28–33. (Discusses solutions to problems of display and storage in the textile study center at the University of Washington, Seattle. Illustrates display case, storage cabinets and "finder's file.")

KECK, CAROLINE K. A handbook on the care of paintings for historical agencies and small museums. Nashville, Tennessee, American Association for State and Local History, 1966.

———. How to take care of your pictures. New York, The Museum of Modern Art and The Brooklyn Museum, 1954.

———, HUNTINGTON T. BLOCK, JOSEPH CHAPMAN, JOHN B. LAWTON, DR. NATHAN STOLOW. A primer on museum security. Cooperstown, New York Historical Association, 1966. (Museum security viewed as a combination of physical security, insurance, environmental security, light and its effect, and other security factors.)

KECK, SHELDON. First aid for art, Museum News, Vol. 43, no. 1, September, 1964, pp. 13–17. (Discusses the nation's first conservation center and its importance for the museums of America.)

LANGAARD, JOHAN H. The Munch Museum, Oslo, Museum, Vol. XVII, no. 1, 1964, pp. 2–9.[3] (Showing storeroom for prints, drawings and paintings.)

LANIER, MILDRED B. Storage facilities at Colonial Williamsburg, Museum News, Vol. 45, no. 6, February, 1967, pp. 31–33.

LUCAS, ALFRED. Antiques, their restoration and preservation. London, E. Arnold & Co., 1932.

LUNDBERGH, HOLGER. Stockholm's new Museum of Modern Art, Museum News, Vol. 37, no. 4, June, 1959. pp. 16–18. (Shows new galleries and wire screens for study storage.)

Myers, George Hewitt. Rugs: preservation, display and storage, Museum News, Vol. 43, no. 6, February, 1965. Technical Supplement, no. 6, Part I, pp. 45–49. (Reprint of the Textile Museum (Washington, D. C.) *Workshop Notes* Number 5, first issued in 1952, with additions by Joseph V. Columbus.)

Oliver, L. L. Storage cases, December 15, 1946, The Museum News, Vol. 23, p. 7.

Plenderleith, H. J. The conservation of prints, drawings and manuscripts. London, Oxford University Press, 1937.

———. The preservation of antiquities. London, The Museums Association, 1934.

———. The conservation of antiquities and works of art. London, Oxford University Press, 1956.

Reid, Norman. Storage and study collections—art galleries, Museums Journal, Vol. 63, nos. 1 and 2, June—September 1963, pp. 64–69.(2) (Discusses temperature, relative humidity, accessibility, good lighting, security. Illustrations showing painting storage in Palazzo Bianco, Genoa and in National Gallery and Capodimonte Museum, Naples.)

Reynolds, Barrie. Some ideas on the storage of ethnographic material, Museums Journal, Vol. 62, no. 2, September 1962, pp. 102–109.(2) (Good illustrations.)

Stout, George L. The care of pictures. New York, Columbia University Press, 1948.

Sugden, Robert P. Care and handling of art objects. New York, The Metropolitan Museum of Art, 1946. (Contains general rules for handling paintings; large objects including sculpture and furniture; small objects including ceramics, enamels, glass, jewelry, etc.; textiles including tapestries, rugs, costumes; works on paper including drawings, watercolors, prints, miniatures, etc.

———. Safeguarding works of art—storage, packing, transportation, and insurance. New York, The Metropolitan Museum of Art, 1948.

Thomson, G. Impermanence: Some chemical and physical aspects, Museums Journal, Vol. 64, no. 1, June, 1964. pp. 16–36.(2) (An article on the chemical and physical conditions inside museums in relation to the conservation of collections. Explains the various accidents caused by variations in heat and moisture.

UNESCO Museum and Monuments IX. The organization of museums: practical advice. Paris, UNESCO, 1960. (Contains "Collections: Their Care and Storage" by Hiroshi Daifuku.)

Volsøe, H. The new Zoological Museum of Copenhagen, Museum, Vol. XVII, no. 3, 1964, pp. 154–155.(3) (Shows storeroom of preserved specimen collection kept in wooden trays on specially constructed steel shelves.) (Storerooms are also described in Vol. XVII, no. 1, pp. 33–35.)

Werner, A. E. The care of glass in museums, Museum News, Vol. 44, no. 10, June, 1966. Technical Supplement, no. 13, pp. 45–49.

Yadon, Vernal L. A portable fumigation chamber for the small museum, Museum News, Vol. 44, no. 5, January, 1966.

Zigrosser, Carl and Christa M. Gaehde. A guide to the collecting and care of original prints, sponsored by The Print Council of America. New York, Crown Publishers, Inc., 1966. (Contains a chapter on the conservation of fine prints.)

Note: For further references see Selected Reference Guide to Historic Preservation, edited and compiled by Frederick L. Rath, Jr. and Merrilyn Rogers respectively, Cooperstown, New York State Historical Association.

(1) Quarterly publication of the American Museum of Natural History, New York.

(2) Quarterly publication of the Museums Association in England, London.

(3) Quarterly review published by UNESCO, Paris.

Chapter 6

LOANS FROM MUSEUM COLLECTIONS

AUTHORIZATION

Loans from the collections of a museum must be authorized by a responsible person. This person varies from museum to museum, depending on the size, staff, type of collections, and value of the individual loans. It is the practice of many museums, large and small, to have all loans approved by the Board of Trustees. Some museums refer only very important long-term, or very valuable, loans from the collections to the Board of Trustees for approval, leaving less important loans to be approved at the discretion of the director. In other museums the director is responsible for approving all loans, and in museums with varied collections, the curator of each department or collection may be responsible for approving a loan from the material in his care.

Before a loan is approved by the director or curator or referred by the director to the trustees for approval, it must be checked for any detail which would prevent its being lent. The records of the curator and the registrar should note whether there is any previous commitment for the object for the dates requested; whether it is in good enough condition to travel; whether there is any stipulation from the donor, if a gift, stating that it is not to be lent; or whether it has been imported under bond and requires permission from U. S. Customs before it can be removed from the museum (see Chapter 8, for explanation of importations under exhibition bond).

The following procedure is suggested for handling outgoing loans after they have been approved by the director, curator, or Board of Trustees. It has proved satisfactory in several museums where the movement of museum objects is handled by the registrar and can, of course, be modified to suit the requirements of each museum.

NOTICE TO REGISTRAR

When a loan has been approved, the registrar should be authorized to release it, and should be given the following information: the name and address of the borrower, the purpose for which it is being borrowed, the period of the loan (the exhibition title and dates, if for an exhibition), the date it should arrive at destination or the date it is to be shipped. He should also be advised of any special packing, shipping, or insurance arrangements. A convenient way of notifying the registrar of outgoing loans is for the director or curator to send him the original or a copy of the initial request and a copy of the reply to the borrower. If the in-

THE ART INSTITUTE OF CHICAGO

LOAN REQUEST

To the MUSEUM REGISTRAR:

The following items have been approved for loan by the Committee on Painting and Sculpture

__________ (meeting) __________ (by telephone)

Accession No.	ITEM	Insurance

Please prepare Shipping Order for loan

To:__________

Name of correspondent responsible for loan:__________

Exhibition:__________

Dates:__________

Date requested for receipt of shipment:__________

Date of shipment:__________ Via: Freight ____ Express ____ Air ____ Truck ____

Express value:__________

Bill to:__________

Copies to: Prepaid ____ Collect ____

____
Curator

Please return Shipping Order promptly to Registrar after signature

Figure 36.—Form authorizing registrar to release out-going loan from permanent collection (size 8½ x 11).

formation needed by the registrar is not available at the time of the first correspondence, it should be brought to his attention as soon as received. The originals or copies of subsequent correspondence concerning the loan should also be sent to the registrar so that he is aware of the status of the loan and of any changes made in the arrangements. The registrar may of course be notified by memorandum or by a form (see figure 36) giving him the information he needs, instead of by copies of correspondence.

The registrar is often responsible for reserving all loans. A convenient way of doing this is by the use of colored flags on the cards. If there should be a group offered from which the borrower is to select, all items should be reserved until the final selection is made.

PACKING, INSURANCE, AND TRANSPORTATION

The lending museum is responsible for preparing the shipment of loans in packing considered to be safe and adequate. If the loan involves a particularly fragile item, the lender should not only pack it accordingly but provide the borrower with special packing instructions for its return. The lending museum may, according to its facilities, request the borrower to engage a commercial packer, experienced in the handling of fragile objects and fine arts, to collect, pack, and ship the loan. The packer must be notified also, of any special packing instructions, value declarations, and the method of shipment. When the loan is returned, the borrower is responsible for packing the object or objects in exactly the same way as received and with the same cases, packages, pads, and other furnishings when possible, unless a change is specifically authorized by the lending institution.

Insurance coverage for loans from museum collections may be placed by the borrowing institution in accordance with the instructions of the lender, or the lending museum may prefer to maintain its own insurance and bill the borrower for the premium from the time the objects to be lent are removed from their normal places of exhibition or storage until they are returned in satisfactory condition.

The lending museum is responsible for determining the valuation of the objects to be lent and also whether a valuation is to be declared to the carrying agency.

Since standard fine-arts policies do not provide coverage for insured material outside the continental United States and Canada, and on Fair Grounds, it should be agreed in advance whether the borrower or lender is to be responsible for providing proper coverage.

The selection of the type of transportation depends on such factors as distance, size, weight, and cost, as well as the type of material to be shipped. If the loan is packed in the building, a work or production order or memorandum should be sent to the superintendent as far in advance as possible. It should state when the work is to be done and, if the superintendent does not have the responsibility for storing boxes, whether boxes are available for the loan or whether they will have to be made; it should also include any special packing instructions. If the building superintendent handles the moving of objects within the building, he should be informed at this time of the location of the reserved loans so that they can be removed from storage or exhibition to be packed. The registrar himself often gives the order to the shipping room and personally oversees the packing and shipping. (See Chapters 7 and 9 for discussion of packing, shipping and insurance.)

RELEASING MATERIAL AFTER AUTHORIZATION

A printed release form is used in many institutions for outgoing material. This form is signed by the registrar and gives the name and address of the borrower, the exhibition title and dates, and the carrier, as well as a list of the objects and the date when the loan is to be shipped. It should be sent to the shipping room well in advance of the time the loan is to be shipped or collected, and if the custodian of the shipping room handles the moving of objects within the building, it can also serve as a notification to him to remove them from exhibition or storage. (A combined release, receipt and pass form for outgoing material is illustrated in Chapter 2, figure 11.) Before the loan is released, the condition of each object is checked by the registrar with the condition as recorded in his file and with a condition photograph if one has been made, and any changes are noted. Sometimes paintings which are glazed have the glass removed and plexiglass substituted for traveling. Sometimes, also, simpler frames are provided for traveling. The braces and backings of paintings should be checked at this time and improvements made, if necessary.

RECEIPTS FROM BORROWERS

To assure notification of the arrival and provide for a signed acknowledgment of the loan, it is a wise policy for the lending museum to send a receipt to the borrower (see figure 37). Two copies of such a receipt are usually sent on the same date that the loan is shipped. One copy is returned with signature and date when the loan is received, and the other is retained by the borrower. Receipts for loans from museum collections should include the following information: name and address of borrower, title, and dates of the exhibition or purpose for which the loan is being made; and the accession number, description, and value for each item lent. The receipt should also list the conditions under which the loan is borrowed from the lending institution.

RETURNED LOANS

When a loan is returned to the lending museum, the director or curator should be notified immediately of its return, and it should be checked immediately for any change in condition or damage. Minor changes not requiring attention are often merely noted in the condition record, but more serious changes or damages should be brought to the attention of

RECEIPT

THE METROPOLITAN MUSEUM OF ART

NEW YORK

The following objects from the Museum collections are delivered to ______________

____

for the purpose of ______________

Authorized by:

______________ Registrar

Approved ______________ Director

NO.	OBJECTS	VALUE

THE METROPOLITAN MUSEUM OF ART

CONDITIONS GOVERNING LOAN OF OBJECTS

1. It is understood that objects covered by this receipt shall remain in the condition in which they are received. They shall not be cleaned, repaired, retouched or altered in any way whatever except with written permission of The Metropolitan Museum of Art.

2. Damages, whether in transit or on the borrower's premises and regardless of who may be responsible therefor, shall be reported to The Metropolitan Museum of Art immediately.

3. The borrower may photograph the objects covered by this receipt only for record and publicity purposes, and for reproduction in an exhibition catalogue. Paintings and drawings must not be removed from their frames for photography. If desired, the Museum will supply photographs of pictures without frames upon request.

4. Borrowers may not reproduce such objects in any media (including photographs) for purposes of sale, nor may such objects be subjected to technical examination of any type whatever without written permission of this Museum.

5. Loans made to other institutions by The Metropolitan Museum of Art for periods of six months or more are subject to the condition that should The Metropolitan Museum of Art desire to recall any object for its own purposes, it may do so on thirty days' notice to the borrower. The Museum, if requested, will exert its best efforts to substitute for any object so recalled another similar object at its expense.

Receipt of the objects summarized above and described in the attached listings, all in good condition, is hereby acknowledged, and the conditions appearing on the reverse side of this receipt are hereby accepted.

Date ______________

______________ Official signature

DO NOT DETACH LOAN LISTINGS FROM ORIGINAL RECEIPT

Figure 37.—Receipt sent to borrower, showing conditions, printed on back, governing loan from museum collections (size 8½ x 11).

the curator or director, who makes the decisions as to repair and whether there should be an insurance claim. The date returned should be noted on the loan receipt and on the registration card recording location or history. Insurance should be reinstated if it was canceled at the beginning of the loan. The objects themselves should be returned to exhibition galleries or to storage.

BILLS TO BORROWERS

Although in many institutions billing the borrower for the charges involved in the loan is handled by the business office, this may be a responsibility of the registrar. Packing charges can be based on an exact record of the hours worked and the amount of materials used, or on a system of flat rates to cover different size boxes and for special packing jobs. Commercial packers very often bill the borrower directly. If the lending institution maintains its own insurance, the charges to the borrowing institution can be figured on the basis of the rate of the policy. Billing for transportation charges can often be avoided by having the loans shipped "collect" and returned "prepaid." However, if this is not possible, the charges for transportation can be added to the bill for packing and insurance.

References:

HATT, ROBERT T., and others. Standard procedure for inter-museum loans, The Museum News, Vol. 27, March 15, 1950, pp. 7–8.

LENDING MUSEUM MATERIALS. Midwest Museums Quarterly, October, 1956.

SHAPIRO, HARRY L. Borrowing and lending, Curator, Vol. III, no. 3, July, 1960, pp. 197–204.

Chapter 7

PACKING AND SHIPPING

The safety of museum collections must be the first consideration in preparing them for shipment and selecting a method of transportation. The type of material involved, its fragility, size, weight, and value, the time it is needed at its destination, the climate or climates to which it is to travel, and the cost, must all be considered in determining how it is to be packed and shipped. The registrar and other staff members concerned with the packing and shipping of collections must know about safepacking techniques and the services offered by various carriers and their packing specifications. They should understand thoroughly the conditions under which carriers accept shipments as well as the rates charged for their services, and they should realize that receipts, bills of lading, airbills and air waybills are contracts between shippers and carriers as well as receipts for the material accepted for shipment. It is, therefore, important that shipments not only be packed in accordance with museum standards of safety, but also that they be properly packed, marked, and addressed so that the contracts of carriers for safe transportation will not be nullified.

Before arrangements are made for packing and shipping curators or conservators should determine that the objects to be transported are inherently sound; and the registrar must see to it that protective materials such as frames, mounts, backing boards etc. are strong and secure. Nothing should be subjected to the strain of travel until these conditions have been met. (See part 2, figures 55-56 and articles 12 and 13 for a discussion of some of the precautions taken to protect art objects during handling and transportation.)

PACKING

Three basic rules should be followed in packing museum objects: provide a strong, closed waterproof container; protect the objects within the container against movement, vibration and shock; plan the packing with unpacking and repacking in mind, making it as uncomplicated as possible. Methods of protecting objects within the container vary for each class of material and should be approved by museum personnel responsible for the safety of permanent and loan collections. It is frequently necessary to discuss individual pieces with the packer and to devise special methods for protecting them during handling and transportation. A conservator or other specialist should also be consulted when insulation against temperature and humidity changes is required.

The application of these basic rules has resulted in the development of standard packing methods for certain types of exhibition material. Current methods are, of course, subject to improvement as new materials are discovered, tested and approved. Procedures for packing art objects for one or many transits and for constructing an insulated box are discussed in part 2, articles 12 and 13. The reader is also referred to basic principles of safe packing in "Packing Problems and Procedures" by Robert G. Rosegrant, which appeared in the January 1942 issue of *Technical Studies in the Field of the Fine Arts.* This guide for packing works of art has been modified and used in *Safeguarding Works of Art* (1948) by Robert P. Sugden and in two UNESCO publications, *Manual of Travelling Exhibitions* (1953) and *Temporary and Travelling Exhibitions* (1963) by Elodie Courter Osborn and others, and has been extremely useful to museums. The packing outline in the American Association of Museums Committee's report "Packing and Handling of Art Objects," published in the September 1, 1948 issue of *The Museum News,* has also been a useful guide for packing museum objects. This outline was also modified and used in the two UNESCO publications mentioned above. (See references at the end of this chapter.)

Although the procedures described in these publications and in part 2, articles 12 and 13 apply mainly to art museums, they should be helpful to all museums with the same basic problems of protecting objects during shipment. The special techniques required for packing the great variety of objects in art, science, historical and industrial museums cannot be described here. The following rules based on the publications listed above and on recent developments should, however, be helpful as a general guide to the packing of all types of objects.

General Rules

The Container

Containers must be closed on all sides and strong enough to hold the objects packed within them and to withstand handling and transit hazards such as dropping or crushing by contact with other boxes. *Open crates should not be used for packing paintings and other valuable or fragile objects.* (See figure 38.)

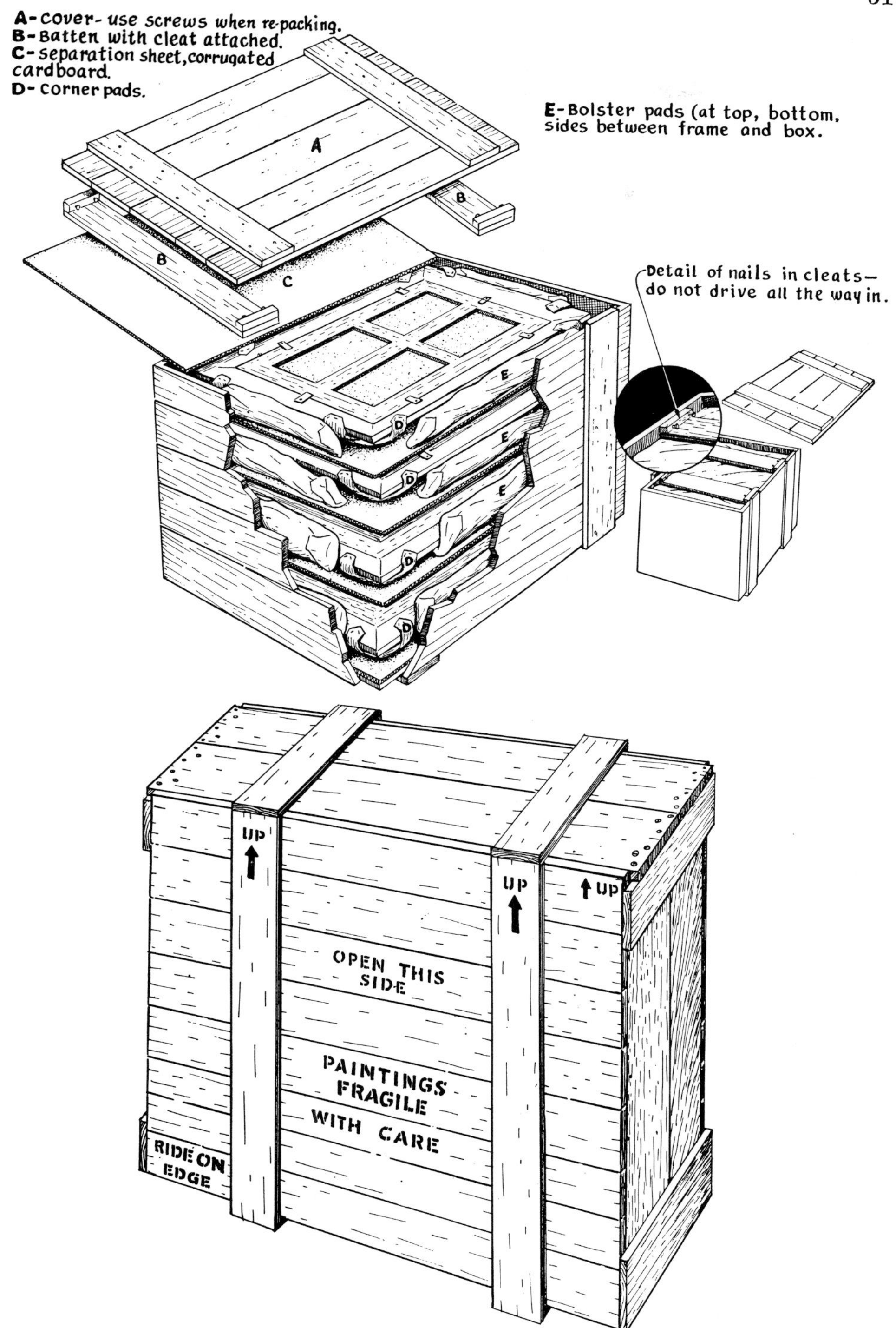

Figure 38.—Packing several paintings in a box, and box packed for shipment, Metropolitan Museum of Art (from Sugden, *Packing Instructions for Paintings;* see references).

1. Boxes should be constructed of the following materials depending on the size, weight, fragility and value of the objects being packed, the destination of shipments and the method of transportation:
   a) Seasoned wood, such as No. 2 Ponderosa pine shelving, at least three-quarters of an inch to an inch thick.
   b) Fir plywood up to one half of an inch thick or for unusually heavy pieces, three quarters of an inch thick. Grade A D and, for some boxes, the waterproof variety of plywood (i.e., marine grade) is recommended. Large plywood boxes (measurements exceeding three by three and one half feet) should be reinforced with strips of wood on all edges.
   c) Corrugated cardboard or fiberboard for long distance shipments of small, light weight, non-fragile objects of moderate value; for long or short distance shipments of more valuable objects when forwarded in a motor van owned and/or operated by the museum or a moving company van hired exclusively for each shipment.
2. Interior measurements should be at least two-and-a-quarter inches larger than the largest objects to be packed. For heavy pieces the interior measurements may need to be larger to allow the works to be removed with ease.
3. Exteriors should be reinforced overall with riding battens and where boxes are oversize there should be adequate diagonal battens as well.
4. Covers should be fastened with screws or bolts instead of nails.
5. Boxes should be lined with waterproof paper stapled or glued to the boxes, NEVER TACKED. *It should be noted that if waterproof paper contains a black substance which becomes liquid when exposed to moth-proofing chemicals it should not be used in boxes containing textiles or other objects which have been moth-proofed.* (See references for technical leaflet "Safeguarding Works of Art" by David B. Little.) The floors of boxes for heavy pieces of sculpture should be covered with masonite so that works can slide out with ease.
6. Boxes for shipments which may be subjected to extreme heat, cold, humidity, or dryness should provide protection against the stress of sudden change and against excessive moisture. Moisture may penetrate a container during prolonged exposure to high humidity, or it may condense out of the enclosed air if the container cools rapidly.
   Porous materials such as wood or fibreboard provide some insulation against sudden changes in temperature; and these same materials when properly pre-conditioned help to stabilize internal humidity by absorbing water vapor from wet air and releasing it when conditions are drier. It is important, therefore, that any waterproofing be near the outer surface of the packing, enclosing as much as possible of these stabilizing materials together with the object to be protected. *Never wrap the object alone in plastic or other vapor-proof material* if there is any chance of its being cooled before the package is opened. (For further information about insulating shipments, registrars should consult conservators and articles such as "Some Studies on the Protection of Works of Art During Travel" and "Controlled Environment for Works of Art in Transit" by Dr. Nathan Stolow. (See also, part 2, article 13.)
7. In so far as possible the gross weight of a packing box should not exceed 400 pounds so that it can be handled by two men.
8. Boxes ready for shipment should be clearly marked with the weights, the names and addresses of consignors and consignees, and caution and handling

marks such as FRAGILE, USE NO HOOKS, and THIS END UP. If old boxes have been re-used, the old markings such as names and addresses of consignors and consignees, REA Express stickers, etc. should be removed. When an off-balanced piece is being shipped, this should be indicated on the box to facilitate handling.

All boxes being shipped to foreign countries should be strapped or banded.

Protection within the Container

Objects should be protected from contact with other objects, from contact with the walls of the container and from the transmission of external shock or vibration during transit.

1. Depending on their fragility, size and weight, works should be "floated" in or be "cushioned" with resilient material or held in place by padded braces. For example: Paintings for shipments to and from a single destination are normally packed with paper-covered excelsior or polyurethane pads fitted around the corners of their frames and are placed face down in the box between sheets of corrugated cardboard or fibreboard or packed in boxes with built-in pads (see figures 38-40, 57-58); sculpture is protected against movement with padded braces and/or loose-fill packing materials (see figures 41-42 and 62-63). Braces can be covered with resilient or soft materials such as cloth-covered sponge or foam rubber, rubberized hair, plastic foams or felt and canton flannel; loose-fill packing materials include among others excelsior, cork chips and plastic foams in the form of flakes or strands.

   The "cushioning" material used within the container should be moisture-resistant as well as shock-absorbant. To protect fragile objects against abrasion or possible harmful effects of some of the artificial foams, it is advisable to make the packing materials into cloth or paper-covered pads unless objects are already wrapped or packed in an inner container. (See part 2, article 12 for more detailed information.)
2. Surfaces of objects are protected with materials such as tissue, glassine or mulberry paper, soft cloth, cotton and mineral wool. Small fragile objects (glass, ceramics, metal etc.) should be protected by wrapping first in tissue, then cotton or other soft material before they are packed.
3. Glass on paintings should be taped (see figure 56) or replaced with plexiglas. If large and replacement with plexiglas is not feasible, glass should be removed, taped and packed in a separate compartment in the bottom of the box or in a separate box.
4. Double boxing should be provided for extremely fragile or valuable shipments, i.e., objects should be packed first in an inner container that is then "floated" in excelsior or other resilient material in an outer box.
5. Heavy and light objects should not be packed in the same container. If this is unavoidable, cross slats or partitions should be made to form separate compartments (see figure 62).

New Packing Materials

New packing materials developed in recent years, particularly plastics such as polyurethane, polyethylene, and polystyrene are being used successfully for "cushioning" commercial shipments. Some of these materials have been used by museums; for example: polyurethane foam has been made into the corner pads for paintings as mentioned above, and also used to line boxes for small fragile objects; expanded polystyrene in the form of strands, flakes or beads has been used for loose-fill packing (see figures 39–40 and 41–42).

Before new materials can be recommended for general use in packing museum shipments, *conservators and scientifically trained consultants should be asked to have them tested to see whether they contain substances or give off vapors that might be harmful to museum objects.* New materials used by the Los Angeles County Museum of Art during the move to the new building in 1965 are described in "New Industrial Packing Materials: Their Possible Uses in Museums" by Frieda Kay Fall in the December 1965 issue of *Museum News* (Technical Supplement No. 10). Information about new materials being used by the packaging industry can be found in *Modern Packaging Encyclopedia,* published by McGraw-Hill in New York and also obtained from the Society of Packaging Engineers in Chicago. (See references.)

Simplified Packing for Motor Van Shipments

Museum shipments carried long distances on a motor van, when combined with cargo from other shippers, should be packed in the seasoned wood or fir plywood boxes recommended for rail, ship, and airplane transportation. Packing in solid wood or plywood boxes, however, may not always be necessary for short trips by motor van, such as local collections and deliveries, or for longer trips when objects are forwarded in vans hired exclusively for each shipment or in vans owned and/or operated by museums. In determining the type and amount of packing, however, that should be used for any particular van shipment, cost as well as safety should be considered. For instance, sometimes it is less expensive to pack in a strong, closed container that can be top-loaded and which takes less space in the van than to have the shipment travel unpacked or lightly packed, top-loading, therefore, not being possible.

For local collections and deliveries, paintings, furniture, non-fragile sculpture and other non-fragile objects can often be carried unpacked but must be protected by the moving company's pads and separation sheets and braced against movement. Small, fragile objects must always be packed in corrugated cardboard, fibreboard or wood boxes. Extremely large paintings (such as a mural 6 feet high x 19 feet long) can be protected with resilient pads around the corners of frames and covered BUT NOT SEALED with polyethylene sheeting or glassine paper. When a frame is not strong, or in the absence of a frame, it may be advisable to attach carrying handles with screws to the back of the stretcher for easy handling and for protection during loading and unloading. These handles, however, should be attached by a skilled person who understands the problems of handling and the structure of the painting. Whenever possible, large, heavy pieces of sculpture whether boxed, crated or unboxed, should travel on pallets or skids constructed to permit handling with fork lift trucks.

For longer trips and for some local trips, it is advisable to provide additional protection. Although solid wood boxes will always be essential for some valuable and fragile works, simplified packing methods may be used for many shipments when the exclusive use of a van is obtained. For example, the methods described below have been used successfully for protecting large groups of paintings of average size, watercolors and drawings travelling in vans hired exclusively for each shipment.

1. *Sandwich-type packages*—Framed works no larger than 46 x 94 inches, to which corner pads have been attached, are covered front and back by pieces of masonite of equal size and at least one inch larger on all sides than the frame. The "sandwich" is then tied securely with rope or heavy twine. (See figure 43.) Unglazed works should be covered with glassine paper before corner pads are attached. (NOTE: The maximum dimension of a sheet of masonite is 48 x 96 inches.)
2. *Fibreboard containers*—Framed works exceeding 46 x 94 inches are packed in a homasote container. The container, which can hold from one to three paintings depending on the size of the work and the width of its frame, has a solid wooden framework. One side is covered with homasote, the other left open. The works to be packed in this manner must have a *protective backing board* (see figure 55) attached to the stretcher with screws and must be covered on the face with polyethylene sheeting or glassine paper. The works are then placed facing the closed side of the container and secured with wooden braces attached with screws (NEVER NAILS) across the open side. Containers should be covered with homasote on both sides, if desirable. (NOTE: The maximum dimension of a sheet of homasote is 8 x 12 feet.)

Figure 39.—Polyurethane corner pads fitted around corners of a painting. Museum of Modern Art, New York.

Figure 40.—Painting cushioned with polyurethane corner pads placed face down in box. Museum of Modern Art, New York.

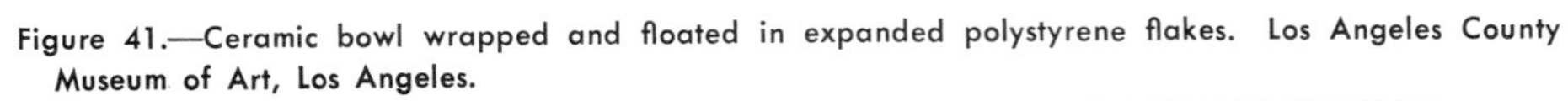

Figure 41.—Ceramic bowl wrapped and floated in expanded polystyrene flakes. Los Angeles County Museum of Art, Los Angeles.

Figure 42.—Sculpture braced in box and surrounded by strands of expanded polystyrene.

Figure 43.—Sandwich-type packing for motor van transportation. Museum of Modern Art, New York.

SHIPPING

A fast (express) and a deferred (freight) service are offered by common carriers for both domestic and foreign shipments whether they travel in railroad cars, motor vehicles, ships, or airplanes. The conditions under which shipments are accepted, packing specifications, documentary requirements, and rates are published by most carriers or can be easily obtained when requested by shippers. The documents required for foreign shipments are discussed in chapter 8. Carriers assume only a limited liability for goods entrusted to them unless a value in excess of the customary or statutory liability is declared by the shipper. In this case, however, there are additional charges based on the value declared. A shipper making such a declaration is, in effect, purchasing insurance coverage through the carrier. This should not be necessary when a shipment is fully covered under another policy. Shippers of valuable material, however, often make a *nominal* declaration of value when considered desirable as a safe handling precaution. Insurance policies sometimes require the declaration of a value to carriers. This must be checked carefully as must the amount that may be shipped in any one conveyance. (See chapter 9.)

The size and weight of the cases to be shipped may determine the method of transportation for some shipments. (See figure 44 showing cases being loaded on a military plane with an opening large enough to receive them.) The weights and measurements of small, medium and large packing boxes are tabulated at the end of this chapter as a guide to registrars planning the method and estimating the cost of packing and transportation.

Various methods of transportation and some precautions which may be taken to insure the safety of shipments are described below. The services described are those offered at the time of writing. Carriers and their publications should be consulted for subsequent changes.

Air Transportation

A rapid means of transportation is offered by the airlines for both domestic and foreign shipments. The airlines are required by law to file classifications, rates, charges, rules, regulations and the services offered with the Civil Aeronautics Board and to make them available for inspection by shippers on request. Shippers can therefore inform themselves of the amount of liability assumed by the airlines without additional cost as well as all other terms and conditions under which shipments are accepted. Documentary evidence of contracts between shippers and carriers is supplied by the airbills and air waybills issued for domestic and foreign shipments.

The passenger and all-cargo planes of the scheduled airlines, which operate over regular routes and according to regular schedules, are recommended for museum shipments. The need for special stowage and the size of boxes may determine the types of planes on which shipments are forwarded. For example: valuable and fragile objects may require shipment on a plane with pressurized and temperature controlled cargo compartments for protection against changes in atmospheric pressure and temperature; shipments containing boxes of great size can only be shipped on planes with door openings large enough to accommodate them. (See Figure 44.) Airline cargo managers should be consulted about the availability and schedules of planes that will meet the requirements of shippers. They should be given the sizes and weights of boxes and asked to reserve space on desired flights. If a valuable exhibition consisting of several boxes is to be forwarded, it is desirable to arrange for staggered shipments. As mentioned previously, insurance policies should be checked for the value that may be shipped on any one conveyance.

Air Freight and Air Express

Depending on the size and weight, transportation by air freight can be less expensive than by Air Express. Air freight rates apply from airport to airport. Delivery to and from airport terminals is arranged by the airlines at additional cost. It should be noted, however, that works of art and other shipments of extraordinary value are sometimes excluded from the normal pick-up and delivery services offered by the airlines. Special service, such as delivery in armored cars, may be provided by the airlines on request but at much higher rates. Shippers and consignees can, however, make their own pick-up and delivery arrangements or have door-to-door transportation arranged by reliable agents. Ideally, all arrangements for the air shipment of valuable and fragile museum objects should be handled by museum personnel or reliable agents who can supervise all movements: 1) from shippers to airports; 2) through terminals into the planes; 3) from the planes to and through terminals; and 4) from terminals to destinations. Supervision of the movement through terminals is advisable particularly in airports where assembly areas and loading and unloading equipment may need to be expanded and improved.

The services offered by domestic and foreign air freight forwarding agents include arrangements for all transportation from the time shipments are collected from shippers until delivered to final destinations. The domestic air freight forwarders, technically known as *indirect* air carriers, issue their own airbills although shipments are carried on planes operated by the airlines or *direct* carriers. Tariffs are filed with the Civil Aeronautics Board and are subject to its regulations. Museum shippers should check with forwarding agents to see if regulations in their tariffs exclude shipments of works of art or other valuable objects. Some tariffs, for example, now exclude works of art but only if a value in excess of $500. is declared for carriage. Museum insurance policies should also be checked in case value declarations in specified amounts are required for shipments forwarded by air freight.

Customs brokers who are foreign freight forwarders and air cargo agents approved by the International Air Transport Association are usually employed to handle foreign shipments for museums. In addition to arranging transportation, including pick-up and delivery, they make import and export arrangements and prepare documents in accordance with the regulations of the United States and other countries. The various documents required for foreign shipments may be found in publications of the international airlines and obtained from customs brokers. (See also Chapter 8.)

Air Express, a division of REA Express, offers an expedited door-to-door delivery service for shipments in the United States, Puerto Rico, and Canada. Shipments are carried on passenger and all-cargo planes of the domestic scheduled airlines. Rates apply from the point where a shipment is collected to the point where it is delivered to the consignee. The Air Express tariff is published by REA Express. A description of air, as well as surface transportation services may be found in the *Directory of Offices and Communities Served,* obtainable on request from REA Express offices.

Highway Transportation

A door-to-door delivery service is offered by commercial motor carriers for shipments moving from one state to another or within a state or city. (See figures 45–46.) In general, moving companies who are household goods carriers are recommended for museum shipments that are forwarded by motor van. Pads and other equipment for protecting shipments in transit are supplied by the moving companies. The conditions under which shipments are accepted appear on the bills of lading issued to shippers.

Companies operating moving vans from one state to another are governed by regulations of the Interstate Commerce Commission and State regulatory bodies. Classifications, rules and regulations, rates and the services offered are published in the tariff circulars issued by the Household Goods Carriers' Bureau, Agent, Washington, D. C.

A delivery service without stops to collect and deliver other cargo can be arranged by hiring the exclusive use of a van. When desirable, arrangements may be made for special guards to ride with the drivers. It is also possible to hire a specified amount of space within a van and contract for expedited service to assure pick-up and delivery on the dates desired by shippers and consignees. The rate charged for expedited service is based on a weight of 5000 pounds or more.

Companies offering motor freight services are also governed by regulations of the Interstate Commerce Commission. Motor freight is not generally used for shipments of high value. This method of transportation may be economical, however, for heavy and bulky shipments of moderate value.

Companies operating motor vans or trucks within a city or state are not governed by the interstate commerce regulations. Rates, regulations, and the services offered must usually be approved, however, by regulatory bodies in each city or state. Small, fragile objects moving short distances should be packed in corrugated cardboard or fibreboard cartons or other containers supplied by the shipper or the moving company, but many large objects may be moved unpacked when properly loaded, padded and braced on the van. (See Chapter 2, Incoming Material, for discussion of local collections and deliveries by van or station wagon.)

Ocean Transportation

Steamship lines offer transportation service for shipments on the fast passenger liners as well as on the slower cargo ships or freighters. Freight rates are usually determined by steamship conferences, voluntary associations of steamship lines. Steamship lines and conferences serving United States foreign trade as common carriers are required by law (Shipping Act of 1916) to file their transportation rates and charges with the Federal Maritime Commission and to make them available to shippers for inspection on request. The Federal Maritime Commission administers the regulatory provisions of the Shipping Act. The obligations, liabilities, and rights of both carriers and shippers are defined in the clauses of bills of lading issued when goods are received for shipment. Bills of lading serve both as receipts for goods to be shipped and as contracts to deliver them.

Since the time in transit is shorter, passenger liners are generally recommended for museum shipments. (See Figure 47.) Many freighters, however, moving between specified ports on a fixed schedule provide efficient transportation. Museum shippers or their agents should request special stowage for valuable and fragile shipments, either in the Strong Room (security area where bullion is kept) or in areas that are well ventilated or air-conditioned to prevent damage from extreme changes in temperature and humidity and other hazards. A Statement requesting special stowage should appear on dock receipts.

Information about the scheduled sailing and arrival dates of ocean carriers, and available cargo space and rates may be obtained from the inward and outward freight departments of the steamship lines or from customs brokers and foreign freight forwarders. Ocean transportation is complicated by the fact that many documents are required by the governments of the United States and foreign countries as well as by the carriers. Customs brokers, who are import specialists licensed by the U. S. Treasury Department, and also foreign freight forwarders licensed by the Federal Maritime Commission, are usually employed by museums to clear incoming shipments through U. S. Customs and to forward outgoing shipments to foreign countries. These agents book cargo space, prepare bills of lading, export declarations, shipping permits, dock receipts, invoices and other customs papers as required, and have shipments delivered to and collected from the docks and cleared through the U. S. Customs. Freight forwarding agents in foreign countries are also employed to prepare the necessary documents and forward shipments to the United States. (See Chapter 8.)

Rail Transportation

REA Express, the new name adopted for the Railway Express Agency in 1960, offers surface transportation on railways and highways for shipments in the United States and to and from Canada. The domestic surface operations are governed by regulations of the Interstate Commerce Commission and state regulatory bodies. Classifications, rates, services offered, and terms and conditions under which shipments are accepted are published in the *Official Express Classification* and supplements, available to shippers on request. (See Air Transportation, p. 100, for Air Express service.)

Museum shippers often declare a value on shipments in excess of the limited liability assumed by REA Express in the hope that boxes will receive more careful handling. Shipments with a declared value of over $550 require a *Uniform Special Contract* (sometimes referred to as the "fine arts contract"). When shipping sculpture, it is advisable to check rates with the REA Express if the declared value exceeds fifty cents per pound.

It should be noted that the following new regulations for shipments of works of art and other articles specified by the Express Company (Items 2220, 2255, 2256) were added to *Official Express Classification 36* in April, 1965 (Item 2219, Supplement 43):

> "If shipper elects to show a declared or released value lower than actual value . . . , satisfactory evidence of the actual value of the shipment must be submitted to the Express Company at time of tender of the shipment for the purpose of establishing applicable class rating. . . . If actual or declared value of shipment is $25,000.00 or more, shipper is required to so notify the Express Company prior to the tender of the shipment."

Higher class rates per 100 pounds are given for shipments of articles listed under Items 2220, 2255, 2256 and 2257 (formerly in 2220) where the actual values are over $1,000. or over a specified amount per pound than for shipments with actual values of $1,000. or less, or less than a specified amount per pound. (Supplements 43 and 45 to *Official Express Classification 36.*)

A protective signature service is offered at an additional charge for all shipments, regardless of the value declared by the shipper. According to the official Express classification, shipments with this service are handled under person-to-person signature from the time of receipt to delivery at destination, but this should be checked by museum shippers. Requests for this service must be made at the time shipments are accepted and express receipts must include the statement, PROTECTIVE SIGNATURE SERVICE REQUESTED. When forwarding large exhibitions, shippers may apply for the exclusive use of a railway express car. Armed guards may also be hired to accompany shipments. Advance arrangements should be made for shipping unusually large boxes as it may be necessary for REA Express to carry them in special "end door" railway cars.

The freight services offered by the railroads are less expensive than those of REA Express. The time in transit is longer, however, and shipments generally must be delivered to and from the rail terminals by the shippers or their agents. Rail freight is not generally used for shipments of high value. Rail freight may prove economical, however, for heavy and bulky shipments of moderate value when the time in transit is not important. Local railroad agents should be consulted about this method of transportation.

Mail Transportation

Both surface and air transportation are available for mail shipments. Regulations, rates and the services offered are published in the *Postal Manual* and the *Directory of International Mail,* which can be purchased from the Superintendent of Documents, U. S. Government Printing Office, Washington, D. C. 20402, or obtained from local postmasters.

In general, transportation by surface parcel post or air parcel post is not recommended for highly valuable and fragile museum objects because of limitations to the size, weight, and value of packages that are accepted for shipment and because of transit and handling hazards. Also, the amounts for which underwriters are willing to insure shipments are limited. For small shipments of non-fragile objects of moderate value, however, parcel post may prove economical and convenient provided containers are strong enough to protect them from the weight of other parcels, from pressure and friction, and from climate changes and repeated handlings.

Small, fragile objects of higher value may be shipped by registered mail. Registry not only provides the shipper with person-to-person signature service but guarantees more careful handling and shipment in guarded mail pouches equipped with special locks. Some foreign countries, however, do not accept all registered mail.

Domestic Shipments

Domestic surface parcel post packages are limited in size to 72 inches (length and girth combined) if going to or from a first class post office (in general, large towns or cities have first class post offices, smaller ones do not); the weight limitation depends upon the distance. Domestic air parcel post packages are limited in size to 100 inches (length and girth combined) and the weight is limited to 70 pounds regardless of distance.

Foreign Shipments

Surface and air parcel post packages shipped to foreign countries are generally limited in size to 72 inches (length and girth combined). The weight limitation depends upon the destination. Certain documents must accompany foreign shipments and these vary, of course, from country to country. (See Chapter 8.)

Figure 44.—The American exhibition from the xxxiind Venice Biennale being loaded on a MATS cargo plane at Aviano Air Base in Italy for return to the United States. Many of the pictures were so large that the boxes would not fit into the hold of any passenger ship sailing to Venice. Special arrangements were made to carry the boxes on these planes, which normally carry tanks and other heavy military equipment.

Figure 45.—Loading furniture on a truck, Metropolitan Museum of Art.

Figure 46.—Unloading sculpture from a van, Cleveland Museum of Art.

TABLE OF MEASUREMENTS AND WEIGHTS OF PACKING BOXES FOR ESTIMATING THE COST OF PACKING AND TRANSPORTATION

This table is for solid wood boxes only; allowance should be made for use of plywood which is lighter in weight. The dimensions below are in the following order: height, width, depth.

OIL PAINTING	*Framed*	*Box*	*Gross Weight*
Small	30 x 42 x 1½″	35½ x 47½ x 7″	70 pounds
Medium	48 x 72 x 2″	53½ x 77½ x 7½″	140 pounds
Large	96 x 144 x 3″	101½ x 149½ x 8½″	230 pounds

The above paintings are oil on canvas with protective backings and "L" frames of approximately ¾″ in width (weight will vary according to the type of support and the size of the frame).

WATERCOLOR, DRAWING OR PRINT	*Framed and Glazed*	*Box*	*Gross Weight*
	24 x 30 x 1½″	28½ x 34½ x 6″	60 pounds

SCULPTURE	*Overall*	*Box*	*Gross Weight*
Small (bust)	11 x 8½ x 8½″	18½ x 16 x 16″	65 pounds
Medium (goat)	46 x 56 x 28″	53½ x 67½ x 39½″	400 pounds
Large (3 figures)	74 x 69 x 30″	79 x 93 x 57″ (with skid)	2,260 pounds

The above sculptures are bronze (weight will vary according to the medium of the sculpture—marble, wood, bronze, etc.—and the extent to which this medium occupies the volume of the sculpture's over-all dimensions). In transporting very large and heavy sculpture, it is helpful to pack it in a box with a pallet or skid constructed to permit handling with a forklift truck.

References:

AMERICAN FEDERATION OF ARTS QUARTERLY, Vol. I, no. 4, 1963. (The entire volume is a handbook on care and preservation of works of art, and deals with problems of traveling exhibitions.)

BARAIL, L. C. Packaging engineering. New York, Reinhold Publishing Corporation, 1954.

BAUHOF, W. A. The package engineer in the museum, Museum News, Vol. 44, no. 4, December, 1965.

BROWN, K. Package design engineering. New York, Wiley and Son, 1959. pp. 139–160.

BUSH, MARGARET F. Comparative methods of transportation and value declarations to carriers. The Museum News, Vol. 28, April 1, 1951, pp. 5–8.

CARMEL, JAMES H. Exhibition techniques, traveling and temporary. New York, Reinhold Publishing Corporation, 1962. (Contains chapters on packaging and transporting.)

DIRECTORY OF INTERNATIONAL MAIL. U. S. Post Office Department. Available for purchase from Government Printing Office, Washington, D. C. 20402.

Figure 47.—Loading into hold of S. S. America—three boxes for the exhibition "Modern Art in the United States" circulated in Europe by the International Program, Museum of Modern Art.

DOMESTIC POSTAGE RATES AND FEES. U. S. Post Office Department, Publication 3. Available free of charge from local post offices. (Contains excerpts from Chapter 1, Postal Manual.)

FALL, FRIEDA KAY. New industrial packing materials: their possible uses for museums, Museum News, Vol. 44, no. 4, December, 1965. Technical Supplement, no. 10, pp. 47–52.

HAYES, BARTLETT H., JR. Traveling boxes, The Museum News, Vol. 23, December 15, 1946, p. 7.

INTERNATIONAL MAIL. U. S. Post Office Department, Publication 51. Available free of charge from local post offices. (Contains general information about international mail. More detailed information is in Chapter 2 of the Postal Manual and the Directory of International Mail.)

LEEMING, JOSEPH. Modern export packing. U. S. Dept. of Commerce, Washington, D. C., Government Printing Office, 1940.

———. Modern ship stowage. U. S. Department of Commerce, Bureau of Foreign and Domestic Commerce, Washington, D. C., Government Printing Office, 1942.

LITTLE, DAVID B. Safeguarding works of art: transportation, records, and insurance. American Association for State and Local History, Technical Leaflet no. 9. History News, Vol. 18, no. 7, May, 1963.

MALKIN, RICHARD. Traffic management, manual no. 31, air freight transportation. Chicago, La Salle Extension University, 1949.

MICHAELS, PETER. Lender beware, Museum News, Vol. 43, no. 1, September, 1964, pp. 11–12. (What happens to art that is loaned, how air conditioning, humidity, packing and unpacking affects objects circulated among museums.)

MILAGE GUIDE AND SUPPLEMENTS. Issued by Household Goods Carriers Bureau, Agent, 1424 Sixteenth Street, N. W., Washington, D. C., 20036. Available for purchase on request. (Contains maps and charts for determining distances in highway miles between points within the United States, to and from points in the United States, to and from points in the United States, Canada and Mexico.) For use with the *Tariff on Household Goods* and supplements.

MODERN PACKAGING ENCYCLOPEDIA. New York, McGraw-Hill, Inc., 1966. (A monthly periodical "Modern Packaging" is also published by McGraw-Hill, Inc.)

OCEAN FREIGHT RATE GUIDE LINES FOR SHIPPERS. U. S. Department of Commerce, Federal Maritime Commission. Washington, D. C., Government Printing Office, 1966. (For sale by the Superintendent of Documents, price 25 cents.)

OFFICIAL EXPRESS CLASSIFICATION 36 AND SUPPLEMENTS. Issued by Director, Pricing, Railway Express Agency, Inc., 219 East 42 Street, New York, N. Y. 10017. Available free of charges on request from REA Express offices. (Contains classifications and rates, rules and regulations; services offered and marking and packing specifications.)

POSTAL MANUAL. U. S. Post Office Department. Available for purchase from Government Printing Office, Washington, D. C. 20402.

REA EXPRESS. Directory of offices and communities served. Available from REA Express offices. (Contains description of surface and air transportation services both domestic and international and principle tariffs.)

ROSEGRANT, R. G. Packing problems and procedures. Technical Studies in the Field of Fine Arts, January 1942.

SMITH, JACK. They broke only a jar, Museum News, Vol. 43, no. 10, June, 1965, pp. 19–23. (Describes the packing and moving of 500,000 objects to the new Los Angeles County Museum of Art.)

STOLOW, NATHAN. Some studies on the protection of works of art during travel. Reprinted from RECENT ADVANCES IN CONSERVATION, Contributions to the IIC Rome conference, 1961. London, Butterworths.

STOUT, GEORGE L.; RICHARDS, CHARLES M.; and SUGDEN, ROBERT P. Packing and handling of art objects (AAM Committee Report), The Museum News, Vol. 25, September 1, 1948, pp. 7–8.

SUGDEN, ROBERT P. Packing instructions for paintings; for supervisors and for packers. New York, The Metropolitan Museum of Art, n. d.

———. Routine museum packing, The Museum News, Vol. 24, September 1, 1947, pp. 7–8.

———. Safeguarding works of art—storage, packing, transportation and insurance. New York, The Metropolitan Museum of Art, 1948.

TARIFF ON HOUSEHOLD GOODS AND SUPPLEMENTS. Issued by Household Goods Carriers' Bureau, Agent, 1424 Sixteenth Street, N. W., Washington, D. C. 20036. Available for purchase on request. (Contains rates, rules, regulations and marking and packing specifications.) For use with the *Milage Guide*.

UNESCO MUSEUMS AND MONUMENTS V. Osborn, Elodie Courter. Manual of traveling exhibitions. 1953 (Out of Print)

———. Museums and Monuments X. Temporary and traveling exhibitions 1963. (Part II is the section on traveling exhibitions and is a revision of the original 1953 manual by Elodie Courter Osborn, *Museums and Monuments V*. The present revision was made by Grace L. McCann Morley and includes additional articles by various authors.)

WILLIAMSON, MONCRIEFF. Shipping small sculpture, Museum News, Vol. 41, no. 6, February, 1963. pp. 34–36. (Discusses and illustrates a combination shipping, display and storage unit for small sculptures.)

Chapter 8

IMPORTING AND EXPORTING

When collections are acquired from foreign sources or lent to exhibitions abroad, museums must comply with import and export regulations of the United States and other countries. The filling out of numerous customs and shipping documents and the complicated procedure which must be followed in forwarding shipments and clearing them through customs require special knowledge and experience. It is therefore recommended that the services of reliable forwarding agents and customs brokers both in the United States and abroad be employed to see that foreign shipments are handled in conformity with all regulations. These agents specialize in preparing the necessary documents and handle all other details connected with foreign freight forwarding and customs clearance. Their fees are usually reasonable compared with the time which would be required if museum importers and exporters were to attempt to handle the details themselves. It is helpful if U. S. Customs brokers are given power of attorney to sign shipping and customs documents.

Particular attention must be given to the packing of all foreign shipments to provide protection during the various stages of transit, loading on and unloading from several different carriers, exposure to moisture, and other hazards. Strong, waterproof, clearly marked boxes must be provided and the material packed within them must be well cushioned against shock. Packing specifications should be issued to the agents employed by museums as well as to museum packers.

The registrar should see that reliable agents are employed. He should also have some knowledge of regulations affecting material imported for and exported from his museum so that he can issue the proper instructions to these agents and supply them with the information they need for customs and shipping papers.

The purpose of this chapter is to describe briefly some of the U. S. tariff laws affecting art and science material and the procedures for handling foreign shipments, so that museum importers and exporters can work intelligently with their agents. The many details connected with forwarding foreign shipments and customs clearance are primarily the business of the commercial agent, and will not all be described here. In preparing it, the writer has received advice from Mr. Percy S. Royals, customs broker, and his import and export managers, Mr. William J. Augerot and Mr. Albert J. Sorrentino, and from Mr. Lewis V. Smith, formerly deputy collector in charge of the entry division, U. S. Customs Office, New York. Their assistance is gratefully acknowledged. (For more detailed information see references listed at the end of this chapter.)

IMPORTS

U. S. Entry Provisions

When the article "Importing and Exporting Museum Collections" was first written in 1958 for this manual, imports were entered by museums or their agents under laws established by the Tariff Act of 1930. Since 1958, provisions for the free entry of antiques, works of art, scientific specimens and other cultural and educational material have been changed by the following legislation: (1) amendments to the bill H. R. 2411 liberalizing the tariff laws for works of art, Public Law 86–262, effective October 31, 1959; (2) Tariff Classification Act of 1962 providing for new Tariff Schedules, effective August 31, 1963; (3) Educational, Scientific and Cultural Materials Importation Act of 1966, Public Law 89–651, effective February 1, 1967.

Amendments to H. R. 2411 Liberalizing the Tariff Laws for Works of Art—Most of the restrictive tariff laws for works of art were removed by the amendments to this bill. Free entry was permitted for the first time to: a) collages, mosaics, and *all* prints made by hand transfer processes; b) *all* sculpture ("made in any form from any material . . ., whether in round or in relief, and whether cut, carved or otherwise wrought by hand, or cast") and the first ten instead of three "castings, replicas, or reproductions made from the sculptor's original model," including those finished after the sculptor's death; c) ethnographic objects in traditional aboriginal styles produced at least fifty years prior to their date of entry; d) *all* handwoven tapestries fit only for use as wall hangings and valued at over $20. per square foot.

The following important addition to the laws provides for the free entry of works not specifically described in other provisions: "Original works of the free fine arts . . . in any media including, but not limited to applied paper or other materials, manufactured or otherwise, such as are used on collages." The Collector of Customs may require proof of the character of these works including, if necessary, "certificates from recognized authorities on art that they represent some school, kind, or medium of the free fine arts." This makes it possible for the status of unprecedented works or media not listed in other provisions to be established by a museum curator or other qualified expert. In addition to collages, specified as free in this provision, assemblages, musical sculptures, and works of kinetic art have been entered free of duty since this amendment was passed. In some instances statements from museum curators supporting the claim for free entry have been furnished to the Collector of Customs.

Before these amendments were passed, antique furniture, including frames whether on or removed from paintings, could only be entered at certain ports designated by the Secretary of the Treasury. Entry of antique picture frames can now be made at any port of entry. (According to a 1966 ruling made by the Treasury Department, T.D. 66–186, *all* antique furniture can now be entered at any port of entry within the customs territory of the United States.) Museum collections will benefit under the liberalized laws that are now available to all importers, not only through their own imports but also through the growth of private collections from which they receive loans, donations and bequests.

Museums may continue to import decorative or applied art objects and other dutiable exhibition material free provided bond is given to pay duties if sold or used contrary to the specified regulations.[1] Exhibition bonds are limited to five years. The registrar's records should indicate the date when the bond will be terminated and the museum's liability canceled. Objects under bond must be kept on the premises of the museum and be available for customs inspection during this five year period. Under the revised laws the Collector of Customs may give permission for their transfer not only to other museums but also, temporarily, to a commercial gallery or other premises for exhibition and not for sale. If they are exported before the bond is terminated, they must be packed and sealed under customs supervision so that the museum's liability under the bond will be canceled. In addition to the exhibition bond, other provisions for the free entry of what would otherwise be dutiable material are available to museums and other cultural, scientific or educational institutions. (See outline at end of this chapter.)

When material held under Exhibition Bond is insured, the insurance value should be increased to include the amount of duty that would become due if any article should be destroyed, lost or stolen.

Tariff Classification Act of 1962—New Tariff Schedules of the United

[1] Museums and other institutions must apply to the Collector of Customs for permission to use this provision He may require a copy of the charter or other evidence of the character of importing institutions.

States—The new Tariff Schedules replace schedules I (dutiable items) and II (free items) of the Tariff Act of 1930. Each item in the new schedules is listed with its number and rate of duty or a notation that it is permitted free entry. These "item numbers", therefore, replace the Tariff Paragraph numbers in the Tariff Act of 1930 under which imports were previously entered. For example, antiques are now entered under item number 766.2500 instead of Tariff Paragraph 1811; and a painting is entered under item number 765.0300 instead of Tariff Paragraph 1807. Objects imported under exhibition bond are entered under item number 862.1000 instead of Tariff Paragraph 1809.

The provisions for free entry in the new Tariff Schedules reflect the liberalized laws resulting from the 1959 amendments to H. R. 2411 described earlier. For example, ethnographic objects (produced fifty years prior to entry) may be entered free under item number 766.2500; original lithographs made by hand transfer processes, under item number 765.1000; and original works of art in any media not specified in other provisions, under item number 765.2500.

Educational, Scientific and Cultural Materials Importation Act of 1966—This act implements an international agreement sponsored by UNESCO, commonly known as the Florence agreement, designed to facilitate the international circulation, free of duty, of visual and auditory materials of an educational, scientific and cultural character. The new legislation, which became effective on February 1, 1967, permits, with certain procedural safeguards, the duty-free treatment of books and other printed or manuscript material, works of art, antiques, scientific material and other educational and cultural material to the extent that they are not already permitted free entry under existing provisions. (Congressional Record, October 7, 1966, Vol. 112, pp. 24697–24699.)

One of the most important changes is the amendment for determining antiques entitled to free entry. Under the previous law antiques must have been produced before 1830. This requirement has been changed to permit free entry for antiques produced more than 100 years prior to their date of entry. Another important change permits free entry to paintings, pastels, drawings and sketches whether or not they are originals. The only requirement is that they must have been produced entirely by hand. Sculpture, mosaics, collages and other works of art in the tariff schedules are still required to be originals or, in the case of sculpture and prints, cast or transferred from the artist's original models or from hand produced plates, stones or blocks.

The former provisions permitting free entry to educational, scientific and other specified institutions have been expanded to include certain visual and auditory materials that were not already duty free and new provisions were made for the duty free treatment of scientific instruments and apparatus, and specimens of archaeology, mineralogy, or natural history.

The liberalized tariff laws that will be most useful to museums, the documents required for free entry, and the new tariff schedule item numbers resulting from the legislation enacted since 1958 appear in the outline of U. S. entry provisions on page 119. Several articles listed in the bibliography at the end of this chapter describe the former restrictions to free entry as well as the liberalized laws resulting from the 1959 legislation.

Arrangements for Packing and Forwarding to the United States

Unless arrangements are being made directly by foreign vendors, donors, or lenders, packing and shipping instructions should be sent by museum importers to their foreign forwarding agents well in advance of the desired shipping date, particularly when a large loan exhibition is being assembled for shipment. These agents will need time to collect from each lender, pack, make export arrangements in accordance with regulations of their governments, and provide the invoices and other documents required by U. S. customs. The agents should be advised of the insurance arrangements, the transportation method desired, the dates shipments must arrive, whether freight charges are to be prepaid or payable at destination, and, if it is the first time the agents' services are being employed, it may be advisable to include a list of documents required by U. S. customs.

Delays may be avoided by having shipments consigned directly to customs brokers for clearance through U. S. customs and delivery to museums. Bills of lading, invoices, and other documents required for entry should be airmailed to the customs brokers in time to arrive in advance of shipments. Copies of shipping papers should also be airmailed to importing museums.

U. S. Customs Clearance and Delivery to Museum

A customs entry must be made by importers or their customs brokers within five working days after the arrival of shipments in the United States. Otherwise, shipments will be sent to a government-bonded warehouse and importers must pay additional charges to withdraw them. If the invoice required by U. S. customs is not available when a shipment arrives, a "pro forma" invoice describing the material must be provided by the importer before entry can be made. Invoices required for imports are described in the outline at the end of this chapter. It should be noted that a "Special Customs Invoice" on Foreign Service Form

5515 is required for shipments exceeding $500. in value, if for sale, and $1,000. in value, if not for sale. (See figure 48.)

Museum importers should advise their brokers how shipments are to be entered. For example, if an import is not allowed free entry, they should either instruct the broker to enter it under exhibition bond, item number 862.1000, or to pay duty. Customs brokers may apply for permission to have shipments delivered to the museum for unpacking and customs examination. When a shipment is destined for a city other than the port of arrival, an "Immediate Transportation Entry" may be made and the shipment forwarded in bond to that city or the nearest designated port of entry for final customs clearance and examination. Copies of customs entry papers should be sent by the brokers to the museum for its records.

Packages imported by mail should have an attached customs declaration showing contents and value. One set of invoices and any other documents required by U. S. customs should be enclosed in the packages and the others sent separately by airmail to the addressee. When values are under $250 an informal entry is made by customs officers, packages are delivered, and the duty, if any, is collected by the Post Office. When more than one package from the same sender to the same addressee arrives on the same ship or airplane, they are combined at the Post Office and considered one shipment. If the aggregate value exceeds $250, a formal entry must be made.

EXPORTS

Preparing Export Shipments

In general, the packing requirements described in chapter 7, and part 2, articles 12 and 13 apply to foreign as well as domestic shipments, except that the method of marking boxes differs. The names and addresses of both consignor and consignee, which must appear on boxes shipped within the United States or between the United States and Canada, are not required for foreign shipments. Instead, identifying marks such as MMA, the city and port of destination, and consecutive numbers are stenciled on each box; for example:

M M A
SAO PAULO
VIA SANTOS
NO 2.

Care should be taken to see that the same number is not duplicated in a shipment consisting of several boxes.

These marks and numbers also appear on the invoices and bills of lading or air waybills which accompany shipments. For museum shipments, it is advisable to have the full name and address of the consignor and consignee appear on a box but not as part of the above-mentioned identifying marks and numbers. Boxes should be marked with the gross weights and measurements, PACKED IN U.S.A., USE NO HOOKS, and other caution marks or symbols. For exports to certain countries the net weight (weight of actual material), legal weight (weight of actual material plus the inner container or wrapper), tare weight (weight of packing case), must be shown in addition to the gross weight which is the weight of the actual material plus both inside and outside containers. It is advisable to show weights and measurements in both metric and the customary U. S. systems and caution marks in English and the language of the country of destination.

Symbols such as arrows indicating "this end up" and champagne glasses or bottles indicating "fragile" should be used for marking foreign shipments which frequently travel through several countries. All marks should be stenciled with waterproof ink on two sides of the box. Box markings should be as simple as possible, so that they can be easily seen and understood. For shipments by air freight it is advisable to attach a label to each box with the following statement typed or printed on it: "This shipment must be protected against the elements at all times."

A list or invoice giving the following information should be prepared for each shipment: the name and address of consignor and consignee, a description of each item with its valuation, and the mark and number of the box in which it is packed. The weights and measurements of each box should also be shown. These invoices are typed on museum letterheads and several copies sent to the agents employed to handle export arrangements. In order to prepare the "export declarations" required by the U. S. Government, forwarding agents will need to know whether the material being exported is of domestic or foreign origin. (See figure 50.) If a temporary export is being made, a note to the effect that the shipment will be returned to the United States should be sent with the invoice so that proof of export may be established when free entry is claimed for material returned after exhibition abroad. (When paintings are exported temporarily, information showing whether they are framed or unframed should be supplied.) Forwarders should also be informed when shipments are being returned to owners abroad after exhibition in the United States.

Forwarding to Foreign Consignees

The U. S. forwarding agents should be notified as far in advance as possible of the shipment to be exported, the transportation method desired, the name of the consignee, the date the shipment is needed at destination, and the insurance arrangements. When loans from abroad are being returned, the same values that were shown on the invoice covering the import shipment should be used on the invoice for the export shipment. Unless they are being returned to another country, they should be consigned to the same agent who forwarded them to the United States.

The forwarding agents should be given specific instructions as to how the charges are to be paid—to deliver to ultimate consignee free of all charges, to prepay charges to port of entry or airport only, or to make all charges payable at destination. An estimate of the total weight and measurement should be given to them so that they can book cargo space in advance and advise the museum of any special information needed for the documents required by the United States and country of destination. United States export licenses are not usually required for the types of material exported by museums; when they are, the forwarding agents should advise shippers so that application can be made immediately.

When a shipment is packed and all customs and shipping papers prepared, the forwarding agents arrange to have the boxes collected and delivered to the carrier. A shipment from an interior city is forwarded to agents at the port of exit, where arrangements are made for delivering it to the carrier. Bills of lading, invoices, and any other papers required are forwarded to the consignee. If insurance is not arranged by the exporter he should notify the consignee or whoever is responsible for insuring the shipment of the date of departure and name of the ship, plane, or other carrier on which it is forwarded.

Foreign Customs Clearance and Delivery to Consignees

Consignees or professional agents abroad clear shipments through the customs of their countries. If agents abroad have been employed by the U. S. exporter, they should be instructed as to the ultimate disposition of shipments. When a shipment consists of objects lent for exhibition abroad, the agent or ultimate consignee should be advised that on the invoice for the return shipment a declaration will be required showing that the objects were imported from the United States for temporary exhibition. This regulation is listed below with other import and export requirements.

OUTLINE OF DOCUMENTARY REQUIREMENTS AND U.S. ENTRY PROVISIONS

The following outline does not include the many forms which must be filled out in making an entry for imports, consular invoices required by foreign countries, and other papers such as shipping permits and dock receipts for exports, as commercial agents are usually employed to prepare them for both incoming and outgoing shipments. The provisions for free entry and documentary requirements summarized in the outline are only those that would apply most frequently to museum shipments. Documents required are listed with the section numbers of the *Customs Regulations of the United States,* as amended. Since the information given at the time of writing (Spring 1967) is subject to change, customs brokers and foreign freight forwarders should be requested to keep their clients informed of subsequent changes in regulations.

DOCUMENTARY REQUIREMENTS AND U.S. PROVISIONS FOR FREE ENTRY

GENERAL REQUIREMENTS FOR IMPORT AND EXPORT SHIPMENTS

IMPORTS

1. **Bill of Lading and Air Waybill**—A contract of carriage between shipper and carrier, receipt for the shipment and negotiable instrument in which title to shipment resides. It serves as evidence of the right of the importer to enter a shipment. For an air shipment, a "carrier's certificate" on an air waybill takes the place of a bill of lading.
2. **Invoice**—On purchased articles, the Bill of Sale. If not purchased, a statement from the exporter showing the name and address of consignor and consignee, an itemized description of the contents and value of a shipment, the marks and numbers of packages and, for some shipments, other information as required by U.S. customs. It is filed with customs when entry is made.
   a. *Commercial Invoice*
   A statement prepared by the exporter giving the information mentioned above for shipments for which a "Special Customs Invoice" is not required.
   b. *Special Customs Invoice on Foreign Service Form 5515* (See figure 48.)
   Required for shipments for sale or for sale on commission if the value exceeds $500. and for shipments that are not for sale or for sale on commission if the value exceeds $1,000. A "Commercial Invoice" may be attached to this form. A "Special Customs Invoice" is not required for certain shipments, for example, exhibition material entered under bond and other material entered for cultural, educational, scientific or exhibition purposes. (Section 8.15, Customs Regulations of the United States.)
   c. *Pro-Forma Invoice*
   Prepared by the importer to describe the contents of a shipment when the "Commercial Invoice" or "Special Customs Invoice" is not available. Bond must be given by the importer to produce the required invoice within six months from the date of entry.

(Sections 8.6 through 8.16, Customs Regulations of the United States and Sections 481 through 484, Tariff Act of 1930.)

3. **Packing List**—A list giving measurements, weights, marks, numbers and contents of each packing box should be sent to the consignee unless this information appears on the invoice.
4. **Customs Declaration for Parcel Post Shipment**—A declaration showing the contents and value of a shipment, prepared by the exporter on a form provided by the Postal Administration in his country, must be attached to the package. An invoice or statement of value and any other documents required by U.S. Customs should be enclosed in the package and copies sent separately to the addressee. (Section 9.1, Customs Regulations of the United States.)

EXPORTS

1. **Bill of Lading and Air Waybill**—See Imports 1. Original ocean bills of lading are sent to the consignees. Air Waybills are not needed by consignees to take possession of shipments.
2. **Invoice**—See Imports 2.
   a. *Consular Invoice and Certificate of Origin* as required by country of destination.
3. **Packing List**—See Imports 3.
4. **Declarations for Parcel Post Shipments** [1]
   a. *Customs Declaration—Form 2966*
   A statement showing contents and value of the shipment, name and address of sender and addressee, description of the parcel (box, package, bag, etc.) and alternate disposition instructions is prepared by sender and attached with cord to the outside of the parcel.
   b. *International Parcel Post Sticker—Form 2922*
   Instructions as to alternate disposition are given on this form which is signed by the sender and pasted on each parcel.
   c. *Dispatch Note—Form 2972*
   As required by countries of destination. Similar to Form 2966 but with space provided for a *Receipt* to be signed by the addressee. Prepared by sender and attached to parcel.
5. **Shipper's Export Declaration**—A declaration on U.S. Form 7525 V showing name and address of consignor and consignee, marks and number of packages, description of material being shipped, values, commodity numbers, etc., must be filed by the exporter or his agent with the Collector of Customs before a shipment is delivered to the carrier. (Export declarations are not required for parcel post shipments unless values exceed $50.) (See figure 50.)
6. **Export License**—As required by the U.S. Government. When an export license is required, application on U.S. Forms FC 419 and FC 420 must be made to the U.S. Department of Commerce, Washington, D. C. Export license numbers will be assigned on forms and returned to the applicant. (Since licenses are not usually required for the types of material exported by museums, the *Export Declaration* listed above should show that material is being exported under *General License*.)

[1] Regulations for International Parcel Post shipments can be found in current issues of the Postal Manual, United States Post Office Department, obtainable from the Superintendent of Documents, U.S. Government Printing Office, Washington, D. C.

7. **Import License**—As required by country of destination. The consignee in country of destination applies for a license when it is required.
8. **Application to Export Exhibition Material Entered Under Bond**—Permission to export under customs supervision must be requested by the exporter or his agent on *United States Form 3495* and sent to the Collector of Customs whenever articles under bond (Tariff Schedule Item Number 862.1000) are to be exported.

SPECIAL REQUIREMENTS AND U.S. PROVISIONS FOR FREE ENTRY

Tariff Schedule Item Numbers are in parentheses. An asterisk indicates that provisions are listed under SPECIAL PROVISIONS FOR CULTURAL, SCIENTIFIC AND EDUCATIONAL INSTITUTIONS. Documents required for free entry are in italics.

ANTIQUES AND ETHNOGRAPHIC OBJECTS

1. **Antiques.**
   a. Antiques made prior to 100 years before their date of entry. (Number 766.2500)
2. **Ethnographic Objects**
   a. Ethnographic objects in traditional aboriginal styles made at least 50 years before their date of entry. (Number 766.2500)

   Proof of Antiquity

   Declaration (on invoice) by the seller, owner or other person having competent knowledge of the facts, stating the place and approximate date of production and, in addition, for articles subject to Foreign Assets Control regulations, the name and address of the person from whom they were acquired and the date acquired. If the declaration is not available, the Collector of Customs may, at his discretion accept a statement from the owner or borrower in this country giving all the facts within his knowledge to show how long the articles have been in existence and where they were produced. (Section 10.53 (a), Customs Regulations of the United States, as amended.)

   Customs Form 3307

   Declaration by importer or attorney in fact on free entry of works of art, artistic antiquities, etc. (Section 10.53 (b), Customs Regulations of the United States.) (See figure 49.)

ART MATERIAL

1. **Paintings, pastels, drawings and sketches** whether or not originals, executed wholly by hand. (Number 765.0300)
   Customs Form and Declaration not required.
2. **Prints, sculptures, mosaics and other works of art**
   a. Engravings, etchings, lithographs, woodcuts, and other prints printed by hand. (Number 765.1000)
   b. Original sculptures made in any form and from any material including the first ten castings. (Number 765.1500)
   c. Original mosaics. (Number 765.2000)
   d. Collages and other original works of the free fine arts not provided for in the foregoing, in any media including, but not limited to, applied

paper and other materials such as are used on collages. (Number 765.2500)

Note: Picture frames, if not produced prior to 100 years before their date of entry, are dutiable. At the time of writing the rate of duty on wood frames is 6% ad valorem. (Number 206.6000)

Declaration of Originality

A declaration in the following form by the artist (or by foreign shipper if it is shown on the declaration why it is impossible to obtain the signature of the artist) attached to the invoice for the shipment:

I, ______________________________, do hereby declare that I am the producer of certain works of art, namely ______________________ covered by the annexed invoice dated ______________________; that any mosaics included in that invoice are originals; that any sculptures or statuary included in that invoice are the original works or models or one of the first ten castings, replicas, or reproductions made from the sculptor's original work or model; and that any etchings, engravings, woodcuts, lithographs, or prints made by other hand transfer processes included in that invoice were printed by hand from hand-etched, hand-drawn, or hand-engraved plates, stones, or blocks.

(Date and place of signing) (Signature of artist, seller or shipper)

The declaration of the artist, or the declaration of the seller or shipper, may be waived upon a satisfactory showing that it is impossible to produce. (Section 10.48, Customs Regulations of the United States.)

Customs Form 3307

Declaration for free entry of original engravings, drawings, sculpture, etc. (See figure 49.) (Section 10.48, Customs Regulations of the United States.)

3. **Tapestries.**
   a. Gobelin and other hand-woven tapestries fit only for use as wall hangings and valued over $20. per square foot. (Number 364.0500)

   Certificate of Authenticity

   Executed by the manager or other responsible employee of the factories producing the tapestries. If the absence of this certificate is satisfactorily explained, other evidence establishing the necessary facts may be accepted. (Section 10.54, Customs Regulations of the United States.)

4.* **Sculpture and statutory**—for educational purposes only.

SCIENCE MATERIAL

1. **Skeletons and other preparations of anatomy.** (Number 190.8000)
2. **Fossils.** (Number 790.2000)

   Customs Forms not required.

3.* **Specimens of archaeology, mineralogy or natural history.**
4.* **Wild animals** (Including birds and fish).
5.* **Scientific instruments and apparatus.**

PRINTED MATTER

1. **Books, tourist and other literature.**
   a. Books not specially provided for. (Number 270.2500)
   b. Printed matter not specially provided for, suitable for use in the produc-

tion of such books as would themselves be free of duty. (Number 274.7300)

c. Tourist and other literature (including posters). (Number 270.7000)

2. **Printed matter produced more than 20 years prior to importation.**

a. Architectural, engineering, industrial, or commercial drawings and plans printed on sensitized materials by any photographic process. (Number 273.4500)

b. Photographs, engravings, etchings, lithographs and woodcuts, and pictorial matter produced by relief or stencil printing processes not specially provided for. (Number 274.5000)

Customs Forms not required.

3.* **Audio Visual material** for cultural, scientific, and educational institutions.

Note: Provisions are also made for free entry of other printed and manuscript material in Tariff Schedule 2, part 5.

PROVISIONS FOR FREE RETURN AFTER EXPORTATION

1. **Products of the United States.**

a. Products returned after exportation without having been advanced in value or improved in condition. (Number 800.0000)

Foreign Shipper's Declaration

Invoice of returned American goods and declaration of foreign exporter if value exceeds $500. stating that articles are products of the United States and that they have not been advanced in value or improved in condition and naming the port from which they were exported and the date of export. (Section 10.1, Customs Regulations of the United States.)

Customs Form 3311

Declaration for free return of American products. (Section 10.1, Customs Regulations of the United States.)

Customs Form 4467

Certificate of exportation—not required if articles are unquestionably products of the United States and have not been advanced in value or improved in condition while abroad. (Section 10.1, Customs Regulations of the United States.)

2. **Miscellaneous articles**—Articles returned after temporary exportation solely for exhibition, examination or experimentation, for scientific or educational purposes, if imported by or for the account of the person who exported them:

a. For exhibition, examination, or experimentation, for scientific or educational purposes. (Number 802.1000)

b. For exhibition in a circus or menagerie. (Number 802.2000)

c. For exhibition or use at any public exposition, fair, or conference. (Number 802.3000)

Customs Form 4467

Certificate of exportation. (Sections 10.66 and 10.67, Customs Regulations of the United States.)

Shipper's Declaration

A declaration made by the foreign shipper on or attached to the invoice for articles returned and entered under 802.1000, 802.2000 and 802.3000 stating that the material described therein was imported from the United States for temporary use in an exhibition or for temporary educational or scientific use and describing the specific use to which they were put while abroad, for example:

I, ______________________________, do hereby declare that the merchandise herein described was imported from the United States, and that it was sent to ______________________________ for temporary use at the Exhibition entitled ____________________ held at ____________________ on ____________________, 19____.

(Date and place of signing) (Signature of exporter or authorized agent)

(Sections 10.66 and 10.67, Customs Regulations of the United States.)

Declaration by Ultimate Consignee

Statement that articles returned and entered under Item Number 802.1000 are those which were exported and that they have not been changed in condition. (Section 10.67, Customs Regulations of the United States.)

Customs Form 3329 (to be replaced by revised Form 4455)

Declaration of the importer for articles (either of domestic or foreign origin) returned and entered under Item Numbers 802.2000 or 802.3000. (Section 10.66, Customs Regulations of the United States.)

SPECIAL PROVISIONS FOR CULTURAL, SCIENTIFIC AND EDUCATIONAL INSTITUTIONS

Articles imported for the use of any public library, any other public institution or any non-profit institution established for educational, scientific, literary, or philosophical purposes, or for the encouragement of the fine arts. (The Collector of Customs may require evidence of the character of institutions using these provisions.)

Except when otherwise stated, articles covered by these provisions must be imported exclusively for the institutions involved and not for distribution, sale, or other commercial use within five years after being entered. They may be transferred to another institution or exported or destroyed under customs supervision within this five year period without duty liability being incurred. If transferred other than as provided by the preceding sentence, or used for commercial purposes within five years after being entered, the importing institution will be liable for the payment of duty.

1. **Audio Visual material.**
   a. Drawings and plans, reproductions thereof, engravings, etchings, lithographs, woodcuts, globes, sound recordings, recorded video tapes, and photographs and other prints. (Number 851.1000)

   Note: Other audio visual material such as developed photographic film, including motion-picture film, is permitted free entry under number 870.3000 when certified by the U.S. Information Agency. (Section 10.121, Customs Regulations of the United States.)
2. **Sculptures and statuary.** (Number 851.2000)
3. **Patterns and models** exclusively for exhibition or educational use. (Number 851.5000)

   Customs Form 3321

   Declaration of free entry for colleges, religious institutions, etc. (Section 10.43, Customs Regulations of the United States.)

   Note: **Models of the inventions and other improvements in the arts,** to be used exclusively as models are also permitted free entry under number 737.0500.

4. **Scientific instruments and apparatus.**
   a. Free entry provided no articles of equivalent scientific value for the purposes intended are being manufactured in the United States. (Number 851.6000)
   b. Repair components. (Number 851.6500)

   Note: Non-profit scientific or educational institutions, whether public or private, wishing to import instruments and apparatus under these provisions must apply to the Secretary of the Treasury in accordance with regulations specified in Sections 10.114–10.118, Customs Regulations of the United States.

5. **Scientific Specimens.**
   a. Wild animals (including birds and fish) for use, or for sale for use, in any scientific public collection for exhibition for scientific or educational purposes. (Number 852.2000)

   Customs Form 332

   Declaration of the ultimate consignee showing that animals or birds were specially imported pursuant to negotiations conducted prior to importation for delivery of animals or birds of a named species meeting agreed specifications of reasonable particularity and that they are intended for public exhibition and not for sale or profit. (Section 10.75, Customs Regulations of the United States.)

   b. Specimens of archaeology, mineralogy, or natural history (including specimens of botany or zoology other than live zoological specimens) imported for any public or private scientific collection for exhibition or other educational or scientific use, and not for sale or other commercial use. (Number 870.2700)

   Declaration of Importer

   Declaration stating that articles entered under 870.2700 are imported for public or private scientific collection for exhibition or other educational or scientific use and are not for sale or other commercial use. (Section 10.47, Customs Regulations of the United States.) Customs Form 3321, while not specifically required, is acceptable evidence of the status of the importing institution.

   Note: Importation of plants and plant products in subject to special regulations of the Department of Agriculture. (Sections 12.10 through 12.15, Customs Regulations of the United States.)

6. **Exhibition material under bond.** (Number 862.1000)
   a. Works of art, photographs, artistic antiquities and copies, collections in illustration of the progress of the arts, sciences, etc., imported under bond by educational institutions for exhibition purposes and not intended for sale.

   Customs Form 3325

   Declaration of entry of works of art, etc., for exhibition. (Section 10.49, Customs Regulations of the United States.)

   Customs Form 7565

   Exhibition bond. (Sections 10.49 and 25.4 a (17), Customs Regulations of the United States.)

TREASURY DEPARTMENT

Attach Additional Sheets Here
Read Carefully Instructions for Preparation of Invoice

Form Approved.
Budget Bureau No. 48-R342.3.

(THIS FORM DOES NOT REQUIRE CERTIFICATION BY A UNITED STATES CONSULAR OFFICER)

SPECIAL CUSTOMS INVOICE

BUREAU OF CUSTOMS

(Original only required for customs purposes)

I. THIS SECTION TO BE FILLED IN FOR EVERY SHIPMENT

1. How were goods obtained by importer? By purchase or agreement to purchase ☐ By some means other than a purchase ☐

DO NOT INCLUDE PURCHASE AND NONPURCHASE GOODS IN SAME INVOICE. USE SEPARATE INVOICE FOR EACH

2. Place (city and country) and date obtained by importer	3. Name of exporting carrier	4. Date of shipment

II. TO BE FILLED IN IF GOODS WERE PURCHASED OR AGREED TO BE PURCHASED	III. TO BE FILLED IN IF GOODS WERE *NOT* PURCHASED
1. Name and address of seller	1. Name and address of person from whom goods were obtained
2. Name and address of purchaser	2. Name and address of consignee
3. Date order accepted	3. Name and address of person for whose account goods are shipped

IV. THIS SECTION TO BE FILLED IN FOR EVERY SHIPMENT

(1) Marks and Numbers on Shipping Packages	(2) Manufacturer's or Seller's Numbers or Symbols	(3) Quantity and Full Description of Goods (State contents of each package and importer's numbers or symbols, if any)	(4) Invoice Unit Price or Value	(5) Invoice Totals and Show Separately Packing Costs; All Other Costs, Charges, and Expenses	(6) Current Unit Price for Home Consumption in Home Currency	(7) Current Unit Price for Export to United States

(8) Country of origin	(9) If rate of exchange is fixed or agreed, give rate	(10) If discount is freely offered, give terms, amount, and whether trade or cash

V. THIS SECTION TO BE FILLED IN FOR EVERY SHIPMENT

1. IF GOODS WERE PURCHASED, have you stated in section IV, column 4, the purchase price of each item in the currency in which the goods were bought? ☐ Yes ☐ No.
2. IF THE GOODS WERE NOT PURCHASED, have you stated in section IV, column 4, the price that you would have received or would be willing to receive now if the goods were sold in the ordinary course of trade for exportation to the United States? ☐ Yes ☐ No.
3. What currency was used in this invoice transaction? ....
4. Whether the goods were purchased or obtained by the United States importer in some other manner, have you stated in section IV, column 6:
   (A) (1) The price at which you are now selling the goods or offering them for sale for home consumption, including all applicable taxes? ☐ Yes ☐ No.
   (2) Is this price freely offered to anyone who wishes to buy the goods for home consumption? ☐ Yes ☐ No.
   (B) (1) Have you stated in section IV, column 7, the price at which you are now selling the goods or offering them for sale for export to the United States and whether this price is f.o.b., c.i.f., c.&f., or whatever the fact may be? ☐ Yes ☐ No.
   (2) Is this price freely offered to anyone who wishes to buy the goods for export to the United States? ☐ Yes ☐ No.
5. Have you listed all charges and stated whether each amount has been included in or excluded from the invoice amount? ☐ Yes ☐ No.
   Is the inland freight included in the invoice price or value? ☐ Yes ☐ No. Is the price or value of the goods the same at the factory as at the point of delivery? ☐ Yes ☐ No. If the answer is No, have any sales been made at an ex-factory price? ☐ Ye
6. Are any rebates, drawbacks, bounties, or other grants allowed upon the exportation of the goods? ☐ Yes ☐ No. If itemized? ☐ Yes ☐ No.
7. If such or similar goods are being sold or offered for sale in the home market for home consumption, what taxes are app in the price shown in section IV, column 6?

Rate .... Kind ....

CUSTOMS FORM JUL 64 5515

SECTION V (Continued)

8. (A) Did production of goods involve costs for "assists" (i.e.—dies, molds, tooling, printing plates, patterns, drawings, blueprints, artwork, engineering work, design and development, financial assistance) *not included* in the invoice price?
   ☐ Yes ☐ No. If yes, identify nature of assist involved ...., and complete Part B.
   (B) (1) Assists valued at .... ("Unknown," if applicable) were supplied by:
   ☐ Manufacturer ☐ Importer ☐ Other (Identify) ....
   (2) Assists were: ☐ (a) Supplied without cost. ☐ (b) Supplied on rental basis.
   ☐ (c) Invoiced separately. If (c), attach copy of invoice.
9. If the price(s) shown in column 6 is (are) higher than those shown in column 7, there is an indication of possible sales at less than fair value within the meaning of the United States Antidumping statutes. If this differential exists, please select one of the following alternatives:
   (A) ☐ To the best of my knowledge and belief the differential between the column 6 and column 7 prices is the result of conditions of sale which would not result in sales at less than fair value within the meaning of the U.S. Antidumping laws.
   OR
   (B) ☐ There is attached hereto an explanation of the differences between the column 6 and column 7 prices.

NOTE.—In his discretion the appraiser may nonetheless require submission of the information called for under item 9. (B).

10. PURCHASE DECLARATION		11. NONPURCHASE DECLARATION	
I declare that the merchandise described in this invoice is SOLD OR AGREED TO BE SOLD; that all the information contained herein is true and correct; and that there is no other invoice(s) except		I declare that the merchandise described in this invoice is shipped OTHERWISE THAN BY PURCHASE OR AGREEMENT TO PURCHASE; that all the information contained herein is true and correct; and that there is no other invoice(s) except	
Explanation of Exceptions		Explanation of Exceptions	
Date	Signature of Seller, Shipper, or Agent of Either	Date	Signature of Shipper or Agent

This form of invoice required generally if rate of duty based upon or regulated by value of goods and purchase price or value of shipment exceeds $500. Otherwise, use commercial invoice.

False statements or willful omissions in any invoice or other documents executed and forwarded for United States Customs entry purposes will subject the goods to seizure and forfeiture or any person involved will be subject to a penalty equal to the value of the goods. Publicity will be given to all seizures and penalties, including the disclosure of the identity of the offenders involved (19 U.S.C. 1592).

Vague or misleading information may result in expensive trouble to importer and delays in customs clearance.

Supplies of this form may be secured from consular offices of the United States and from The Director, Customs Information Exchange, 201 Varick Street, New York, N.Y., 10014. Privately printed forms must conform in all respects to the official form.

U.S. GOVERNMENT PRINTING OFFICE: 1966—O-727-488 GPO 945-880

Figure 48.—Special Customs Invoice, obverse and reverse, required for import shipments with values in excess of $500, if for sale, and $1,000, if not for sale. (Size 8½ x 11 inches.)

DECLARATION FOR FREE ENTRY OF WORKS OF ART, ARTISTIC ANTIQUITIES, ORIGINAL PAINTINGS, STATUARY, ETC.

(Items 765.05—765.30, incl., 766.20, 766.25, Tariff Schedules of the United States)

BUREAU OF CUSTOMS

Entry No. ....

....
(Date of entry)

....
(Importing vessel or carrier)

PORT ....
(Date) (Name of consignee)

I, ..., the undersigned, am the ☐ owner ☐ artist ☐ ultimate consignee, of the articles described on the reverse side of this declaration or identified by the letter (A) and my initials in the entry noted above or on the invoice attached thereto, and that:

☐ 1. **ORIGINAL PAINTINGS, ENGRAVINGS, DRAWINGS, SCULPTURES, ETC. (Items 765.05—765.25, incl., T.S.U.S.)**

The articles described or identified are, to the best of my knowledge and belief,* .... and were produced by .... at ....

* State whether originals, or, in the case of statuary, whether the original model or one of the first ten castings, replicas, or reproductions, and in the case of etchings, engravings, wood cuts; lithographs, or prints made by other hand transfer processes, whether printed by hand from hand-etched, hand-drawn, or hand-engraved plates, stones, or blocks.

☐ 2. **WORKS OF ART PRODUCED BY AN AMERICAN ARTIST RESIDING TEMPORARILY ABROAD (Item 765.30, T.S.U.S.)**

I am a citizen of the United States of America, and by profession .... (artist or sculptor); my permanent residence is ....; I departed from the United States of America on or about .... to take up temporarily my residence at ....; I have not given up, and it is not my intention to give up, my residence in the United States, and it is my purpose to settle ultimately in the United States. The articles described or identified are my own production, having been produced at .... during my temporary residence abroad.

INSTRUCTIONS: In describing or identifying the articles, state title of each work and, if the work is framed, state separately the value of the work and the value of the frame.

☐ 3. **WORKS OF ART, ARTISTIC ANTIQUITIES, ETHNOGRAPHIC OBJECTS, ETC. (Items 766.20 and 766.25, T.S.U.S.)**

I have investigated the origin and history of the articles described or identified and believe they were produced, if rugs or carpets, prior to the year 1701, if violins, violas, violoncellos, or double basses, prior to the year 1801, if ethnographic objects made in traditional aboriginal styles, 50 years prior to their date of entry, or if other articles, prior to the year 1830.

The articles involved are being imported for..............................
(State whether for sale or personal use)

(See Sec. 10.53 (b), C. R.)

....
(Signature)

....
(Address)

....
(City-State-ZIP Code)

INSTRUCTIONS: Check square opposite applicable paragraph and insert information necessary to complete declaration.

CUSTOMS FORM June 1964 3307 GPO 947-947

Figure 49.—Declaration by importers required for the free entry of works of art, antiquities and ethnographic objects. (Size 8 x 10½ inches.)

Form No. 29—Printed and Sold by Unz & Co., Inc., 24 Beaver St., New York 4, N. Y.—U 36793

Form 7525-V
(Rev. July 1962)
(See Instructions on Reverse Side)

U. S. DEPARTMENT OF COMMERCE
BUREAU OF THE CENSUS—BUREAU OF INTERNATIONAL COMMERCE

SHIPPER'S EXPORT DECLARATION

OF SHIPMENTS FROM THE UNITED STATES

Export Shipments Are Subject To U. S. Customs Inspection

READ CAREFULLY THE INSTRUCTIONS ON BACK TO AVOID DELAY AT SHIPPING POINT

For shipments to foreign countries, the export declaration (*a*) must be presented to and authenticated by the Collector of Customs before the goods are placed on pier or dock or other place of loading for the purpose of exporting by water or air; (*b*) must be presented to and authenticated by the Collector prior to exportation where the goods are exported by other means.

Declarations Should Be Typewritten Or Prepared In Ink

Form approved. Budget Bureau No. 41-R397.5.

CONFIDENTIAL For use solely for official purposes authorized by the Secretary of Commerce. Use for unauthorized purposes is not permitted. (Title 15, Sec. 30.5 (b) C.F.R.; 50 U.S.C. App., 2026c.)

Customs Authentication (For Customs use only.)

Do Not Use This Area	District	Port	Country (For customs use only)

FILE NO. (For Customs use only.)

1. FROM (*U. S. Port of Export*)

2. METHOD OF TRANSPORTATION (*check one*): ☐ Vessel (incl. ferry) ☐ Air ☐ Other (Specify)______

2a. EXPORTING CARRIER (*If vessel, give name of ship, flag and pier number. If air, give name of airline.*)

3. EXPORTER (*Principal or seller—licensee*) ADDRESS (*Number, street, place, state*)

4. AGENT OF EXPORTER (*Forwarding agent*) ADDRESS (*Number, street, place, state*)

5. ULTIMATE CONSIGNEE ADDRESS (*Place, country*)

6. INTERMEDIATE CONSIGNEE ADDRESS (*Place, country*)

7. FOREIGN PORT OF UNLOADING (*For vessel and air shipments only*)

8. PLACE AND COUNTRY OF ULTIMATE DESTINATION (*Not place of transshipment.*)

(9) Marks and Nos.	(10) Number and Kind of Packages, Description of Commodities, Export License Number, Expiration Date (or General License Symbol) (Describe commodities in sufficient detail to permit verification of the Schedule B commodity numbers assigned. Do not use general terms. Insert required license information on line below description of each item)	(11) Shipping (*Gross*) Weight in Pounds[a] (required for vessel and air shipments only)	(12) Specify "D" or "F"[b]	(13) Schedule B Commodity No.	(14) Net Quantity in Schedule B Units (*State unit*)	(15) Value at U. S. Port of Export (Selling price or cost if not sold, including inland freight, insurance and other charges to U. S. port of export) (*Nearest whole dollar; omit cents figures*)

These commodities licensed by the U. S. for ultimate destination__________Diversion contrary to U. S. law prohibited.

16. WAYBILL OR MANIFEST NO. (*of Exporting Carrier*)

17. DATE OF EXPORTATION (*Not required for shipments by vessel*)

18. THE UNDERSIGNED HEREBY AUTHORIZES__________ (Name and address—Number, street, place, State) TO ACT AS FORWARDING AGENT FOR EXPORT CONTROL AND CUSTOMS PURPOSES.

EXPORTER__________ BY (DULY AUTHORIZED OFFICER OR EMPLOYEE)__________

▶ 19. I CERTIFY THAT ALL STATEMENTS MADE AND ALL INFORMATION CONTAINED IN THIS EXPORT DECLARATION ARE TRUE AND CORRECT. I AM AWARE OF THE PENALTIES PROVIDED FOR FALSE REPRESENTATION. (*See Paragraphs I (c), (e), on reverse side.*)

Signature__________ (Duly authorized officer or employee of exporter or named forwarding agent)

For__________ (Name of corporation or firm, and capacity of signer; e.g., secretary, export manager, etc.)

Address__________

▶ Declaration should be made by duly authorized officer or employee of exporter or of forwarding agent named by exporter.

[a]If shipping weight is not available for each Schedule B item listed in column (13) included in one or more packages, insert the approximate gross weight for each Schedule B item. The total of these estimated weights should equal the actual weight of the entire package or packages.

[b]Designate foreign merchandise (reexports) with an "F" and exports of domestic merchandise produced in the United States or changed in condition in the United States with a "D." (*See instructions on reverse side.*)

CARRIERS, FORWARDERS AND EXPORTERS ARE REMINDED THAT IF A DESTINATION CONTROL STATEMENT IS REQUIRED ON A SHIPPER'S EXPORT DECLARATION COVERING A GIVEN SHIPMENT, SUCH STATEMENT MUST ALSO APPEAR ON ALL COPIES OF THE BILL OF LADING AND COMMERCIAL INVOICE. (*See Comprehensive Export Schedule.*)

Do Not Use This Area

Figure 50.—Shipper's Export Declaration which must be filled in by exporters or their forwarding agents and filed with the Collector of Customs. (Size 8½ x 11 inches.)

References:

BUDD, JOHN F., editor. Custom House guide. New York, Import Publications, Inc. (Annual publication; contains tariff schedules of the United States annotated in accordance with the Tariff Classification Act of 1962; lists of articles subject to duty with rates, articles free of duty, customs regulations, alphabetical import commodity index, trade agreements, and other information for importers.)

DERENBERG, WALTER J. and BAUM, DANIEL J. Congress rehabilitates modern art. New York University Law Review. Vol. 34, no. 7, November, 1959, pp. 1228–1253.

DUDLEY, DOROTHY H. Problems of importing and exporting works of art, The Museum News, Vol. 26, October 15, 1949, pp. 5–7.

———. Report on passing of bill (H.R. 2411) to revise the tariff laws for works of art, Museum News, Vol. 38, no. 4, December, 1959, p. 13.

HENIUS, FRANK. Dictionary of foreign trade. New York, Prentice-Hall, Inc., 1946. (Contains explanations of foreign trade terms, practices and procedures, and illustrations of customs and shipping forms.)

HORN, PAUL V. International trade principles and practices. New York, Prentice-Hall, Inc., 1951.

JAVITS, JACOB K. Art needs a new passport, Museum News, Vol. 37, no. 1, March, 1959, pp. 14–15. (The Senior Senator from New York discusses proposed revisions in U. S. Customs regulations.)

ROSENTHAL, MORRIS S. Techniques of international trade. New York, McGraw-Hill Book Co., 1950.

Trade barriers to knowledge. Paris, UNESCO Publication 847, 1951. (Available through Columbia University Press, New York; contains regulations affecting educational, scientific and cultural materials in 43 countries.)

The following are publications of the U. S. Government. For information about them, consult issuing agency or the Superintendent of Documents, Government Printing Office, Washington 25, D. C.

Correct way to fill out the shipper's export declaration. U. S. Dept. of Commerce, Bureau of the Census.

Schedule B: Statistical classification of domestic and foreign commodities exported from the United States, January 1, 1965, with supplemental bulletins and insert pages. U. S. Dept. of Commerce, Bureau of the Census. (Available through Department Field Offices, Collector of Customs; contains the specific commodity information necessary for the preparation of the *Shipper's Export Declaration* required by the U. S. Government for export shipments.)

Postal manual. U. S. Post Office Dept.

Customs regulations of the United States. U. S. Treasury Dept., Bureau of Customs.

Summary of United States Export Control Regulations. U. S. Dept. of Commerce, Office of Export Control.

Tariff Schedules of the United States, annotated, 1963. U. S. Tariff Commission (T. C. Publication 103.)

Chapter 9

INSURANCE

This chapter is directed to registrars who are responsible for administering insurance policies covering loan and permanent collections. It is intended as an elementary guide to help them work intelligently with museum insurance representatives, conservators, curators and other members of the staff, and it suggests procedures for handling insurance reports and claims for damage. Museum insurance representatives should be consulted for more detailed information. For precise definitions of insurance terms, readers are referred to the glossary at the end of this chapter, prepared by Huntington T. Block, an insurance broker-agent whose Washington, D. C. firm specializes in fine arts insurance. Mr. Block's assistance in preparing this chapter is gratefully acknowledged.

FINE ARTS INSURANCE

Insurance is not a substitute for the precautions taken by museums in safeguarding their collections, but it is a means of compensating them financially if loss or damage occurs. Despite the best preventive and protective measures in museums occasional losses or damages occur, owing to a variety of causes, such as bursting steam and water pipes, vandalism in the galleries, fire, theft, or accidents while objects are being handled, particularly when they are away from the museum or in transit.

Insurance offers financial protection against these unexpected or "fortuitous" losses. When damages can be repaired, insurance will cover the cost of restoration and depreciation. In the case of total loss, museum objects which are unique can never be replaced; but the payment of the insured value makes it possible to purchase new acquisitions which may to some extent substitute for the lost item in the collection. (See "Insurable Interest," "Insurable Loss" and "Insurance" in glossary.)

Fine arts insurance is normally handled as so-called "inland marine" or "inland transportation" insurance which came into use after the liberalization and extension of coverage in ocean marine policies. Unlike underwriters for other insurance companies, marine and inland marine underwriters were not restricted to narrow lines of coverage but made it possible for property to be insured against "all risks" under one policy instead of under several separate policies. Eventually, property could be covered under these policies whether or not it was subject to transportation risks. (See "All Risk Policy," "Inland Marine Insurance," and "Marine Insurance" in glossary.)

The fine arts policy was first written in answer to the need for a broad coverage for art collections, and is now used by museums to insure a variety of objects. It may cover permanent collections as well as the property of others which is on loan to exhibitions or held for study and possible acquisition. It may be written on an "all risks" or "named peril" basis. It may be used to insure objects: 1) only while on the premises; 2) only while in transit; or 3) while on the premises, in transit and at other locations.

When insurance covers objects only while on the premises, individual trip transit insurance may be arranged if occasional shipments are made. When frequent shipments are made from the permanent collections, or if objects are being continually borrowed for exhibition, broader "floater coverage" is advisable. Fine arts floater policies cover insured objects against all risks, or certain specified risks, from the time they leave the hands of owners until they are returned, whether in storage, on exhibition, in transit, or at other locations. The term "floater" means that objects are covered anywhere within the territorial limits of the policy. The protection "floats" with the property. This coverage, often referred to as "wall-to-wall" or in Europe as "nail-to-nail" is valuable protection. (See "Floater Policy," "Named Peril Policy," and "Wall-To-Wall" in glossary.)

Floater policies do not normally cover property outside the continental United States and Canada, or on fair grounds or the premises of national or international expositions unless special arrangements are made and the policies endorsed accordingly. Also, they may include limits of liability (i.e. a limit to the amount covered on any one conveyance or in any one location or on any one object). In order for them to cover trans-oceanic shipments, specific arrangements must be made. (See "Endorsement" and "Rider" in glossary.)

The amount and kind of insurance protection purchased by museums varies, as does the rate, which is expressed in "X" cents per $100. of value per month or per year. Some museums do not insure their own collections unless they leave the premises. The decision not to insure them when at home is usually made when it is felt that a sound, fire-proof building, fire watches, gallery guards, night watchmen, alarm systems, carefully trained and supervised handlers, and conservation facilities provide sufficient protection. Budget considerations may, of course, be another reason for not insuring permanent collections unless they leave the premises.

When collections are insured, policies are generally written with one or both of the following types of coverage:

1) *Coverage based on a stated or flat amount* (i.e. a fixed amount of loss that can be claimed in any one occurrence). Museums calculate the amount for which they wish to be protected, and buy insurance accordingly. With a loss limit of $1,000,000, for example, claims for loss or damage to one or several objects in a given incident would be covered up to the stipulated amount of $1,000,000. Policies with this type of coverage have proved feasible in museums with large and extremely valuable permanent collections when the cost of full coverage would be prohibitive. Museums with this type of coverage must of course accept the risk for any losses beyond the limits specified in their policies.
2) *Coverage based on the value of individual objects.* Policies with this type of coverage are called "scheduled policies" because they are based on a list maintained in the museum's records giving a specified value for each object, or on a list or schedule furnished to the insurance company.
   Scheduled policies are used by some museums for insuring both permanent and loan collections. If the insured values of objects in the permanent collection are based on current market values, these values must be kept up to date and increases and decreases reflected in amounts reported to the insurance company.
   When written with floater coverage, scheduled policies are particularly useful for insuring objects borrowed for temporary exhibitions. If the objects in the permanent collection are insured only when on the premises or are not covered at all while on the premises, outgoing loans can, of course, be insured either under a floater policy arranged by the lender or the borrower, or individual trip transit insurance can be arranged as mentioned previously. (See chapter 6 for discussion of insurance coverage for loans from permanent collections.)

Policies are often written with deductible or franchise clauses. Deductibles are agreed amounts which are deducted from the total loss claimed; therefore if the amount of a loss is less than the deductible, no claim at all is made. Franchises are similar to deductibles except that the insurance company pays the entire amount if a claim equals or exceeds the amount of the franchise. Both clauses reduce the number of small claims and the paper work necessary in processing them, and also are influential in reducing premiums. If deductibles and franchises are included in their policies, museums should budget funds to cover the cost of losses or repairs not amounting to a claim. (See "Deductible," "Franchise Clause," "Limit of Liability," "Loss Limit," "Scheduled Insurance Policies" and "Valued Insurance Policies" in glossary.)

PURCHASING INSURANCE

It is customary for brokers or broker-agents who are experts in the insurance field to be selected to advise museums on their insurance problems and to act for them in placing their insurance with reliable companies. The amount and kind of coverage to be purchased is usually determined by the administrative head or business manager in each museum with the advice of these experts and in consultation with members of the staff who are familiar with the number and variety of risks that should be covered. The registrar may be called upon to help determine the coverage needed. (See "Insurance Agent," "Insurance Broker" and "Insurance Broker-Agent" in glossary.)

A registrar with the responsibilities described in previous chapters becomes familiar with the hazards to which objects are subjected and is in a good position to work with the insurance representative in administering the permanent and loan collection policies. His control of the entry and exit of objects, his responsibility for their safe handling and safekeeping while in his custody, his records of their condition, and his registration files identifying and recording the location of each object in the permanent and loan collections are an important part of the security provided by the museum.

Working with the insurance representative, the registrar should see that he is informed not only of the curatorial and registration procedures but also of all the museum's security regulations and protective measures, such as guarding and alarm systems, its packing and shipping methods, its conservation program, and its loss experience so that this information can be given to the underwriter for the company insuring the collections. This information as well as the physical condition and location of the building and its published fire rate will influence the underwriter in determining the amount of risk he can accept for the insurance company and the rates to be charged. (See "Fire Rating," "Insurance Underwriter" and "Loss Experience or Loss Ratio" in glossary.)

There is no one form of policy or established rate for insuring a museum's permanent and loan collections.[1] Standard fine arts policies are adapted to fit the requirements of each museum. Museums may decide to purchase more than one type of fine arts coverage to provide varying amounts and kinds of protection for permanent collections, loans to temporary exhibitions and "Extended Loans." Some may decide to purchase separate policies to cover each loan exhibition. All policies, however, should provide coverage against all risks, or certain specified risks, of physical loss or damage from external cause. Damage or loss resulting from the following are customarily excluded in all policies:

a) Wear and tear, gradual deterioration, moths, vermin, inherent vice

[1] A fine-arts insurance form suggested as a standard policy for museums is illustrated in A Primer on Museum Security by Caroline K. Keck, Huntington T. Block, Joseph Chapman, John B. Lawton, Dr. Nathan Stolow. (See references at end of this chapter.)

b) Repairs, restoration or retouching

c) Acts of government: war, insurrection, confiscation

d) Nuclear reaction

Inherent vice means "the quality which an object has to deteriorate or damage itself without external help." For example: paintings finished in tempera over oil which results in the peeling away of the tempera; the checking of inadequately cured wood sculpture; and the deterioration of cheap paper. (See "Inherent Vice" and "War Risk" in glossary.)

Before a final decision on coverage is made, the policy or policies being considered should be checked carefully and the insurance representative asked to explain all of the provisions, particularly any other exclusions that appear. It may be desirable to request the removal of certain exclusions. For example: 1) clauses excluding breakage of fragile objects can and should be removed; 2) if higher rates are being charged for insuring fragile objects, it may be desirable to request that rates be averaged to avoid the necessity for totalling valuations for separate groups; 3) "fidelity exclusions" (concerning the possible dishonesty of museum personnel) should be removed or, if removal is not possible, employee bonds should be checked to see if they are adequate and, to avoid conflict in the event of a loss, issued by the same company that is covering the collections. (See "Fidelity Exclusion" in glossary.)

Policies should also be checked to see if provisions that would be to the advantage of the museum could be added. For example: 1) the payment of the current market value of objects at the time of loss; 2) the insurance of the museum's interest in remainder gifts and jointly owned property; 3) the insurance of trans-oceanic shipments (ocean and air transit coverage); 4) coverage during strikes, riots and civil disturbances; 5) bailee or legal liability (protection in case lenders' insurers subrogate against borrowing museums; see section below "Subrogation and Waiver of Subrogation"). It may also be desirable to include deductibles or franchises to reduce the number of small claims as well as the premium. (See "Bailee," "Bailee's Liability," "Legal Liability," "Strikes, Riots and Civil Commotion," "Subrogation" and "Valuation Clause" in glossary.)

It should be made clear in policies that the museum, at its discretion, can release insured objects to its packing, forwarding and carrying agents either without value declarations or with nominal value declarations when considered desirable as safe handling precautions. A limited amount of liability is assumed by these agents, and insurance companies can subrogate against them and collect a percentage of a claim if damages have been caused by their negligence. If a warranty on the use of competent packers is included in the policy, it would be advisable to phrase it so that the museum "to the best of its ability" will provide for insured objects to be packed and unpacked by competent packers. Any clauses restricting the protection of the museum should be reworded if possible. For example, the museum should not be required to report a loss or damage "immediately after it occurs," but to report it "as soon as practicable" or "immediately after its discovery."

When a large amount of insurance protection is purchased, policies are written by several insurance companies to spread the risk. The museum deals with one company through the insurance representative, but that company, known as the "lead company," reinsures with at least one other company. The "lead company" establishes the rate and, with the museum's insurance representative, services the account. It may sometimes be advisable to arrange a special policy for an individual exhibition with an extremely high value instead of covering it under the museum's existing policy. Rates for this special coverage should be favorable. (See "Lead Company" and "Reinsurance" in glossary.)

Objects in trans-oceanic shipments forwarded either by ship or airplane are covered by marine insurance. This can be arranged as automatic coverage under a floater policy and the value of each shipment reported periodically. It may be desirable to broaden the marine coverage by including in the policy a "marine extension clause" to protect the objects insured against delays, deviation, forced discharge or other variation in the trip. The rates are higher than those paid for overland shipments and should be discussed with the insurance representative. Rates by air are usually lower than by ship. Certain clauses such as "general average" and "particular average" appear in marine insurance policies. It is advisable to ask the insurance representative to explain them. (See "Marine Extension Clause" and "Marine Insurance" in glossary.)

After the insurance coverage has been determined it is helpful for the registrar and other staff members concerned to meet with the insurance representative periodically to discuss problems that arise, the adjustment service, the possible revision of rates, future plans and other matters relating to the museum's insurance program.

INSURANCE REPORTS

Policies based on a stated or flat amount of coverage (a loss limit) do not require a report of individual values as the objects are covered up to the fixed limit for any loss or damage in a given incident. They may, however, require periodic re-evaluations. With this kind of coverage it should be understood that museums can determine the valuations of objects in case of loss or damage. These "loss limit" non-reporting policies eliminate the necessity of frequent revision and detailed reporting as values increase or decrease.

Scheduled policies based on the specified values of individual objects require the periodic reporting of amounts at risk. Reports, however, may be made with a minimum of detail. For example, it may be possible for reports of total amounts at risk, instead of itemized values, to be made for periods varying from every month to every three years with adjustments to premiums after each report. When lists with itemized values are not made, museums permit the insurance company to have access, if necessary, to their records of insurance values. For reporting additions and cancellations for temporary exhibitions, it may be advantageous to report each month the total amount at risk on the last day of the preceding month and pay a monthly premium. If, for budgetary purposes, it is desirable to break down the total amount at risk, the total value of additions and cancellations for each loan exhibition may be shown. For example:

MUSEUM OF ART — DATE ____________

INSURANCE REPORT — POLICY NO. ____________

Exhibitions	*Previous Report*	*Added*	*Cancelled*	*Balance This Report*
Eight American Sculptors	$150,000.		$100,000.	$ 50,000.
Landscape Paintings	60,000.	$ 50,000.		110,000.
Twentieth Century Drawings		$75,000.		75,000.
	$210,000.	$125,000.	$100,000.	$235,000.
Other Museum Exhibitions at Risk	$200,000.			200,000.
	$410,000.			$435,000.

The total value of new acquisitions to the permanent collections or of objects cancelled, if any, may also be shown on this report if they are covered on the same scheduled policy.

INSURANCE CERTIFICATES

Occasionally a packing agent, freight forwarder or lender requires a certificate of insurance stating that the object or objects being packed, forwarded or lent are fully insured by the museum. In some instances they ask to be named as insured. Normally, this certificate is written evidence of insurance in force signed by the insurance company or its agent. It is helpful, however, if the insurance representative can supply a form which can be filled in and signed by the registrar for this purpose (see figure 51). (See "Additional Insured Clause," "Certificate of Insurance" and "Cover Note or Certificate of Insurance" in glossary.)

SUBROGATION AND WAIVER OF SUBROGATION

The subrogation clause in a policy allows the insurance company to assume the rights of the insured to collect from a third party if a loss or damage is caused by negligence of the third party and not by an "Act of God" (i.e. an event over which man has no control). A waiver of subrogation is an agreement whereby the insurance company waives this right to subrogate against a third party. A waiver is sometimes requested by borrowing museums when lenders wish to maintain their own insurance. The museum's packing and carrying agents who are legally liable to certain extents may also request that subrogation against them be waived. When this request is granted, the insurance company may agree to "waive subrogation beyond their common law or statutory liability." (See "Act of God," "Subrogation" and "Waiver of Subrogation" in glossary.)

INSURANCE CLAIMS

It is customary for an insurance adjuster to be appointed by the insurance company to settle claims for loss or damage exceeding a specified amount or when subrogation is involved. The registrar should request that the company choose in advance an adjuster who has some understanding of fine arts or other objects covered by the museum's policy. (See "Insurance Adjuster" in glossary.)

Before reporting a loss or damage the registrar must understand the following conditions under which a claim can be made:

1) The object damaged must have been covered by the policy at the time of loss.
2) The damage must have resulted from a peril insured against.
3) The total loss or amount of repairs plus depreciation, if any, must exceed the amount of the museum's deductible or equal or exceed the amount of a franchise if included in the policy.

He must also understand and explain to the museum's staff or lenders concerned that if total loss is claimed and paid, the insurance company owns the salvage. (See "Depreciation," "Insurable Loss" and "Salvage" in glossary.)

Reporting a Loss or Damage

If an insurance claim is justifiable, the insurance representative must be notified in writing of the loss or damage as soon as possible after it is discovered and given a description of its extent and of the circumstances surrounding it. The report of loss or damage does not in itself constitute a claim. It is simply a notification that conditions have been recorded that may lead to a claim. If a damage has occurred in transit, it is also reported to the carrier, and whenever possible, inspected by the carrying agency's representative. As mentioned previously, carriers have a limited liability, and insurance companies can subrogate against them and collect a percentage of the claim if damages have been caused by their negligence. (See Chapter 7 for a discussion of the liability of carriers and value declarations made by shippers.)

If an object has disappeared and theft is suspected, a report should be made immediately to the local police and, if the value is over $5,000., also to the Federal Bureau of Investigation, as well as to the insurance representative. It is important that a photograph and complete description of a stolen object be supplied to the investigators as soon as possible.

If an object has been damaged a condition photograph should be made as soon as possible and a conservator consulted and asked to estimate the cost of repairs. If a serious damage is involved, it is reported to the insurance adjuster and inspected by him in consultation with the conservator and any others concerned. It may not be possible to determine the amount of depreciation until restoration has been completed.

In so far as possible, damaged objects should be left as they are until the adjuster has made his examination. This does not preclude whatever action may be necessary to prevent further loss. First-aid treatment, however, should be made only by a trained conservator. No repairs should be made without the consent of the owner, and the insurance adjuster must approve the conservator's estimate of the cost of final restorative repairs.

The Actual Claim

When final costs of restoration are known and the amount of depreciation, if any, has been agreed upon by all concerned, the total amount is reported to the insurance company. When an adjuster has been employed, he prepares a *Proof of Loss,* a document which must be signed and notarized to substantiate the claim. Settlement is made either with the lender, if the damaged object is a loan, or with the museum, either as owner or borrower. If there is disagreement between the museum or lender and the insurer as to the amount claimed, settlement may be based on the decision of a third party mutually acceptable to all concerned. (See "Proof of Loss" in glossary.)

When processing claims the registrar should understand that provision is made under the "Sue and Labor Clause" in the policy, for the insurance company to reimburse the museum for expenses incurred while attempting to recover lost or damaged property. This clause makes it "lawful" and "necessary" for the insured "to sue, labor and travel" in order to assist the insurance company in recovering a loss.

SUMMARY

Working with the insurance representative, the registrar must be familiar with all precautions taken by the museum to prevent loss or damage and maintain its collections in good condition. His files must identify each object in the permanent and loan collections and show its location or disposition. He must keep records of the condition and valuation of all objects or he must have access to them in the conservation or curatorial offices. Above all, he must read and understand the insurance policies covering the loan and permanent collections, including the obscure clauses in fine print, and ask the insurance representative to explain anything that is not clear.

CONCISE GLOSSARY OF INSURANCE TERMS

Prepared by HUNTINGTON T. BLOCK INSURANCE, Washington, D. C.

ACT OF GOD: a happening, such as a tornado, a hailstorm, etc., over which man normally has no control.

ADDITIONAL INSURED CLAUSE: an agreement, often limited as to term, whereby a third party, with a valid insurable interest, is made an insured under the policy. (Note: Museums often request Certificates of Insurance naming them as "Additional Insureds." The museum's insurable interest is the extent of its legal liability for loss caused by its own negligence to the object in its care or custody.)

ALL RISK POLICY: covers against "all risks of loss or damage . . . except as herein provided." The exceptions or exclusions are specifically listed. (Note: Most Fine Arts policies are on an "All Risk" basis.)

ASSURED: and Insured are synonymous.

BAILEE: a person to whom goods, the property of others, are entrusted for a special purpose and for a limited period.

BAILEE'S LIABILITY: a Bailee is normally liable for a loss due to his own negligence. (Note: A so-called "Act of God" could not be construed as due to the negligence of a Bailee.)

BINDER: a memorandum or temporary contract of insurance issued in anticipation of the issuance of the policy itself. A binder, either oral or written, is a valid contract. A binder must include the risk to be insured, the time the protection commences, the name of the insured, and the amount.

CERTIFICATE OF INSURANCE: written evidence of insurance in force signed by the

POLICY

____

____

CERTIFICATE OF INSURANCE

This is not a policy of insurance. It is issued as a matter of information only on the understanding that it is only a Certificate of the issuance of the policy named herein and confers no rights on the holder and imposes no liability upon the Companies named herein. Said policy is subject to endorsement, alteration, transfer, assignment and cancellation in accordance with its terms and conditions.

The following is information from the policy:

ASSURED - THE MUSEUM OF MODERN ART

ADDRESS - 11 West 53rd Street, New York, N.Y.

TERM - July 1, 1962 Until Cancelled

COVERAGE - All risks of physical loss or damage from any external cause except wear and tear, gradual deterioration, moths, vermin, inherent vice, damage resulting from any repairing, restoration or retouching process nuclear reaction, radiation or radioactive contamination and risks of war, confiscation or seizure.

PROPERTY-INSURED-	LENDER	DESCRIPTION OF PROPERTY	AMOUNT

POLICY - Policy referred to herein is a Joint Subscription Policy subscribed to by the Companies indicated below.

COMPANY	COMPANY

____________, Agent

Signed by: ________________ Registrar

Figure 51.—Certificate of Insurance. (Size 8½ x 11 inches.)

insurance company or its agent. (Note: Museums often require Certificates of Insurance from borrowers before releasing works of art on loan.)

COINSURANCE CLAUSE: a provision in a policy whereby the insurance company's liability or payment is limited to that proportionate part of the loss which the total insurance purchased bears to the total value at risk or to an agreed percentage of the total value at risk. A clause to be avoided in dealing with Fine Arts.

COVER NOTE OR CERTIFICATE OF INSURNACE: a document issued by a representative of the insurance company confirming that insurance has been effected. It is most important that all insurance transactions be confirmed in writing, and since actual policies often take some time to prepare, a Cover Note or Certificate is employed prior to policy issuance.

DEDUCTIBLE: an agreed amount of loss which an insured must suffer before his policy will pay. A deductible often serves as a device to substantially lower the premium and should not be overlooked.

DEPRECIATION: the difference between the value new and a lower value at a subsequent time. In Fine Arts insurance, depreciation is an important factor in a partial loss. It represents the difference in value, if any, before damage and after restoration.

ENDORSEMENT: A modification of an insurance policy by means of a written, typed, or printed addition either to the policy itself or on a piece of paper which should be attached to it. An endorsement is sometimes referred to as a "rider".

EXCESS INSURANCE: a term used to identify insurance which is not operative until a loss exceeds a stated amount. In Fine Arts insurance, it is sometimes possible, when dealing in high values, to reduce premiums by arranging your insurance in layers, one excess of the other.

FIDELITY EXCLUSION: sometimes found in Fine Arts policies, this clause normally excludes protection for losses caused by the infidelity or dishonesty of the insured's employees or those of a concern to which the property is entrusted. Be certain that you carry an adequate bond and, to avoid conflict in the event of a loss, see that it is in the same insurance company as the one carrying your Fine Arts insurance.

FIRE RATING: a term used to identify the established cost per $100. value of fire and lightning insurance on a building or its contents. This rate is normally promulgated by a local Rating Bureau and is used by all insurance companies as a basis for establishing the "all risk" Fine Arts rate.

FLOATER POLICY: covers anywhere including in transit, in storage, or at any location. The protection "floats" with the property.

FRANCHISE CLAUSE: similar to a "deductible" except that once a loss equals or exceeds the amount of the franchise, the insurance company must pay the entire loss.

INHERENT VICE: the quality which an object has to deteriorate or damage itself without external help. A very important concept in Fine Arts insurance.

INLAND MARINE INSURANCE: generally refers to the protection of property which is floating in nature and not limited to one location. Buildings would not be a subject for Inland Marine Insurance. The protection of Fine Arts, on the other hand, is normally handled as Inland Marine Insurance.

INSURABLE INTEREST: in order to make a valid contract of insurance, the buyer (insured) must have something to lose, otherwise his contract of insurance would be nothing more than a wager.

INSURABLE LOSS: to an insurance underwriter such a loss must be of a fortuitous nature. Fortuitous means accidental, unexpected, or occurring by chance.

INSURANCE: a promise by an insurance company to indemnify or make whole a financial loss.

INSURANCE ADJUSTER: the representative appointed by the insurance company to settle claims in a manner satisfactory to the insured and in accordance with the protection afforded by the insurance contract.

INSURANCE AGENT: the agent of the insurance company and, as such, his acts, ommissions and knowledge are those of his principal. His authority, rights and obligations are defined by agency contract and by law. He normally has the authority to *bind* (attach protection on behalf of his principal).

INSURANCE BROKER: normally defined as the representative of the insured, the broker advises on and negotiates for the best insurance contracts on behalf of his principal. He normally does *not* have the authority to bind.

INSURANCE BROKER-AGENT: modern-day practice requires that most insurance be arranged through an individual who may be an agent for some companies and broker for others. (Note: It is most important that a museum's insurance representative have the authority to *bind.*)

INSURANCE UNDERWRITER: an employee of the insurance company charged with the responsibility of accepting or rejecting risks presented to the company by brokers or agents, and establishing on what terms acceptable risks will be insured.

LEAD COMPANY: a term used in connection with subscription policies (those in which several insurance companies participate for a specified percentage). The Lead Company normally establishes the rate and, with the broker/agent, services the account—the other companies normally follow the "lead" for their percentage.

LEGAL LIABILITY: is the same as Bailee Liability.

LIMIT OF LIABILITY: the most the insured may collect under various circumstances as specifically outlined in his policy. In Fine Arts insurance, you might have a limit for transportation, another while on your premises, and still another at someone else's premises. It is extremely important to know what these limits are, so that they are never exceeded.

LLOYD'S: world famed as a source for unusual or hard to place insurance. Lloyd's is a place of doing business rather than an insurance company. Insurance may be arranged only by approved brokers through underwriters representing syndicates of private investors. An insurance arrangement at Lloyd's may require several days as each underwriter (or syndicate) usually commits himself for but a small proportion of the total risk, and many underwriters must be seen before a risk is 100% "complete."

LOSS EXPERIENCE OR LOSS RATIO: usually expressed as a percentage showing the amount of losses to the amount of premiums in a given time period. A consistently low Loss Ratio should result in lower premiums.

LOSS LIMIT: is the same as Limit of Liability.

MARINE EXTENSION CLAUSE: certain special insurance provisions which normally apply when property is undergoing transport by vessel. These provisions contain standard wording (established in Admiralty Law) which afford important extra protection.

MARINE INSURANCE: Has to do primarily with property in transit. Originally confined to coverage of risks of ocean transportation, but now extended to cover transportation over inland waterways and on land generally—thus we refer to Ocean Marine and Inland Marine.

NAMED PERIL POLICY: the perils insured against are so stated in the policy. Any perils not stated, whether by intent or otherwise, are not insured. (Note: This type of policy is normally to be avoided in arranging Fine Arts insurance.)

PROOF OF LOSS: the burden of proof is on the insured to demonstrate that a loss has occurred. The policy usually specifies the manner in which this must be accomplished, including the time required for a notice of loss to be filed. In practice the Proof of Loss is prepared by the adjuster and states the total amount to be claimed; it must be signed and notarized.

REINSURANCE: a device used by the original insurer to spread or *reinsure* among other insurance companies the risk which he has accepted. (Note: In Fine Arts insurance, because of the tremendous values involved, reinsurance is often employed.)

RIDER: and Endorsement are the same.

SALVAGE: property "salvaged" from a loss. Remember that if an insurance company pays a total loss, it has in fact "purchased" the salvage.

SCHEDULED INSURANCE POLICIES: these are policies based on a list or schedule giving a specified value for each object insured.

STRIKES, RIOTS AND CIVIL COMMOTION: important protection to purchase, particularly for traveling exhibitions. Covers all manner of civil disturbances short of war or act of war. A demonstration similar to a sacking of one of our USIA libraries would not be considered an act of war.

SUBROGATION: under insurance contracts, the insurance company is entitled to any rights of the insured to collect its loss from a third party under the rules of legal liability, to the extent, of course, of the indemnification afforded by the contract of insurance. (Note: Important in Fine Arts insurance; for example, insurance companies will *subrogate* against carriers if loss is caused by negligence in transit.)

VALUATION CLAUSE: the most important clause in any Fine Arts policy—it tells exactly what you will be paid in the event of a claim, or how the amount of your claim will be determined.

VALUED INSURANCE POLICIES: these are policies in which specific values of the property insured are made a part of the policy, and the amounts so stated are payable by the insurance company in case of total loss. (Note: Many Fine Arts policies are written on a "valued" basis, but normal escalation of values calls for institutions to re-examine declared values often.)

WAIVER OF SUBROGATION: an agreement whereby the insurance company or the insured waives his right of subrogation against a third party. (Note: Often required by borrowing museum when lender maintains own insurance.)

WALL-TO-WALL: a clause in a Fine Arts policy which extends protection from the wall (or normal repository) where the shipment originates until it is returned. An important concept because the period of packing and unpacking is automatically insured. The British refer to this extra protection as "nail-to-nail."

WAR RISK: protection normally available only during an ocean or air shipment. Virtually unobtainable while property is on land.

WAREHOUSE-TO-WAREHOUSE: the same concept as wall-to-wall, but obviously more limited, and to be avoided when dealing with Fine Arts.

References:

BLANCHARD, RALPH H. and ALBERT H. MOWBRAY. Insurance, its theory and practice in the United States. New York, McGraw-Hill, 1961. (Fifth edition)

CARMEL, JAMES H. Exhibition techniques, traveling and temporary. New York, Reinhold Publishing Corporation, 1962. (Contains chapter on insurance.)

DUDLEY, DOROTHY H. Insurance, Museum News, Vol. 45, no. 6, February, 1967, pp. 29–31. (A condensed version of chapter in this book.)

HUEBNER, S. S. and KENNETH BLACK, JR. Property insurance. New York, Appleton-Century Crofts Inc., 1957. (Fourth edition)

KECK, CAROLINE K., HUNTINGTON T. BLOCK, JOSEPH CHAPMAN, JOHN B. LAWTON, DR. NATHAN STOLOW. A primer on museum security. Cooperstown, New York State Historical Association, 1966. (Museum security viewed as a combination of physical security, insurance, environmental security, light and its effect, and other security factors. Contains a model form for fine arts insurance.)

LAWTON, JOHN B. and HUNTINGTON T. BLOCK. Museum insurance, Curator, Vol. IX, no. 4, December, 1966, pp. 289–297.

LITTLE, DAVID B. Safeguarding works of art: transportation, records and insurance. American Association for State and Local History, Technical Leaflet no. 9. History News, Vol. 18, no. 7, May, 1963.

RODDA, WILLIAM H. Fire and property insurance. Englewood Cliffs, New Jersey, Prentice Hall, Inc., 1956.

———. Inland marine and transportation insurance. Englewood Cliffs, New Jersey, Prentice Hall Inc., 1958. (Second edition)

SUGDEN, ROBERT P. Safeguarding works of art—storage, packing, transportation and insurance. New York, The Metropolitan Museum of Art, 1948.

UNESCO. Museums and Monuments V. OSBORN, ELODIE C. Manual of traveling exhibitions, 1953. (Contains a chapter on insurance which has a sample Insurance Policy for Fine Arts Coverage.)

UNESCO. Museums and Monuments X. Temporary and Traveling Exhibitions, 1963. (Contains chapter VII on insurance. Part 2 is the section on traveling exhibitions and is a revision of the original 1953 manual by Elodie C. Osborn now out of print. The present revision was made by Grace L. McCann Morley.)

Part Two

SPECIAL INFORMATION

Article 1

A PROCEDURE FOR ACQUIRING OBJECTS—INCLUDING REMAINDER AND FRACTIONAL INTEREST GIFTS

BETSY JONES

Associate Curator, Department of Painting and Sculpture; Executive Secretary of Museum Collections, Museum of Modern Art, New York

Members of the public often ask art museum employees how a museum goes about acquiring its collections. Sometimes, especially where modern art is concerned, the question comes from a visitor who has been outraged or puzzled by a particular work and wonders how it ever managed to reach the museum's walls. Usually, however, the asker just wants to know how he can bring to the museum's attention an object he thinks it may want to acquire. The following article outlines the steps through which every work passes on its way to becoming part of the collection of The Museum of Modern Art, and treats briefly special procedures for works in which a donor retains life interest and works given to the Museum in fractional interests. Many museums doubtless have similar procedures, but as there is no handbook for guidance in these matters, this outline may be useful to both curators and registrars of new museums. It is important to note at the outset that the need for constant communication between the curators of collections and the registration department cannot be over-emphasized. At The Museum of Modern Art a position called "Secretary of the Museum Collections" was created many years ago. Among functions of this job is that of providing this kind of liaison. (The following article was written August 1965)

BASIC PROCEDURE

As is customary in most art museums, acquisitions by all collections at The Museum of Modern Art (except the Film Library which, for legal reasons, has its own procedures) must receive formal approval from the Board of Trustees before they are accessioned as part of the collections. This applies equally to painting and sculpture, drawings and prints, architecture and design (including graphic design) and photography. Since the Trustees themselves cannot review each proposed acquisition personally, this responsibility is delegated to the Committee on the Museum Collections composed of Trustees and friends of the Museum, most of them collectors themselves. The Committee has the professional advice of members of the staff including the Director of the Museum Collections—who has general responsibility for all collections and specific charge of the painting and sculpture collection—and the curators of each collection. In addition, the Director of the Museum and other curatorial staff serve as advisors.

Before the Committee is shown an object, however, it is first seen by the curator within whose province it falls. He has discretionary power to turn down works he feels are not appropriate or desirable for his department's collection or which, if offered for sale, are beyond the limits of available purchase funds. However, the owner of a work turned down by a curator may, if he wishes, ask to have that decision reviewed by the Committee.

Before each Committee meeting the curators, after consultation with the Director of the Collections, draw up a list of the works they wish to propose for acquisition and send to the Secretary of the Museum Collections enough copies for each person attending the meeting. These lists contain all pertinent data about each object which may affect the Committee's decision. The agenda for the meeting is then drawn up by the Director of the Museum Collections. A list of all works to be presented to the Committee is given by the Secretary to the Registrar who sees that they are delivered in good time to the meeting room, since the Committee must see each work. (If for good reason it is not possible to have a work at the meeting at a time when a decision is needed, it must be shown in photograph. In such a case, however, the Committee may elect to accept it tentatively or in principle only, until it can actually be seen.)

Along with the agenda and the lists the Committee is also provided with a mimeographed report, prepared by the Secretary, of the balances in all purchase funds. After the Committee has studied a proposed acquisition, heard the recommendation of the staff—which is its principal guide—and discussed the work, it votes whether or not to acquire it. (Sometimes, when a large group of like objects is under consideration—for instance a collection of Tiffany glass or prints or photographs by one artist—a subcommittee of specially qualified or interested Committee members is asked to consult with the curator of the collection involved and the Director of the Collections and make a recommendation to the Committee.)

Certain works may be accepted only for the Museum's Study Collection. Each department except the Film Library has a study collection composed of works which are acquired not so much for their esthetic interest as for their historical importance or value to scholars and teachers. They are not catalogued with the Museum Collection and are not usually exhibited in the public galleries, though there is no rule preventing it. The study collections of architecture and design, and photography, which are very large, are not accessioned, but are recorded intra-departmentally. Other works may be accepted only if they can be sold to provide purchase funds or exchanged for other works. If works are accepted for the Study Collection, or for sale or trade, the donors are so informed and given the opportunity to withdraw them if they wish. Works acquired by exchange or with funds realized through the sale of an object always bear the name of the donor of the work disposed of. (The credit line of the new work might read, for instance, either "John Doe Fund" if it is a purchase, or "Gift of John Doe (by exchange)" if it was acquired through trading.)

The Committee is also shown every work already in the collection which the staff feels should be disposed of either because similar but better works have been added to the collection in the meantime, or because it no longer appears to be appropriate to the collection or of sufficient quality. Before any such work can be disposed of, however, a formal motion of approval must be passed by the Board of Trustees. The work itself must be shown to them when this approval is requested. (This permission need not be secured, of course, for works accepted for sale or exchange in the first place.)

The Committee's meeting is regularly held two days before the monthly Board meeting so that its decisions can be passed on to the Board promptly by means of a report made to the Trustees by the Committee Chairman. The most important acquisitions of each department are shown and discussed by the Director of the Collections and the curators. Following the Trustee meeting, the Chairman sends a formal receipt, usually accompanied by a letter of thanks on behalf of the Trustees, to the donor of every gift accepted. The Director of the Collections and the various curators are responsible for acting on other decisions of the Committee, such as those involving purchase negotiations, or notification to a donor that his gift was not accepted, was accepted for the Study Collection, or for sale or exchange.

Immediately after the Trustee meeting a marked agenda showing decisions on all works considered by the Committee is sent to the Registrar who assigns accession numbers to all new acquisitions.

The Secretary of the Museum Collections writes the minutes of the

Committee's meeting, and prepares the final list of acquisitions which is appended to the minutes. This list, which constitutes the formal record of acquisition, is sent to the Registrar and all curatorial departments concerned and, in slightly abbreviated form, to other members of the staff not directly concerned but who should be kept informed of new acquisitions. It contains the basic data about each work: accession number, name of artist, title of work, date of execution, medium, form for credit line, price paid if a purchase and insurance value (which is set by the appropriate curator). Since the list is usually issued before each item has been fully studied, some information such as date of execution, medium or even credit line is subject to change, but it serves as the basis for fuller documentation and provides an immediate inventory of acquisitions with accession numbers—extremely helpful to the Registrar as well as the curators. In addition to acquisitions, the list includes works which have been approved for elimination from the collection (which are finally listed again when they have actually been disposed of); extended (i.e. long-term) loans received and returned; works accepted in principle or tentatively; works considered but not approved for acquisition; and those on which decision was postponed.

The Registrar then proceeds to record each acquisition as fully as possible on a worksheet which is sent to each curator. The curators are responsible for adding pertinent data not available to the registration department and returning the worksheets so that final records can be prepared.

ACCESSIONING OF GIFTS OF REMAINDER AND FRACTIONAL INTERESTS

Revenue Rulings 57-293 and 58-455 (promulgated in 1957 and 1958) made tax benefits available to donors giving to qualified educational institutions remainder (i.e. future) interests in works of art, as well as fractional interests future and present (i.e. outright). The tax deductibility of gifts of any remainder interest whether fractional or entire was discontinued under the Revenue Act of 1964, though it is to be hoped that the Congress may soon be persuaded to reinstate it. Up until June, 1964, however, many museums received remainder and partial remainder interest gifts, in which the donor, by sacrificing some tax benefits, retained for himself the right to full use and control of a work during his lifetime while transferring ultimate title in it to the museum. The gift of a present fractional interest in a work of art is still deductible.

In accessioning such gifts it has been the practice to assign an accession number on receipt of the first deed of gift, even though the Museum's share in it may be small. A Museum label is attached to the stretcher or protective backing, if it is a painting, or in any inconspicuous spot on a piece of sculpture, identifying the work, giving its accession number and stating what the Museum's equity in it is at the date of accession. (If the work cannot be brought to the Museum the label is mailed to the donor with the request that he attach it to the work.) Filed together with the original copy of the deed of gift is a photograph of each work to which the Museum does not have full title so that at the death of the donor there will be no question as to the identity of the work given to the Museum. The Registrar maintains a separate card file of all works in which the Museum has a remainder or fractional interest.

Fractional interests must be conveyed by a duly acknowledged deed or equivalent document, and each additional fraction given requires a new deed. In an optional paragraph of the deed the donor may undertake to execute a codicil to his will bequeathing the museum any remaining fraction still owned by him at his death. This is clearly a valuable guarantee since without it the museum may find itself involved in joint ownership—and possibly controversy—with the donor's heirs in spite of the fact that a fractional gift to a public institution would seem to imply an intention to give full title eventually.

Under Revenue Ruling 57-293 an institution receiving a fractional interest in a work of art must have the right to possess it for that part of each year proportionate to its ownership. The museum is not obligated to do so, however, and is entitled to weigh the desirability of having the work in hand for parts of each year against the risk it might incur through frequent trips and consequent atmospheric changes.

INSURING PARTIAL GIFTS

Insurance of works in which a museum has a remainder or fractional interest will be handled differently according to each museum and its insurance company. The Museum of Modern Art's insurance policy, which is non-reporting, permits us to insure only our share of any such gifts (unless of course the work is temporarily in our possession, in which case the donor's share is automatically covered by the Museum). This arrangement seems practicable and reasonable. Since the Museum has no physical control over a work in which the donor retains a life interest, it should not be liable for insuring his life interest. In the case of a fractional gift, where both parties share outright ownership, the museum should of course be consulted about the use and treatment of the work in the same way that joint owners of any other kind of property would act in concert.

Article 2

CLASSIFYING PAINTINGS, DRAWINGS AND PRINTS BY MEDIA

LAWRENCE J. MAJEWSKI

Chairman, Conservation Center,
Institute of Fine Arts, New York University

The descriptive terms involving media, used in classifying objects of art, can be of considerable value, particularly to the student interested in the creative process and to those responsible for maintaining the good health of the work of art.

Medium is a term used by artists in a variety of connotations; it is, variously, (a) the mode of expression or technique employed by an artist, e.g., etching, painting, sculpture; (b) the actual instrument or material used by an artist, e.g., oil paint, metal, chiseled stone; (c) the technique or method of application involved in using these materials (this definition seems almost synonymous with (a) but is rather a subdivision of it, wherein painting might be subdivided into such techniques as palette knife, splatter, impressionism; this connotation will not be discussed here); or (d) the binding agent of a paint, that is, a liquid in which pigments are suspended and which dries after application, and in this sense is practically synonymous with vehicle—it is this meaning of the word that is significant in classifying works of art.

Of the modes of expression employed by the artist, only painting, drawing, and graphic arts are discussed here. The materials employed in any of these modes of expression all have the following in common:

The support is the paper, canvas, wood panel, plaster wall, sheet of metal, or other material which acts as a base upon which the expression is executed.

The ground (not always used in some expressions) is a preliminary coating given to the support to make a more desirable surface for rendering the expression, e.g., gesso, sizing, lead white.

The design layer consists of the pencil, chalk, ink, paint film, etc., applied to the ground and support, to form a painting, drawing, or print.

In classifying an object by medium, therefore, one must include first of all the broad terms—painting, drawing, and graphic arts—and be able to distinguish one from the other.

Painting is characterized by the more or less manual application to a surface of pigments, ground or mixed in a medium.

Drawing is characterized by the application to a surface of pigments or coloring material, such as charcoal, pencil, or silver point, by friction or rubbing or by the use of pens and inks; sometimes thin washes in a vehicle are used in drawings; obviously, there are bound to be border-line cases when a wash drawing might be called a painting and vice versa.

The graphic arts are characterized by the fact that they are printed from another surface or through the use of stencils, plates, or other means of mechanical reproduction.

PAINTINGS

A painting may be classified according to its design layer, ground, and support. In considering the design layer, the vehicle, or medium, with which pigments are mixed is the important factor, as it is the variable.

The Vehicle or Medium

The numerous vehicles or binding media available for the artist's use generally consist of one or more of the following:

SIZES: a term used more or less synonymously with the word glue. The most common glues, or sizes, are gelatin, skin glue, and casein.

GUMS: a group of noncrystalline materials occurring in plants and forming viscous solutions or mucilages. They are soluble in water and form a clear solution. Gum Arabic is the most common of the gums and is often used in the manufacture of water colors.

WAXES: complex organic compounds (esters of monohydric alcohols) obtained principally from animal secretions and from hydrocarbons; e.g., beeswax, parafin.

OILS: belong to the class of chemicals known as esters. Certain oils such as linseed oil, poppyseed oil, and walnut oil, are of a drying type; they become a jelly or polymerize when heated or when exposed to atmospheric oxygen; when spread out in thin layers they form a hard solid.

RESINS: secretions or excretions of certain plants, mostly living trees, although resins from fossil trees might also be used. These natural resins form the basis for all natural varnishes and sometimes are used as a paint medium, either alone or mixed with oil.

Synthetic Polymers (also called Synthetic Resins): complex organic semisolids made from chemical reactions on a variety of raw materials; the chemical process is that known as polymerization (the production of large or chain molecules by the union of molecules of the same kind, i.e. the monomer). These artificial products possess some of the physical properties of natural resins; they also have certain distinct characteristics, such as ease of manipulation, controlled setting or drying time, controlled gloss and transparency, that have made them popular with contemporary painters both as paint media and as coating or varnish materials.

Lime Water: used in fresco painting, and here the carbonate of lime binds the pigment to the plaster.

Mixtures and Emulsions: a mixture is a combination of two or more of the above elements, as in the mixture of linseed oil and a resin. An emulsion consists of drops of one liquid suspended in another liquid. Nonmiscible liquids such as oil and water (i.e., liquids which normally will not mix) may be suspended in each other if the droplets of either the oil or the water are surrounded by an emulsifying agent. Egg yolk is a natural oily emulsion in which the oil particles are suspended in a solution of albumen and the lecithin in the egg acts as an emulsifying agent.

Medium and Technique

In describing the final product of the artist, a list of terms has been adopted which connote the technique employed as well as the medium used. These include the following:

Pastel: a chalk or crayon made from pigments and fillers held together in stick form by a weak gum medium. It is applied dry usually to a support of paper and may be fixed with a thin spray of film-forming material such as bleached shellac in alcohol.

Water Color: used to describe a standard preparation of pigment ground in water-soluble gums. The typical water color painting is executed with paint applied thinly and with a degree of transparency on a support, usually paper.

Gouache: (also called distemper); actually a water color (or gum tempera). The word is used more to describe the opacity obtained with such paints than to define a different material. Ordinarily it is applied on a paper support but with thicker layers than in a water color technique and is further distinguished by the use of mixed tints of white for the light colors instead of transparencies of color. This term is synonymous with the terms poster paint and also opaque water color.

Tempera: has a wide variety of meanings and until the 15th century may have meant all painting media, although it most generally refers to a medium prepared from egg. For specification a second term should be used; e.g., gum tempera, glue tempera, egg tempera, casein tempera.

Glue Tempera and Gum Tempera: almost identical in appearance and are commonly called *gouache* paintings.

Egg Tempera: (in the traditional manner) generally painted on a wood support with a gesso ground. Egg yolk is mixed with pigments ground in water and the mixture is applied to the smooth gesso surface in thin layers. Gesso is a mixture of chalk or gypsum and glue and is applied in several thin coats over a sized wood panel to produce a ground that is smooth and white. Gold and silver leaf are frequently used in egg tempera paintings. In making an egg tempera painting a drawing is first made on the gesso with ink and brush; the gold or silver leaf is laid on where needed, and the layers of pigment mixed with egg yolk and water are then applied. The water evaporates quickly and the oil in the egg hardens slowly, producing a hard, strong paint film.

CASEIN TEMPERA: casein, usually referred to as a glue, is an organic protein compound generally made from the curds of milk. In casein tempera the medium is made from skim milk and lime or from powdered casein dissolved with ammonia. Pigments are mixed with this medium and applied to a variety of supports including paper, canvas, plaster, and wood panels. It somewhat resembles gum tempera in application of paint to support and in its final appearance. However, the distinguishing difference is that casein tempera dries to a very hard finish not soluble in water.

OIL: painting using a standard preparation of pigments ground in a drying oil, usually linseed oil. The oil dries first to a jelly and then to a hard film in the presence of oxygen in the air. Oil painting may be applied to a variety of supports including wood panels, masonite, paper, glass, metals, and canvas. Oil paintings are usually varnished after a period of drying to increase the index of refraction of the pigments (i.e., the amount of light reflected by pigments) and this varnish imparts to the painting a greater luminosity as well as a somewhat glossy finish.

ENCAUSTIC: a method of painting with wax that was more or less common in ancient times. The word refers, literally, to the process of melting or burning the color mixed with wax into the surface on which it is applied. Generally, encaustic paintings are on a rather absorbent support or ground, such as a gesso panel, paper, or plaster wall.

FRESCO: painting on plaster with lime water as a medium. It is of two types: true fresco or buon fresco, and dry fresco or fresco secco. Both types are often finished in egg tempera.

BUON FRESCO: or true fresco, the method of applying pigments to a freshly laid coat of wet plaster before it has had time to absorb much, if any, carbonic acid from the air. In the process, a thick layer of fine plaster is laid over a section of a rougher plaster so as to cover only the area that an artist can paint in one day. The artist then mixes his pigments, ground in water with lime water, and applies this mixture of pigment and lime water to the wet plaster. The carbonate of lime binds the pigment to the wet plaster, producing a quite permanent colored plaster surface.

FRESCO SECCO: or dry fresco, a process similar to buon fresco except that the plaster coat is allowed to dry. The plaster is then drenched with lime water the night before painting is to take place and again in the morning. The colors are mixed with a little lime water and are applied as in buon fresco. Fresco secco is not as permanent or durable as buon fresco but it is a faster method of decoration. The term fresco secco is also used to describe buon fresco with egg tempera revisions. Egg tempera and casein tempera are sometimes done on plaster but these paintings should be referred to as egg tempera on plaster or casein tempera on plaster, and not as fresco unless there is a fresco foundation (see fresco).

ENAMELS: hard gloss paints varying somewhat in composition with the manufacturer.

Generally the medium is a heat-treated oil combined with either natural or synthetic resins.

SYNTHETIC POLYMER PAINTS: or synthetic polymers used for painting are thermoplastic (may be softened with heat) and are dissolved in a solvent when used as a medium for mixing with pigments. Polyvinyl acetate, polyvinyl alcohols, polyvinyl chlorides, polyesters, epoxies, and acrylic resins are among the synthetic polymers used by painters as media. Paints using acrylic resins have become especially popular.

Medium, Ground, and Support

In classifying paintings, then, by media, it is most desirable to include the name of the technique employed, the material component of the support, and sometimes the ground, as, for example: egg tempera on gessoed wood panel; oil on canvas; gouache on paper; or casein tempera on plaster.

In some instances the artist employs different techniques and media in the same painting. These might be classified as: mixed technique—egg tempera with oil glazes on paper; or, mixed technique—casein tempera with oil glazes on canvas.

If the support is of a complex structure or has undergone a major change, this might be noted as follows: egg tempera transferred from wood panel to canvas; or oil on paper attached to canvas; etc.

Often it is most difficult to decide exactly the technique that has been used, especially in modern experimental painting. Whenever it is possible to obtain the exact process or technique from the artist himself, this is most desirable. Such information can be extremely valuable in determining the kind of treatment the painting should have to preserve it in the best manner.

The most common media used in painting have been discussed. Mention should be made of unusual elements found in paintings, such as metal foils, metal paints, sand and small stones, jewels, wood chips, plastic strips, strings. Generally these substances are used in connection with one or more of the above mentioned techniques and might be classified somewhat as follows: egg tempera with gold leaf on gessoed wood panel; oil mixed with sand on canvas; casein tempera with brass filings, leather, and feathers on paper.

Also it should be noted that as a result of experimentation and scientific discovery, new products are appearing on the market which contemporary artists are employing in their paintings. These include the enamels and some of the plastics. If possible, one should secure from the artist the type of enamel or plastic medium used. These might be classified: duco enamel on paper; synethic polymer paint—acrylic resin—

on canvas; synthetic polymer paint with oil glazes on masonite.

DRAWINGS

The classification of drawings usually involves the type of material used as a pigment rather than a vehicle or medium with which pigments are mixed. So we have drawings in pencil, pen and ink, brush and ink, charcoal, crayons of colored wax, colored chalks, and points of metals such as silver, gold, and lead. Paint of various kinds is also used in making drawings but the paint is used in a technique that would suggest more the technique that might be employed by sketching with the above mentioned materials.

The classification of drawings then might include the word "drawing" and the coloring material used as well as the support; e.g., drawing—pencil on paper; drawing—silver-point on paper; drawing—charcoal on paper.

Occasionally a drawing becomes rather complex and the result might be referred to as a painting as in the case of pastel drawings by Degas and Lautrec. However, technically when a dry-pigment process is used, that is, when the coloring substance is rubbed into the ground or support, the result should be referred to as a drawing. The classification of works in pastel as drawings or paintings is more or less a matter of opinion and, hence, in this classification pastel is listed as a type of painting as well as a drawing medium.

Graphite Pencils: (commonly called lead pencils) consist of graphite (crystalline carbon) compressed with fine clay.

Charcoal: the residue from the dry distillation of wood made by heating sticks of wood in closed chambers or kilns.

Chalk: a natural form of calcium carbonate largely composed of the remains of minute sea organisms. It is often used on tinted surfaces for the light areas while charcoal is used for the darks. (Conté crayons are a variety of chalk.)

Pastels: (or colored chalks) crayons made from pigments and fillers and held together in stick form by a weak gum medium. Some color pencils are of a pastel type but may be held together with a stronger gum.

Wax Crayons: made from pigments and fillers held together with wax. Color pencils are often a type of hard wax crayon.

Color Pencils: usually, as stated above, pigments in a stick held together by either a gum or wax. Some gum pencil drawings may have been worked over with a brush and water to achieve something of a water color effect by redissolving the gum, as in making a water color; these pencils are sometimes called water color pencils. Wax pencil drawings and wax crayon drawings are sometimes heated, as by ironing, so that the wax melts; such a technique is really an encaustic technique and more properly belongs under the classification of paintings.

Silver-point, Lead-point, and Gold-point: thin wires of lead, silver, and gold or sharpened points of these metals may be drawn across paper that has been coated with a pigment, usually white (to provide a tooth); a small deposit of the metal is rubbed into the porous or granular surface of the coating. Of these drawings, referred to as silver-point, lead-point, or gold-point, the silver-point tends to darken as the silver tarnishes; this is generally desirable.

INKS: made from dyes and from pigment suspensions. India ink is carbon black suspended in a water solution of a gum or suspended in a water solution of borax and shellac. Ink drawings may be made with pen or brush and most inks may be diluted with water to give lighter shades or tints.

Painting materials may be used in a sketching or drawing technique and should be referred to as to the type of paint used (see paintings); e.g., drawing—water color on paper; drawing—oil on paper; drawing—egg tempera on paper; etc.

Any combination of the above media might conceivably exist in a single drawing. In such drawings, the various media should be listed in the order of their importance in the design; e.g., drawing—wax crayon, pencil, and ink on cardboard; drawing—pen and ink and water-color washes on paper; etc.

GRAPHIC ARTS

The term graphic arts is in general use for designating all processes for the production of multiple-proof pictures on paper on a hand-made basis, the work being done either wholly or in most part by the original artist, and the editions limited. The processes are also referred to as print making and the resultant pictures as prints.

In classifying prints it is of value to know something about the various processes in use today, as the technique in use is the important factor in the classification of the graphic arts. These processes may be grouped into four types based on the type of surface that holds the printing ink or coloring substance for the print: i.e., relief, intaglio, planographic, and stencil.

Relief Processes

In the relief processes part of the surface of a flat block is cut away so that the design stands up to provide a printing surface. Woodcuts, wood engravings, and cuts of linoleum, lucite, cardboard, chipboard, and composition board as well as plaster blocks.

WOODCUT: a block of wood cut plank-wise is cut away with knives, gouges, and chisels to leave that part of the surface which is the design. The surface is then inked and the print made on soft paper. Several different woodblocks may be used for the same print and several colors may be used on these blocks, as in the case of the Japanese woodcuts. Generally a woodcut is characterized by angular direct, coarse lines and black and white areas in sharp contrast. Linoleum cuts, lucite cuts, and cuts of such materials as masonite, plywood, etc. are variations of the woodcut process. The cellocut, also a variation of the woodcut process, is made by coating a smooth block or plate with coats of a plastic varnish composed of celluloid dissolved in acetone; when this varnish has set, the resultant surface is worked as a woodcut.

WOOD-ENGRAVING: crosscut sections of box wood or similar fine grained wood are glued together to form an absolutely smooth cutting surface. Burins or gravers of various sizes are used to cut out the design. The burin is a very hard steel shaft with a V-shaped cutting edge and rounded wooden handle. Because the wood is cross-cut, the artist with great skill can achieve delicate lines of surgical precision and grey tones through crosshatching. Wood engravings are printed on soft paper.

PLASTER BLOCK PRINT: Smooth blocks of plaster of Paris are obtained by casting the plaster in a frame on glass. The plaster block is then engraved or worked and printed like a woodcut. Since the plaster is rather soft, a somewhat limited edition of about 30 prints is possible.

Intaglio Processes

The principle of the intaglio process is the exact opposite of that of the relief process. The printing line is a groove or furrow below the nonprinting surface of a metal plate. In other words, the lines which are etched or cut away from the plate carry the ink rather than the high standing areas, as in the relief processes. Engravings, etchings, soft-ground etchings, aquatints, mezzotints, and cellocuts are examples of this process. New techniques are described in *New Ways of Gravure*, by Stanley William Hayter (Pantheon Books, New York, 1949).

ENGRAVING: a steel, copper, or zinc plate (today usually copper) is worked with the burin—the V-shaped hard-steel graver. Sharp, clean-cut lines with tapering ends are characteristic. The engraved plate is inked so that the lines are filled, and the surface is wiped clean. The paper support for the engraving is then dampened and the print is made under pressure in an etching press. The cellocut (see above) can be printed in the same manner, and thus is a variation of the engraving as well as of the woodcut.

ETCHING: in making an etching, a clean copper or zinc plate is covered with a varnish or other substance impervious to acid. Lines are then drawn with an etching needle to penetrate this substance and expose the copper or zinc. The plate is immersed in an acid bath, the acid attacking the drawn lines of the bare copper or zinc. The length of time the plate remains in the acid determines the depth of the etched line. Etching lines are flowing and threadlike. The plate is printed in the same manner as an engraving, in an etching press under pressure on dampened paper.

SOFT-GROUND ETCHING: a process similar to etching except that a softer coating is used on the plate; paper is laid over this soft ground plate and the drawing is done on the paper. Pressure from drawing on the paper picks up part of the ground and exposes the copper or zinc so that it can be etched with acids. The resultant lines are coarse, grainy, and pencillike—no sharp lines are obtainable by this process.

Aquatint: the plate is carefully and evenly covered with a powdered resin dust and heated, so that each particle of dust becomes crystallized and adheres firmly to the plate. The particles leave small exposed sections of the plate which are then bitten by immersion in acids. Through a series of resin treatments delicate gradations of tone can be produced. The aquatint is characterized by a fine or coarse grainy texture of tones and no lines. It is printed like an etching.

Mezzotint: similar to an aquatint in appearance but the plate is prepared by scraping, tooling with special tools, and burnishing the metal surface until the desired gradations of tone are achieved. The mezzotint is characterized by a grainy stippled texture with fine gradations of tone. It is printed like an etching.

Drypoint: made by applying a sharp tool or diamond-pointed needle directly to the copper plate. The needle tears into the smooth copper plate leaving a rough edge known as a "burr" along the side of the line. This burr gives a character of fuzziness to the drypoint line but quickly wears away in the etching press so that the first prints from a drypoint plate are most characteristic. It is printed under pressure on dampened paper as in an etching.

Inkless Intaglio or Embossed Print: These are prints made from engraved or etched intaglio plates without ink. The design is created in relief through embossing the paper by running the dampened paper and plate through a press under pressure.

Planographic Processes

In the planographic process there is only one technique—lithography.

Lithograph: a technique of surface printing achieved through a change in surface structure of the printing stone or zinc plate rather than through a change in the physical contours of the block or plate as in the relief and intaglio processes.

In the lithograph the design is drawn directly on a smooth limestone slab with a grease crayon or with tusche, a liquid ink. The design is fixed on the stone by a wash of acid gum Arabic solution so the grease crayon does not spread. When this solution is completely dry the stone is washed with clear water and inked. The water wets that part of the stone where there is no grease crayon and the greasy ink adheres to that part of the stone where there is no water. The stone is placed face up on the traveling bed of the lithographic press and printed on slightly dampened paper under pressure.

Stencil Processes

In the stencil processes ink or color is applied to the perforated or cut-out sections of especially treated paper or other thin material so that the desired pattern comes through to the paper or surface below the stencil.

Serigraph: the most recent development of the stencil process and primarily a color technique, the serigraph is a fine silk-screen print. In simple terms a stencil or series of stencils are placed on one or more screens of pure silk. A support (usually paper) is placed beneath the silk screen and paint is forced through the silk in the design areas where the stencil is cut away. Through the use of several screens (as many as 50 or more although usually many less) different colors and gradations of tone may be achieved in the serigraph.

Allied Processes

In addition to the four types of processes mentioned above, certain allied processes are often included in the category of the graphic arts.

MONOTYPE: or monoprint, unique print made from a painted plate. It stands halfway between painting and print making. Any smooth surface as glass, metal plates, or plywood may be used as a support for the design, and the transfer is usually made to a sheet of paper with the aid of a press, a hot iron, or merely by rubbing the back surface of the paper as it is placed on the painted plate.

PLASTER-MOLD PRINT: an engraved or etched plate usually of bold design is well inked and placed face upward on a sheet of glass. A frame ¾-inch deep, with a margin of a few inches, is placed around the plate and plaster is poured over the plate to fill the frame. After the plaster has set, the plate of glass is removed and the etched or engraved plate is removed from the plaster by heating slightly. The resultant print on plaster has the smooth surface of polished marble and the engraved or etched line stands in relief.

COLLAGE: composition of various materials such as small pieces of paper, textiles, strings, wire screen, or wood. Since the design is composed of ready-made elements and often of printed matter such as labels, bits of newspaper, or photographs, there is a tendency to classify collages under the general heading of graphic arts, although this is somewhat a matter of opinion.

Selected References to Aid in Classifying Media

CENNINI, Cennino d'Andrea, "The Craftsman's Handbook," Trans. by D. V. Thompson, Dover Publications, New York, 1954.

GETTENS, R. J. and Stout, G. L., "Painting Materials, A Short Encyclopedia," D. Van Nostrand Co., New York, 1942. Dover Publications, N. Y., 1966.

JENSEN, Lawrence N., "Synthetic Painting Media," Prentice Hall, Inc., Englewood Cliffs, N. J., 1964.

MAYER, Ralph, "The Artist's Handbook of Materials and Techniques," Viking Press, New York, 1957.

PETERDI, Gabor, "Printmaking," The Macmillan Co., New York, 1961.

"Synthetic Materials Used in the Conservation of Cultural Properties," published by the International Centre for the Study of the Preservation and the Restoration of Cultural Property, Rome, Italy, 1963.

WATROUS, James, "The Craft of Old Master Drawings," University of Wisconsin Press, Madison, 1957.

Article 3

THE INSPECTION OF ART OBJECTS AND GLOSSARY FOR DESCRIBING CONDITION

RICHARD D. BUCK

Conservator, Intermuseum Laboratory
Oberlin, Ohio

Condition refers to the state of preservation of an object. It can be said that there are three basic aspects of condition. An object may be insecure because of weakness of material or construction brought about by deterioration or mechanical stresses. It may be damaged because the deterioration has advanced to a state of actual losses or ruptures, or it may be damaged through subjections to mechanical or physical violence or chemical change. Lastly an object may be disfigured by dirt, stains, discolored coatings, poor restorations, or by damage. Condition, comprehensively, must be described in these three aspects.

Condition in all its aspects should be familiar territory for a registrar because his office is a check point in the traffic of museum objects, a place where all points of condition should be observed and comprehended, even if they are not all recorded. On the other hand, the full record of condition belongs in the curator's dossier and in the records of periodic inspections carried out by the conservator. These more detailed records should be available to registrars.

The practical need for information on condition is apt to arise when objects are to be handled or arrangements made for their exhibition, storage, or shipment. It is the function of the registrar or whoever is performing the registrar's duties to inspect an object upon its arrival at the museum. This first inspection is important in view of possible damage claims, and for that reason insecurity is a primary matter of concern to a registrar. He should also be able to recognize and describe recent or unrepaired damage. The questions of an old damage that may be hidden under restorations, or of disfigurement, are in general of less immediate importance to the registrar; they are more properly the concern of the curatorial or conservation departments.

To some extent the limits of the registrar's concern with condition may be defined by the equipment that is available for inspections. A registrar should have available a good-sized table over which are fitted at least two strong lights; a hand lens should also be available. Some museums have such a facility located at a strategic point and reserved for inspections alone. If the lights are so switched that both can be used for general illumination, or one can be used for cross lighting, most of the necessary evidence about condition should be apparent. The table should be well padded, not only to protect frames, but also to make it possible to turn paintings and drawings face down safely for a scrutiny of their backs. It would also permit solid objects and ceramics to be up-ended for study. With this equipment it is possible to find the small inconspicuous defects, such as cleavage in paintings, checks or splits in the backs of wood panels (which usually appear on the backs of panels before they break through to the front), scratches or dents in metals, stone, and ceramics, foxing on paper, etc., all of which may be signs of new damage or insecurity.

Commonly, the arrival of objects is one occasion for an inspection. Another inspection is advisable at the time an object leaves a museum. Presumably an object will have been carefully examined before its shipment is authorized, but there are other reasons for the registrar to make a final check. Mountings should be checked to see that drawings have frames that are sound; that the backings are stiff enough to take a moderate accidental blow without bursting the glass; that the back is sealed to exclude dust; that paintings are secure in their frames but not bound; that the stretcher keys are all present and firm, and none have fallen down behind the lower stretcher stick; and even that in larger paintings a small wad of cotton is lightly taped between the canvas and the center of the middle stretcher cross-member to prevent vibration of the canvas during shipment. In short, the registrar makes the final check to see that an object is fit to travel, to be handled by another staff, to endure another climate, and make a safe return. This is an insurance that gives protection not offered by any underwriter. After the last inspection it is advisable to keep objects in some safe storage area until they are ready to be put into their packing cases, thus keeping them out of the shipping room traffic as long as possible.

Failure to follow this procedure can bring serious consequences. For example, a museum painting is returned from a loan with a bad tear. The borrowing museum denies knowledge of the damage, and the carrier can find no evidence of damage or inadequacy in the box or packing. There remains the embarrassing question as to whether the damage had occurred after the last inspection, but before the painting left the lending museum.

Having briefly considered the aspects of condition that are pertinent, and a method of inspection, the next point is the method of recording condition. The actual form of the records used necessarily varies, as each registrar knows best where and how notes on condition may be included. However, it is well to mention the nature of the notes to be made. There is a need for brevity and accuracy. Every attempt should be made to describe three attributes of any defect: its nature, its location, its extent. Its nature should be described in a word or two that have specific meanings, "moderate," "marked," and "extreme." The word "slight," for instance, thus has some meaning because it refers to a defect more serious than "negligible" and less serious than "moderate." The location may be described a number of ways, and a review of some of these seems pertinent in spite of the fact that all may be common practice.

A defect, such as grime, may be generally distributed, in which case the word "general" will suffice. Occasionally stains or scars may be described as being "scattered generally."

A defect can be located in terms of the design, as in the background, in or near a figure or other design feature. It may be located in reference to the eye, arm, or leg of a figure; but in so locating it, the point of view must be clear. It has been found useful to adopt the heraldic terms "dexter" and "sinister" to designate the subject's right or left, respectively, as distinguished from the viewer's right or left.

In paintings, an approximate or an exact method can be used. In the approximate method the surface can be divided into nine zones like those of a tic-tac-toe figure. By naming the three horizontal positions left, center, and right, and the three vertical positions top, center, and bottom, any zone can be designated by capital letters such as TL, C, BR, etc. In the exact method the coordinates of the defect are measured in height (H), i.e., vertical distance above the bottom left corner, and width (W), i.e., horizontal distance from the same point, just as one would plot a point on a graph. Always, unless otherwise stated, the point of reference is not the corner of the frame but the bottom left corner of the stretcher or panel.

The extent of defect has to be gauged according to its nature. There are some exact methods that can be applied, but there are no entirely satisfactory ways of approximating the extent of a defect. A split, a tear, a hole, or stain can be measured in length or area. But abrasion, grime, cleavage, weakness, brittleness, dullness, etc., are not easily measured, and adjectives must be used. A standard sequence of five adjectives that represent arbitrary degrees have been used with fair success: "negligible," "slight," "moderate," "marked," "extreme."

The use of any cast-iron terminology makes very dull reading but it saves time in writing records, and it has been found that it automatically increases accuracy. Such entries as "slight general dullness," "flaked loss of paint, size of a dime, H. 6½ in., W. 8¼ in.," or "disjoin at dexter elbow" all have reasonably clear meanings.

The question of describing the nature of defects still remains. Much misunderstanding found in print and in verbal communication about condition seems to be traceable to a casual use of terms. The glossary here offered represents a step toward some standardization. The writer takes responsibility for the selection of these terms from many others that might have been included, and realizes that there are gaps that may need to be filled.

One class of defects, insecurity, mentioned earlier, merits some final emphasis because it is of particular interest to the registrar, and is often the most difficult aspect of condition to detect and describe. Insecurity covers a wide range of symptoms, in the past largely ignored, that may be taken as omens of damage.

Insecurity comes from the weakening of materials. Fabrics, paper, bone, leather, varnishes, almost all organic materials, tend to become weaker and more brittle in time, and signs such as tiny splits and breaks are the beginning of larger ruptures. Insecurity comes from weakness of constructions. Joins and repairs should be examined to see if they are sound; repaired breaks are particularly vulnerable. There are certain types of objects, such as Greek vases, that suffer abnormally high casualties during shipment.

Insecurity comes from mechanical stresses. The mounting of paintings in their frames has already been referred to. Wood and fabric both move in response to seasonal changes; it is safer to permit some movement than to thwart it by nailing paintings into their frames, or by using any other rigid fastenings. This is particularly important with panel paintings. On the other hand, there should be no risk of inadequate mounting. Metal clips or board backings should be props, not levers exerting great pressures against the painting. In this connection, the fit of the painting into the rabbet of the frame should be checked to see that there is no danger of the painting falling through the frame, and that the thin step of the rabbet is not cracked or broken and threatening to give way. The free members of the cradle might be tested to see that they are not locked; the looser they are, the better for the panel.

Insecurity can be an attribute of an object because of its design, e.g., the fragility of glass, ceramic, or stone, and especially objects with free-standing elements. But there is one aspect of fragility that is sometimes forgotten. Stone is usually heavier than commonly thought, and only half as strong. A cubic foot of marble weighs about 175 pounds; a statue of several cubic feet in volume may seem easy to handle, particularly if there is an arm, head, or other projection to grasp, but often these handles will be too weak to stand the lifting stress. It is therefore suggested that the weight of stone sculpture be recorded if possible. Points of possible weakness in stone objects can and should be checked; the presence of real weakness is revealed by identifying hairline cracks.

Insecurity is normally described in detail by the curator and conservator. It is taken into account before an object is cleared for shipment or handling. But there are occasions when a registrar may discover some evidence of insecurity that has not been previously noticed. It is then the registrar's implicit responsibility to recommend that special precautions be taken in the handling of an object, or even that an object be withheld from shipment.

CONCISE GLOSSARY OF TERMS USED TO DESCRIBE CONDITION OF WORKS OF ART

Incorporating suggestions made by members of the Committee on Terminology, IIC-American Group.

ABRASION: a surface loss apparently caused by friction on the varnish, paint or ground in a painting, the design material or the support of a drawing or print, the finish of furniture, sculpture or other objects. Other terms: scrape, wear, rub

ACCRETION: an accumulation of extraneous material on the surface of an object which alters the original texture conformation and usually the color, either generally or locally. Other term: incrustation

BLANCHING: irregular, abnormal, pale or milky areas in paint or varnish; not a superficial defect like bloom, but a scattering of light from microporosities or granulation in aged films.

BLEEDING: the suffusion of a color into adjacent materials, often caused by water or other solvents.

BLOOM: a milky cast or iridescence that may develop on the surface of varnish causing some loss of transparency. Local bloom may result from handling.

CHECK: a rupture in wood along the grain and less than the length of a board. Usually caused by the accelerated drying of wood at the exposed end grain (*cf.* Split). In plywood and in wood that has been too rapidly dried, checks may appear anywhere along the grain due to surface shrinkage.

CLEAVAGE: separation between or in any of the layers in a stratified construction. In paintings, a division parallel to the surface in the paint, ground or support, or between two of these layers. Several forms of cleavage are recognized:

BLIND OR FLAT CLEAVAGE: a separation that is not evident in surface examination. Such areas may "sound" under light tapping.

BLISTER: a separation of a paint surface or coating layer appearing as an inflated semiglobular bulge (*i.e.*, convex in section) and usually caused by excessive heat. An inflated pocket in a film produced when the film is made plastic, by the action of solvents, heat, or both. A rare form of cleavage.

BUCKLED CLEAVAGE or BUCKLING: in a paint or coating, a condition in which loosened layers are lifted from their normal position and take a conformation characterized by low peaks or ridges (sometimes called "tenting") with slopes at either side, usually caused by compressive forces from the support acting on layers that have lost plasticity.

CUPPED CLEAVAGE or CUPPING: in old paint and ground, polygonal islands inside of cracks and concave in section, accompanied by cleavage along the island edges. Cupped paint on canvas often draws the fabric into the same cupped conformation without actual cleavage.

COCKLING: a broad wrinkle or system of wrinkles without creasing, usually referring to the conformation of paper or parchment.

CORROSION: The chemical alteration of the surfaces of metals caused by agents in the environment or by reagents applied purposely. Hard nodules or crusts are formed on metal surfaces if there is an increase in the volume of the corrosion products. The color and texture of a metal surface may be changed without alteration of the form if there is no increase in the volume of the corrosion products, as in the gray-green corrosion of Chinese bronzes. Other terms: patina, eruptive patina, noble patina *Cf.* Efflorescence

CRACKLE: a system of fissures in varnish, paint, or ground or in all of these layers of a painting, or in the glaze of ceramic ware, caused by tensions which develop in drying or aging. Two principal types are distinguished: an aged brittle layer may fracture to form cracks with sharp edges and fine apertures. This type may be called *fracture crackle* (other term: age crackle). A slow-drying plastic film may fail to maintain its continuity as it dries and shrinks. The edges of such cracks are rounded, sloping to a relatively wide aperture. This type of crackle may be called *traction crackle* (other terms: alligator crackle, youth crackle).

DENT, DIG, GOUGE, CHIP: each is caused by a blow. A dent is a simple concavity; a dig implies that some material has been displaced; a gouge that material has been scooped out; a chip that material has been broken away.

DISHING: a stretcher defect caused by the torque of a drawn fabric. If the stretcher members are twisted out of a common plane, a shallow dihedral angle is formed at the corners. Dishing is a common cause of corner wrinkles in stretched canvases (*cf.* Draw).

DISJOIN: the partial or complete separation of a join between two members of an object, as distinguished from a CRACK, TEAR, CHECK or SPLIT.

DRAW: a wrinkle or system of wrinkles in stretched fabric radiating from corners or edges, usually caused by uneven tension. Corner draws may also be caused by various stretcher defects, especially dishing, *q.v.*

EFFLORESCENCE: although efflorescence has a specific chemical meaning referring to the change from a crystalline salt to a powdery mass with loss of water, the term is often used more broadly to describe powdery or crystalline crusts on the surface of stone, plaster, ceramics or metals, resulting from other interactions. Efflorescence has been used to refer to crystalline accumulations on the surface of paint, a relatively rare phenomenon not yet fully investigated, which seems to involve certain ingredients in the paint interacting with each other or with agents in the environment. The bright green spots of powder sometimes found on bronzes and called "bronze disease" are an efflorescence caused by the transformation of cuprous chloride corrosion into cupric chloride. This reaction requires moisture and can be controlled by maintaining a dry environment, *i.e.*, below 60% R.H. *Cf.* Corrosion.

FLAKING, FLAKED LOSS: a loss of islands of paint, ground, or both, following cleavage or weakness in or between layers (*cf.* Cleavage). Other terms: lacuna, void

FOXING: yellow or brown spots on paper, occasionally pale spots on toned paper, which follow the degradation of cellulose by mold. Similar brown spots are sometimes caused by the rusting of iron particles in the paper.

MOLD, MILDEW: a large group of small fungi, the vegetative structures of which invade many organic substances. Provided sufficient moisture is present, these structures or hyphae produce enzymes which dissolve or degrade the host material. This chemical action may leave wastes which stain the hosts, as foxing marks on paper. On maturity reproductive structures will appear on the surface of the host as visible and often colored, furry, or web-like excrescences. Until mature, mold or mildew may not be detectable except by the characteristic musty odor. Because mold requires moisture for growth, mold activity may usually be arrested by maintaining a dry environment, *i.e.*, below 65% R.H.

PENTIMENTO: literally, repentance or a change of mind. In painting, the visible evidence of an early design below a revised design. If the upper paint has become slightly translucent, either through an increase in the refractive index of an oil medium or through other causes, a ghost of the earlier design may be seen. Evidence of the earlier design may also consist of brushmarking in the surface conformation unrelated to the visible design.

SOIL: a general term referring to any material that dirties, sullies or smirches an object.

DUST distinguishes loose soil generally distributed on surfaces.

GRIME distinguishes soil tenaciously held on surfaces.

SMEAR, FINGERPRINT refer to types of local GRIME. (FINGERMARK may refer to local bloom on varnish, or occasionally to an interruption in general varnish bloom.)

SPATTER, RUN, STREAM refer to dried droplets or splashes of foreign material.

STAIN is a discoloration caused by an agent which has penetrated a porous or absorbent surface.

SPLIT: a rupture running along the grain of a piece of wood from end to end, usually caused by exterior mechanical stress.

STRETCHER CREASE: a crease or line of cracks in the ground and paint layers of a painting on fabric following the inside edges of stretcher members or the edges of cross members, caused by the flexing of the fabric against the edges of these members.

Article 4

CARD RECORDS—THEIR ORGANIZATION AND DUPLICATION

DAVID B. LITTLE

Director, Essex Institute
Salem, Massachusetts
Formerly Secretary-Registrar
Museum of Fine Arts, Boston

Card records in a museum are intended to convey information about the collections to the museum staff. They are tools which, to be effective, must be simple to prepare, to understand, to maintain, and, when necessary, to replace. They are only tools and must be subordinated to the collections they serve.

Few people will disagree with these criteria, yet many museums are hampered by card records which do not meet them. Some systems are so complicated that only a few members of the staff can operate them; others are so expensive that they infringe upon funds which might better be spent on the collections. Such systems as these often lag behind the growth of the collection and so add "incompleteness" to the list of their sins.

ORGANIZATION

Card records in the general files of an art museum have four basic kinds of information to furnish concerning the objects to which they pertain: What it is, where it is, when it was acquired, and who gave it or from what fund it was bought. In a file of limited objectives, specialized headings may be chosen to accomplish the specific task determined for the file. With care this list of major headings may be kept down to not more than four or five titles. For example:

DATE	DATE
AUTHOR	ARTIST
SOURCE	COUNTRY OF ORIGIN
SUBJECT	TECHNIQUE

To provide this information, any one of several filing systems may be set up, such as an alphabetically coded category system, a decimal system of classification, a straight numbering system based on sequence or date of acquisition or a punched card system. Each system involves the use of a numerical or combination of alphabetical and numerical coding. This coding is the root of any registration system, because only in the symbol attached are object and record card identical.

Alphabetically Coded Categories

In a category system the emphasis is upon what the object is. A series of categories are chosen arbitrarily into which the arts, with all their infinite variety, are divided. These categories are made as comprehensive and as mutually exclusive as possible. Nevertheless, they tend to multiply and to overlap one another. Examples of these categories are arms and armor, pottery and porcelain, sculpture, oil paintings, textiles, coins and medals. Objects are assigned consecutive numbers within their category in the order of their acquisition. The 750th piece of pottery or porcelain to enter the collection, for example, is accessioned as P.750, "P" being the category code letter for pottery and porcelain.

The system works well with a homogenous category like oil paintings but fails wherever there is a choice, and the heading "Miscellaneous" is often overworked by a cataloguer who does not know either the object or the available categories well enough to decide in which compartment the object belongs. If an accession book for each category is maintained in addition to the card records, the labor of making entries is increased by the number of books to be handled.

Decimal Classification

In a decimal classification system the emphasis is again upon what the object is. The choice of categories is greater than it is with the straight category system, since numerical coding allows for more variations than an alphabetical system does. As the number of categories increases, so does the difficulty of making the right choice of category. Complicated charts or indexes must be mastered by the cataloguer who puts the information into the files, and also by the staff member who wishes to get this information out of the file later on. The numbers are long, complicated with decimal points, hard to remember, hard to file, and hard to read when painted on the bottom of a small clay pot. Yet, to the skilled practitioner of this system, the number on the object conveys to him most of the catalogue information without recourse to the files. The setting up of accession books based on each separate category is not practical.

Numbers Based on Sequence or Date of Acquisition

In a straight numbering system the identification marking either depends upon when the object was acquired or is determined by the arbitrary sequence of accessioning. It has no other significance whatsoever. Consequently the choice of number is an administrative rather than a scholarly function. The accumulation of objects through the years reaches into the thousands in a small museum and into the millions in a large one. If a system of consecutive numbers were set up starting at one and heading toward infinity, it would soon become unwieldy. To avoid this problem, therefore, many museums start afresh each year with the number one, identifying the year by placing it to the left of the consecutive number with a decimal point between them. Thus the 510th object acquired in 1951 bears the number 51.510 or 1951.510 if a full year-designator is preferred. With this system only a single series of accession books is required. Of all the systems, this one is least susceptible to errors in judgment by the person putting information into the file. It is also the easiest system for extracting information from the file.

PUNCHED CARDS

Punched-card systems are playing an increasingly important part in science, business, and industry, making readily available information whose extraction from a large conventional file would be tedious and often incomplete. The bulk of a filing system may also be reduced, as one card properly coded and punched will give the information which would require four ordinary cards to locate. Punched-card systems are not the final answer to all problems of record searching, however, although they can open up vast stores of accumulated knowledge for the use of those who need it. They supplement but do not replace conventional filing systems, which are still the best available means for accomplishing certain tasks. Punched cards are primarily sorting tools, not filing systems.

The first step in setting up a punched-card system is the writing of a clear declaration of intent. What precisely is this file meant to accomplish? What sort of information is to be extracted from it? The second step is the preparation of the coding scheme. These are the two essential intellectual steps upon which the success of the mechanical operation of a punched-card file depends. Experience has shown that the simplest coding scheme which will accomplish its purpose is the best. The initial setting up of broad yet well-defined topics allows for the establishment of subheads as the need for them is proved. An elaborate sorting system which will pinpoint an individual card is too cumbersome in operation to have much practical value. It is far better to design a simple code which will eliminate nearly all unnecessary material and leave a small number of cards for visual scanning.

The decimal systems of classification are well adapted to use with punched cards since their coding may be expressed physically by the punch slots on the cards. Indeed, since the cards must be coded anyway, it would seem wise to apply the same code as identification symbols on the objects that the cards describe.

Since the purpose of a punched-card file must be clearly defined, the establishment of a system which embraces the whole of a museum's collections is not an easy task. It is better to have several simple systems each with a precisely stated and limited objective.

Punched-card systems are divided into two main groups, the marginal-punched and the center-punched. Marginal-punched cards are hand sorted by means of a needle resembling an ice pick. The center-punched cards are sorted by machine. Hand-sorted cards may be any size or proportion so long as a rectangular shape is retained. Machine-sorted cards are limited in shape and size by the machines that sort them. Both types can be and usually are specifically printed to conform to the purpose and coding of the files in which they serve.

The possibilities of punched-card systems are too vast to be expressed in a short note. The published literature[1] on their use is constantly expanding, and should be consulted by anyone interested in setting up a punched-card file. Then, if the staff can prepare a precise statement of the task it intends to accomplish, the salesmen for the various systems should be consulted. Their experience will save much time and effort in the acquiring and establishing of an efficient system best suited to the museum's needs and pocketbook.

Net even the punched cards, however, can answer directly the four basic questions with a single file card, since all methods but the straight numbering system are coded, and codes require some sort of index to translate them. This is not the place to enter into the ramifications of an index. Suffice it to say that methods other than the punched-card system operate well with four full cards, one to answer each of the four basic questions.

[1] Recommended as a starting point is *Punched Cards, Their Applications to Science and Industry,* edited by Robert S. Casey and James W. Perry, Reinhold Publishing Corp., New York, 1951. Mr. T. J. Sullivan, assistant manager of the McBee Company's Boston office, who provided the writer with this reference and much sound advice, is in no wise to be held responsible for this brief sketch about punched cards, but it could not have been written without his help.

DUPLICATION

The use of four duplicate cards in a file of any size makes the task of preparing them a sizeable one. If the cards are typed by hand, proofread, and corrected, this can be a time-consuming and thereby expensive process which usually lags well behind the acquisition of the objects described. Clearly, mechanical methods of reproducing card records must be considered. What are the basic requirements of such a method?

1. The results must be permanent: that is, the record must be made with non-fading ink on good quality paper and capable of withstanding erasure and of receiving corrections or additions by typewriter.
2. Preparation of the master, from which the copies are made, should be a simple process: that is, the typist should be able to produce it at her desk with a minimum of special equipment, and corrections to the master should be simple to make.
3. Operation of the reproducing machine should be simple and convenient enough to make using it to produce frequent small lots worthwhile.
4. The reproducing machine must be flexible. It should be able to do other jobs for the museum in addition to the printing of cards.
5. The cost of the equipment, and of its operation and maintenance, should be in proportion to the tasks assigned.

Since the cards are permanent records, it would be false economy to use other than high-quality card stock because, regardless of the method of preparation, the labor costs are greater than the cost of the materials. The cards should be stiff enough to stand up in the file drawers without wrinkling but not so thick as to add unnecessary bulk. A stock possessing the strength and durability equivalent to 36-pound linen ledger bond is required.

What are the reproduction processes commercially available? Irvin A. Hermann[1] lists ten, of which seven are either already in use by museums or are potentially useful.

Carbon Paper

Carbon paper is the reproduction process most commonly used for a wide range of copying in any office. It is made in many grades of quality, weight, and finishes. The best results are obtained by using a paper designated for each specific task. These general rules must be observed: For quality results use quality grade paper; use the heaviest carbon paper that will produce the number of legible copies desired; and use

[1] "Office Reproduction and Imprinting Methods," *The Office Magazine of Management, Equipment, Methods,* April 1951.

the carbon paper with the hardest finish that will produce the number of legible copies wanted.

While carbon papers have long since proved their value as a reproducing medium, they do not produce clear copy through paper heavier than 20 pounds. Since a 36-pound stock is recommended for file cards, the use of carbon paper in making one or more duplicates of these cards is not satisfactory.

Automatic Typewriter

An automatic typewriter produces typewritten copy without the intervention of any printing process other than the typewriter keys and ribbon. It operates at twice the speed of the average typist. This machine is most useful in preparing from 50 to 500 copies of form letters on which the operator may type the name, address, salutation, and any other special information manually. Two types of automatic machines are on the market: one operates from a perforated record roll, the other from a perforated paper tape.

As weighed against the basic requirements, the automatic typewriter rates "yes" on 1, 2, and 4; 3 is debatable; 5 must be decided on an individual basis.

Hectograph Duplicating

Two types of hectograph duplicating equipment are in general museum use. One employs the gelatine process, the other a spirit process. The masters may be prepared by writing, typing, or drawing. The best copies are made on a special hectograph paper, of sulphite stock. Hectograph and stencil duplicating equipment are probably the most flexible reproducing machines within their price range on the market.

As weighed against the basic requirements, the hectograph rates "yes" on all but the first.

Stencil Duplicating

Stencil duplicating shares with the hectograph the major portion of all museum printing tasks. Stencils print best on an absorbent sulphite paper, although a careful operator, with the judicious use of slip sheets and a fast-drying ink, can produce satisfactory results on a hard-surface bond paper. The range of printing tasks which can be accomplished on a stencil is great enough to make the machine useful to all departments of a museum.

As weighed against the basic requirements, the stencil duplicator rates "yes" on all except possibly the first.

Offset Lithography

More expensive than the stencil duplicator and usually considered more complicated to run, an offset lithography machine brings high quality printing into the museum. Its range of uses covers all of the printing needs of a museum on short or long runs, whether four copies of a file card or five thousand copies of an exhibition catalogue. Preparation of the master is accomplished by typing, drawing, or writing with oil base materials designed for the job. Masters may also be preprinted in reproducing inks, nonreproducing inks, or a combination of both, thus reducing or eliminating the stocking of blank forms. Corrections to the master are made with a soft pencil eraser. No correction fluids are needed.

As weighed against the basic requirements, it rates "yes" on all.

Photography

Photography is employed where exact copies are required. Seals, signatures, marginal notes, or any other mark that appears on the original are faithfully reproduced.

There are five steps in the photographic method: expose, develop, fix, wash, dry. The camera may be used in the conventional manner to produce a negative which is entirely the reverse of the subject, or it may operate through a prism and lens arrangement to produce a negative opposite only in color value. In the latter case negative copies are rephotographed to obtain positive prints. The results are as permanent as any photograph. No master need be prepared. Any kind, size, or shape of record, transparent, translucent, or opaque, black and white or colored, one side or both, may be photographed onto film or sensitized paper. Processing requires a darkroom.

Since the image is chemically reproduced in the coating of the paper, it cannot be erased without tearing the coating. It can, however, be typed or written upon.

Contact Printing

Contact printing processes depend upon the transmission of light through the original material to be copied onto a sensitized surface. They avoid the heavy expense of a camera lens and are therefore able to introduce refinements in the five inevitable steps—exposing, developing, fixing, washing, and drying—which speed up the operation considerably. By means of mirrors some contact printing machines are able to copy such opaque materials as pages in a book.

Contact printers are manufactured in two basic types, those requiring wet development and those requiring dry. Most, but not all, wet development methods also require a darkroom. Dry development methods operate with ammonia vapors contained in the unit.

The most practical applications of contact printing center upon the use of translucent materials for all office purposes. Translucent papers of high quality are commercially available and are finding a growing market wherever the advantages of contact printing for easy duplication of records is realized.

Within the size limits of the machine, copy of various sizes can be accommodated. By starting with translucent originals, no masters are needed. These are the two big advantages of photographic or contact printing over other printing processes. However, they lack the speed desired for long printing runs.

Electrostatic Printing

When this article was first written in 1955, electrostatic printing was not widely known in the museum profession. By 1960 it had gained widespread acceptance in the business world as a means of producing excellent facsimile copies. The printing of a second edition of *Museum Registration Methods* provides an opportunity to include electrostatic printing with the other seven reproduction processes described in the original article.

Electrostatic printing machines, though rugged, are far more sensitive than their salesmen will admit. They do not require skilled operators but they do require skilled maintenance if their prints are to be as permanent as advertised.

When they are working properly they will produce a dry facsimile of any original up to 9″ x 14″ in size within thirty seconds, six or seven copies a minute, on ordinary paper, although their own special stock is preferred. They will also print on offset paper masters for long-run production. They thus bridge the gap between the instant few copies and the rapid many.

Electrostatic printers will use any ordinary paper, offset paper master and card stock up to .0076″ thickness in sizes from 7″ x 7″ to 10″ x 15½″. They will reproduce in black originals in every color.

The Museum of Modern Art in New York reports that it is now printing its catalogue cards by electrostatic means on 8″ x 14″ sheets of 100% rag content paper .0076″ thick. Each sheet contains four 4″ x 6″ cards and a two-inch trailing edge to cope with the distortion caused by the weight of the paper. After reproduction the cards are cut from the sheet on a very precise disc type paper cutter.

The full potential of electrostatic printing remains to be discovered.

Other ingenious experimenters, spurred on by dire necessity, will undoubtedly broaden its usefulness even further.

As weighed against the basic requirements, it rates "yes" on all. It is particularly valuable as an adjunct to an offset lithography machine, thus making possible any number of copies from one to 2,000 or more without retyping the original material.

SUMMARY

Of the eight reproduction processes weighed against an arbitrarily chosen list of standards, each is found to have advantages and disadvantages that must be further weighed against the work load it would be expected to carry in a specific installation. Of the eight only carbon paper may be considered really inexpensive to buy. The qualification of flexibility, how many jobs a duplicating machine can do for the museum besides the printing of cards, is therefore of great importance. These machines earn their keep and pay dividends only when they are working at or near two capacities, their own and that of the job. A small machine struggling with a big job is as uneconomical as a big machine loafing on a small job. The Museum of Fine Arts, Boston, for example, installed an offset lithography system in 1948 as an answer to its own duplicating needs. This machine has paid for itself many times over in increased production and lowered unit costs.

The salesmen of office machinery[1] in any city are glad to study the duplicating needs of a business or a museum to determine the type of installation best suited to their over-all needs, and most are quite willing to explain and demonstrate the capabilities and limitations of their machines.

[1] This paper, for example, could not have been prepared without the generous assistance of Bernard Cerier of Thorp and Martin, Williams Office Supply Corp., and George Martin, the Ozalid Sales Representative of Spaulding-Moss Company, both of Boston, Massachusetts.

Article 5

CATALOGUING IN THE METROPOLITAN MUSEUM OF ART

MARCIA C. HARTY

Formerly Supervisor of the Catalogue,
Office of the Registrar
Metropolitan Museum of Art, New York

The catalogue is a card file record of information on each object in the museum arranged in the order most useful to the institution. Cataloguing is generally considered a curatorial function, but in a large museum with many curatorial departments, ten curators may develop ten different systems. To maintain uniformity of records for such diverse materials as laces and arms and armor, centralized cataloguing is done in the Metropolitan Museum of Art in the office of the registrar, where each cataloguer does the work for several departments under the supervision of the respective curators. This work, of course, could be done in curatorial offices or elsewhere, subject to the museum's needs. Because a card system is flexible, it is preferred to a book catalogue. It reflects the fields represented in the museum and allows for the growth of the collections as well as for changes in classification or for any reorganization of curatorial departments in the future.

The flexibility of the catalogue is counterbalanced by the permanence of the accession number, which should never be changed. If this number were based on classification it, too, would be subject to change and there would be no fixed point of reference in the system. Such a numbering system, furthermore, would necessitate partial cataloguing before the number could be assigned.

An accession number based on the year and the sequence of transactions during the year can be assigned immediately, since it does not depend upon curatorial study and decision. In the event that two large collections arrive at the same time they can be worked on simultaneously, because the numbering of one is not dependent upon the completion of the numbering of the other. The accession number 53.19.2 signifies that the item was acquired in 1953, that it was part of the 19th transaction of the year, and was the second item in that paricular transaction. When a single object is obtained from one vendor or donor only the first two parts of the number are used, as 50.4.

The classification system is determined by the nature of the collection and the way it is to be used. Paintings will naturally fall into geographical categories divided by century, school, or artist. A collection of porcelain might be arranged the same way. The use of the collection might, however, make it preferable to have the primary classification by shape so that all cups or all pitchers would be grouped together, subdivided by technique or decoration, or by color. The information about geographical origin, period, and maker might then be subordinated to the position ordinarily given to the description. It is possible that a highly specialized collection would have its basic classification by use. For example, a group of ecclesiastical vestments might be arranged by the church year with all chasubles, dalmatics, and copes placed according to the services for which they are used, under Advent, Pentecost, Easter, and so on.

Large and diversified collections such as those in the Metropolitan Museum of Art require a more complex classification system. There the primary break-down is by civilization:

Far Eastern
Egyptian
Near Eastern
Greek and Roman
Western art

Western art was divided into European and American when the latter field was placed under a separate curatorial department.

Within these fields the classification is by material, such as ceramics, textiles, and woodwork, with such self-evident exceptions as arms and armor, coins, paintings, and sculpture.

These are arranged alphabetically as follows:

Arms and armor
Ceramics
Coins
Costumes
Drawings and water colors
Enamels
Fans
Glass
Horology
Ivories
Lacquers
Lapidary work
Leatherwork

Medals and plaquettes
Metalwork-brass (or: bronze, gold, silver, etc.)
Miniatures
Musical instruments
Natural substances (amber, straw, wax, etc.)
Paintings
Sculpture
Silhouettes
Textiles (embroidered, laces, tapestries, woven, etc.)
Wallpapers
Woodwork (architectural, furniture)

Special classifications are used for some departments and not for others, as seals and sealings for Near Eastern antiquities, vases for Greek and Roman, because these categories have special significance within these civilizations.

Arms and armor is broken down into a classification based on use, for example, armor for man, armor for horse, firearms, weapons. Musical instruments are divided into stringed instruments, wind instruments, vibrating membranes, and sonorous substances.

A separate file, the subject index, replaces the added entries for subject headings that are used in library catalogues and brings to the fore those facts about an object which cannot be shown by the classification system alone.

In a large catalogue the basic classification is shown by labels on the outside of the drawers and by the guide cards inside them; hence, the classification information is placed on the bottom line of the card, because it needs to be read only when the card is actually being filed. And as all the cards for an individual object are tied together with string through the bottom hole, this line can be omitted from all but the first card.

CATALOGUING PROCEDURES

To register an object is to record the data necessary to identify it, and to summarize the transaction by which it was acquired. To catalogue an object is to record the full information about it, abbreviating the acquisition data to suit the uses of the classified catalogue. As the registration of objects has been discussed in chapter 2, only the records made for the classified catalogue will be discussed here; however, an adaptation of these records is suggested later for a small institution.

At the Metropolitan Museum of Art, registering and cataloguing are done by the same person, and the catalogue record is duplicated for the curatorial office files. Each object is carefully examined when it arrives. It is measured, any visible damages and repairs are noted, and the accession number is assigned.

The cataloguer then gathers and organizes all available information about the object, preparatory to making a set of catalogue cards. This information comes from notes made by the cataloguer when examining the object for signatures or maker's marks, colors, and technical details; from the curator, including records of collections and exhibitions of which it has been a part and publications in which it or related pieces have been described; and from library research. The curator assists by verifying and evaluating the material thus obtained.

When all the information has been gathered and integrated, the cataloguer types a draft in final form, making certain that authors' names, titles, page and plate numbers are accurate, and that inscriptions have been copied and translations typed exactly as the curator wants them. The draft and a photograph of the object are then sent to the curator for final approval. A carbon copy of the draft is kept in the unfinished-work file in the registration and cataloguing office for an interim record.

After the original draft has been initialed by the curator and returned, the final cards are typed or reproduced mechanically for the central classified catalogue and the duplicate file in the curatorial office.

The original draft is then filed in the completed-work file by accession number and the carbon in the unfinished-work file is thrown away. Notations are made on the back of the original draft of all sets of cards sent to the other departments (curatorial, study rooms, or overlapping curatorial interests), of the number and sizes of photographs supplied to the photo sales department, and of all index entries made. Changes and additional information subsequently received from the curators are filed with the original draft as an authorization for the supplementary work done by the cataloguers, and notations are made to identify the records changed in consequence. Thus all records can be found and changed whenever a title or attribution is changed, or all cards can be cleared from the files when an object is de-accessioned.

These catalogue cards, compiled with curatorial help and approval, form the official records for all objects owned by the museum. Therefore the information on them must be correct and there must be absolute accuracy in spelling, typing and proofreading. If the cataloguer does not understand everything to be recorded, the curator should be consulted. This may eliminate, in years to come, days of research checking inaccurate or confused information. Good cataloguing cannot be done by lazy minds, nor by rigid ones.

DESCRIPTION OF CATALOGUE CARDS

The catalogue record is made on a standard library card (100% pure rag content, 7.5 cm. x 12.5 cm., .080 thick, which is slightly smaller than the usual commercial 3- x 5-inch card). This record contains all information about each accession, gathered together from the various administrative and curatorial departments. This information, compiled in a useful and consistent order, is arranged to bring the most important facts to the first card. Basic data which must appear on this card are: accession number, heading, material and measurements, source from which the object was acquired, classification, century and country. As many of the following items as apply, and for which there is space, are placed on the first card in the following order:

Accession number (in upper left corner)
Heading: artist and title, or descriptive heading, followed by a short descriptive text
Heraldry
Inscription
Signature and date, or maker's mark
Material and measurements
Name of donor or vendor (latter with price and name of fund)
Ex collections
Provenance
Period
Designer (decorator, etc.): name and dates
City or place: maker and dates (for ceramics, silver, etc.)
Classification, century, country

The photograph, printed on stock of the same size and weight as the catalogue card, is filed immediately behind the first catalogue card. Additional cards, each with the accession number typed at the top left corner, bearing further description, notes, exhibitions, and references, are placed in that order behind the photograph, and all the cards are tied together.

Examples of various types of catalogue cards are shown on the following pages. For Gauguin's painting "Ia Orana Maria" the complete catalogue set totals 15.

DE-ACCESSIONING

De-accessioning is registration and cataloguing in reverse. When the trustees authorize the disposal of an object all records for it are removed from the active files. The accession card and photograph from the registrar's accessions file are placed in a numerical file of de-accessioned objects to form a cumulative record of all objects ever disposed of from

52.170ab
CUP, LOVING: cup (a) with scrolled handles, leaf-shaped thumbpieces; coat of arms on one side, cipher of William Cave on other side; domed cover (b).
Arms: Cave impaling Petit
Inscribed: (in cipher on side) (C.W.C.?)
Marks: (top of cover) HURD ; (underside of foot) Jacob Hurd ;
(below midband) Hurd
Silver ab) H. 10-3/8; a) Diam. 5-15/16 in.
Purchase, 1952 Graham & Sons Morris K. Jesup Fund

Mass: Boston: Jacob Hurd, 1702-1758
Metalwork-Silver XVIII century American
(prior to 1741)

FIRST CARD: Descriptive heading entry, showing place and maker

52.170 ab
154134

SECOND CARD: Photograph

51.112.2
Gauguin, Paul 1848-1903
Ia Orana Maria

Inscribed: (lower left) IA ORANA MARIA
Signed and dated: (lower right) P. Gauguin '91 [1891]
Oil on canvas H. 44-7/8, W. 35-3/8 in.
(114.0 x 89.7 cm.)
Bequest of Samuel A. Lewisohn, 1951

Paintings French

FIRST CARD: Artist and title entry

51.112.2
150398

SECOND CARD: Photograph

THIRD CARD:

Ex collections—names and dates of ownership; dealers' names in brackets

51.112.2
Ex collections
Michel Manzi, Paris (ca. 1893-1919); [M. Knoedler & Co., New York (1919)]; Adolph Lewisohn, New York City (1919-1938); Samuel A. Lewisohn, New York (1938-1951)

FOURTH CARD:

Notes

51.112.2
Notes
Gauguin wrote to his friend, de Monfreid, that "Ia Orana Maria," or "Hail Mary," was the first work of importance as distinct from sketches and studies which he executed after his arrival in Tahiti. He added that he was "rather pleased with it." (See ref. Gauguin, 1920.)

The fruit at the feet of the Virgin is placed on a "fata," an altar of the type once used to make offerings to the Tahitian gods.

FIFTH CARD:

Exhibitions

51.112.2
Exhibitions
New York. Museum of Modern Art. New York private collections, 1946. [No catalogue published]
Paris. Orangerie. Gauguin, 1949, no. 25, pl. VIII (ill.; lent by S.A. Lewisohn).
New York. Paul Rosenberg & Co. Nineteenth century heritage, 1950, no. 8 (lent by Mr. and Mrs. S.A. Lewisohn). [Not in M.M.A. Library, 1953]
M.M.A. The Lewisohn collection, 1951, no. 34 (lent by Mrs. Sam A. Lewisohn).
M.M.A. Art treasures of the Metropolitan, 1952-1953, check list no. 152.

SIXTH CARD:

References (arranged by publication date, showing book entry, periodical entry, and museum publication)

51.112.2
References
Gauguin, Paul. Lettres à Georges-Daniel de Monfreid, Paris, 1920, p. 86 (March 1892-describes the picture fully), p. 254 (June 1899-says he would like it to be included in an exhibition of his works), p. 281 (refers to it as one of my good old canvases).
Dorra, Henri. Ia Orana Maria, <u>in</u> M.M.A. Bulletin, N.S., vol. X, 1952 (May), pp. 255-260; ill. p. 254.
M.M.A. Art treasures of the Metropolitan, 1952, p. 159 (ill. in color), p. 234, no. 152 (described).

the collections. A cross-reference card is placed in the registrar's file to maintain the numerical sequence. The carbon of the accession card filed in the alphabetical donor and vendor file is stamped "De-accessioned" and returned to keep that file intact. The catalogue card is also stamped and put in a separate classified file for de-accessioned objects, but no cross-reference is inserted in the catalogue itself. The subject index entries for the artist or maker and title of the object are stamped and left in the index, but all other entries are destroyed. All pictures of the object are withdrawn from the photo sales department. Original drafts made when the object was being catalogued are stamped and returned to the finished-work file. Duplicate cards are stamped and sent back to the curatorial offices for their de-accessioned files.

THE SUBJECT INDEX

The subject index was developed to deal with those aspects of an object which do not appear in the material breakdown of the classification system in the catalogue. This index is an alphabetical card file containing entries for artists and makers, subject matter, title, ex collections, and provenance. Each of these entries will lead the inquirer to the cards for the object in the catalogue. At present, the subject index in the Metropolitan Museum of Art encompasses only objects in the fields of Western Art.

For example, Gauguin's painting "Ia Orana Maria" is indexed under:

Gauguin, Paul
Ia Orana Maria
Hail Mary
Virgin and Child
Christ Child and Virgin (cross reference)
Manzi, Michel (ex collection)
Lewisohn, Adolph (ex collection)
Lewisohn, Samuel A. (ex collection)

The silver loving cup made by Jacob Hurd is indexed under:

Hurd, Jacob
Cup   loving
Heraldry   Cave
Heraldry   Petit

Cards illustrating the various types of entries for these works are shown on the page following (read from bottom up):

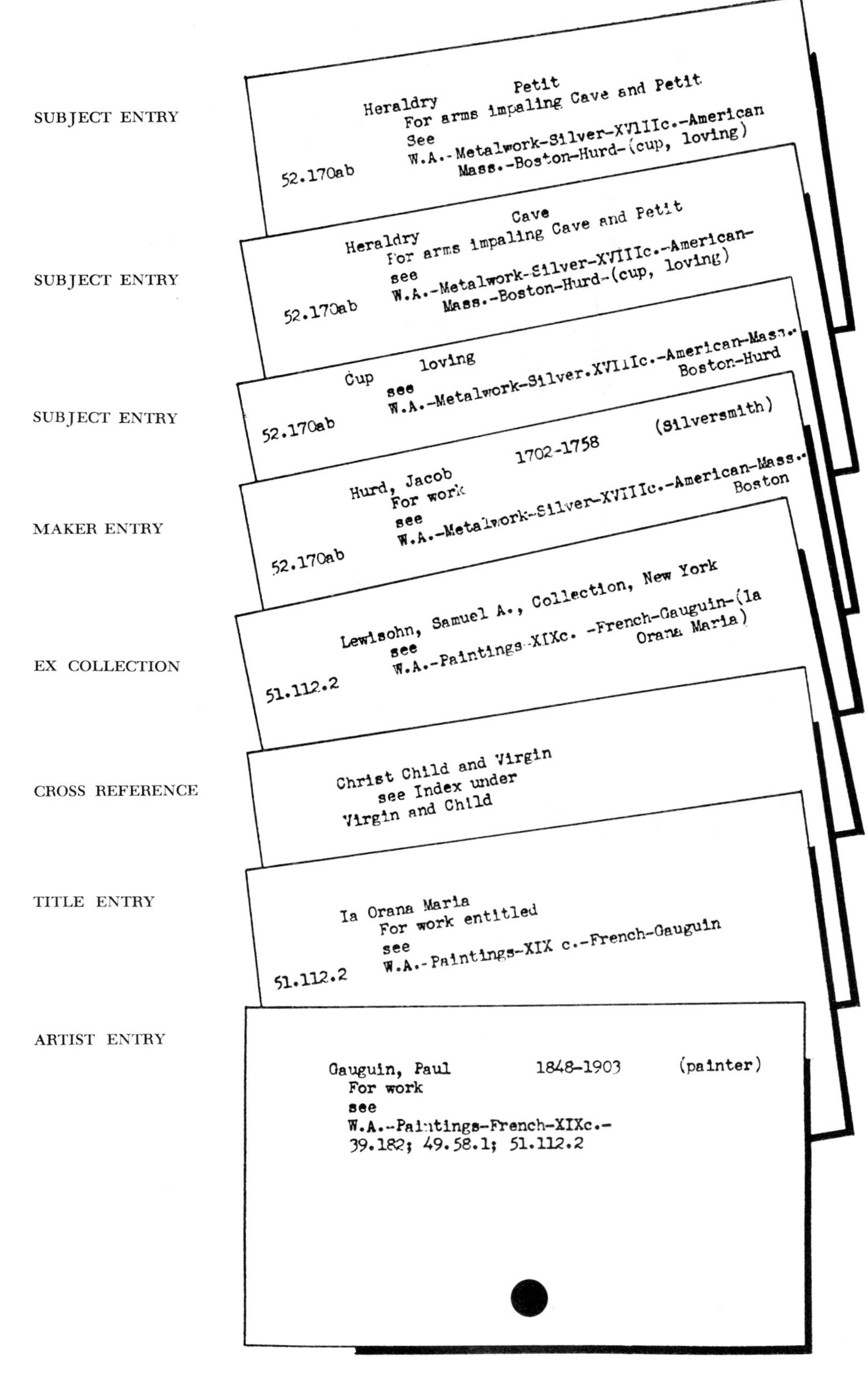

READ FROM BOTTOM UP

SIMPLIFIED RECORDS FOR SMALL INSTITUTIONS

To have complete sets of records on objects of art, one set for curatorial use and another for the central records file, to be used for a general information service, is ideal for an institution the size of the Metropolitan Museum of Art. It may, however, be too expensive to maintain or otherwise unnecessary for a smaller institution, in which case a system based on one set of simplified records can be employed. In such a system curators would keep a file of folders, one for each object, in which they could place bibliographies, large photographs, lists of negative numbers, correspondence, and their own work notes, etc.

One advantage of this system is that if a museum at some time finds it feasible to expand the simplified records into a full catalogue, the additional cards can be made from the curators' files. It is obvious that a full set of records for the information-giving services saves the curators' time and adds to the efficiency of serving the museum and the public. Each institution must choose the method which best fits its needs.

Examples of cards for simplified records are given below.

1. Accession card—identifies each object by its accession number; filed numerically
2. Source card—identifies each donor, bequeathor, vendor, and all objects acquired from each person, filed alphabetically in one file, then by accession number under each name
3. Catalogue card—records each object by its classification, filed with all other objects of the same type, as Furniture, Glass, Paintings, Sculpture, etc. Filed by country, century, then by artist, school, maker, or title of object
4. Finding card—gives location for each object at the present moment, each change should be recorded as soon as object is moved; filed by accession number
5. Location card—duplicate of Finding card, identifies each object by the position it occupies, filed by gallery, storeroom, office, and specific location within that space, so that if object disappears its identity can be quickly determined
6. Photograph—identifies each object and its physical condition in the most positive and definite way. The number of prints of the photograph will depend upon the use and location of the files. Ideally there would be one for the accessions file, one for the catalogue, and one for the public to see

Note: If the institution has a typewriter with interchangeable platens, a plain one for ordinary office use, and a card-holder platen for cards, the Accession and Source cards can be typed in one operation by using carbon paper, and the Finding and Location cards in another, thus reducing the manual labor involved to three instead of five steps.

The Finding and Location cards could be done on different color cards, so that they would never be placed in the wrong file.

1. Accession card—pale blue

65.10.3
Textiles-Woven XIX century American
Bedspread: handwoven, blue and white wool; signed and dated: Nancy Brown/1853

Vendor: John Green
31 White Avenue
Redding, Conn.

Rec'd 1 Ap. 65
Condition: frayed on top edge, hole darned lower right

Price: $65.

Size: L. 96, W. 80 in.

Fund: Smith
Authorized: Purchasing Comm. 15 Mar. 65

Neg. no. 1673
Size 3x4 8x10

2. Source card—carbon copy of above, on white stock; name "Green" underscored in red for filing

3. Catalogue card—white

65.10.3
Textiles-Woven XIX century American
Bedspread: handwoven, blue and white wool; variant of Wheel of Fortune pattern; double fringe on four sides.
Signed & dated (lower left corner) Nancy Brown/1853
Wool L. 96, W. 80 in.
Purchase, 1965 William T. Smith Fund

Bibliog.: Atwater. Shuttle-craft of American hand-weaving, 1928, p. 156 (cf. Wheel of Fortune design)

4. Finding card—locates object, filed by accession number. In a small institution where all records are kept in one office this could be filed behind the Accession card; otherwise it

would be kept in Curatorial office in a separate numerical file.

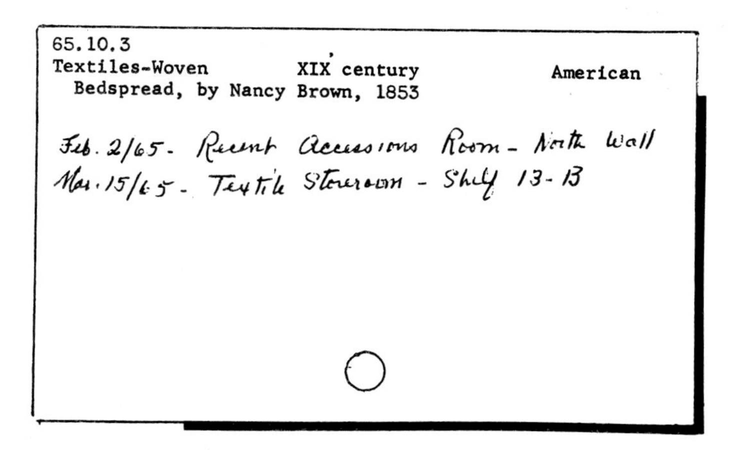
65.10.3
Textiles-Woven XIX century American
Bedspread, by Nancy Brown, 1853

Feb. 2/65 - Recent Accessions Room - North Wall
Mar. 15/65 - Textile Storeroom - Shelf 13-B

5. Location records: Guide cards

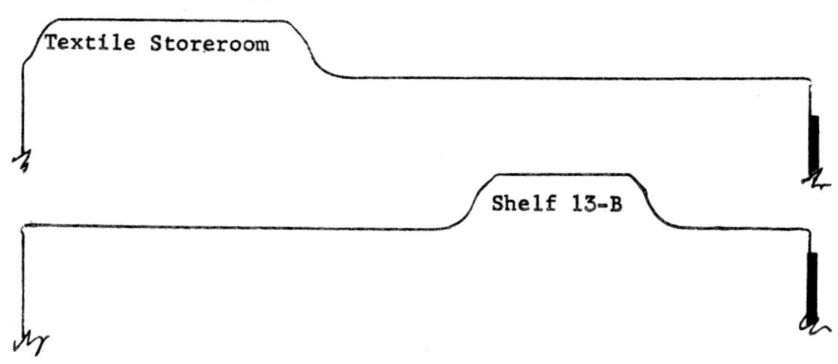

Location card (Duplicate of Finding card; same data added to each)

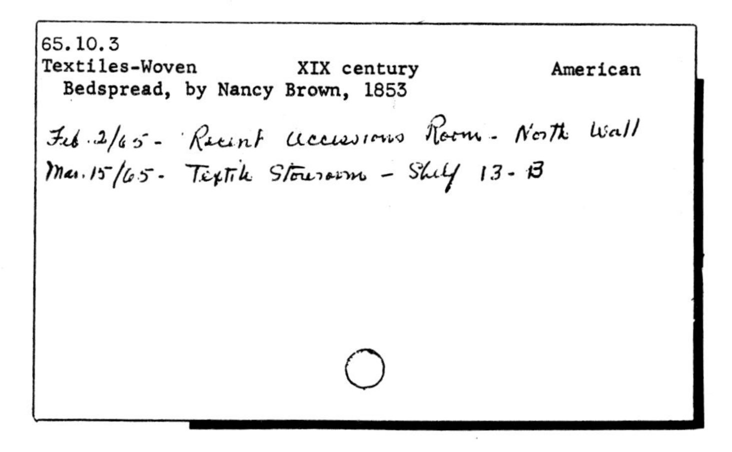
65.10.3
Textiles-Woven XIX century American
Bedspread, by Nancy Brown, 1853

Feb. 2/65 - Recent Accessions Room - North Wall
Mar. 15/65 - Textile Storeroom - Shelf 13-B

References:

AMERICAN LIBRARY ASSOCIATION. A.L.A. cataloguing rules for author and title entries, 2nd ed., edited by Clara Beetle. Chicago, American Library Association, 1949.

CHAMBERLIN, Mary Walls. Guide to art reference books. Chicago, American Library Association, 1959.

Article 6

CATALOGUING PRINTS IN THE MUSEUM OF MODERN ART

DOROTHY L. LYTLE

Registrar
Museum of Primitive Art, New York
Formerly Associate Curator of Prints
Museum of Modern Art, New York

The system of cataloguing prints in the Museum of Modern Art was set up by the late Carl O. Schniewind, curator of prints and drawings at the Art Institute of Chicago, working with the registration department of the Museum of Modern Art. It is of course only one of many possible systems and can be modified to suit other requirements. Some museums, particularly those whose print collection is not open to the public, may not need such extensive records.

The accession number is assigned by the registration department. Vertical prints which are hinged along the back of the left side (that is, verso, right side) are marked in pencil on the back of the lower right corner so that only the one corner need be lifted in checking a number. Horizontal prints, which are hinged at the top, are marked on the back of each of the free corners, though it is necessary to mark only one corner.

The cataloguing is done by the print room staff, and a carbon copy of the catalogue sheet is sent to the registration department, which takes from it such information for their records as is required.

In cataloguing a print, the following records are made. Each will be described in turn with "typical" samples in cases where this may make the procedure seem a little less formidable.

Catalogue sheet and artist's sheet (these are master records, and are filed in lock-post binders)
Catalogue card and artist's card (these are for use of the public)
Mat label
Donor card
Subject file
Photograph albums and file

PRINTS: CATALOG DATA

Accession No. 133.49

Artist KLEE, P.

Negative No. Leica-3456-D.

Credit Line Purchase Fund. (Mrs. John Doe)

Accepted 3-24-49

1. Title The One in Love
(Der Verliebte)

2. Date and Place Executed "1923" lower left, in pencil; lower left on stone

3. Medium Lithograph, printed in black

4. Dimensions 10 3/8 x 7 1/2 in. (263 x 190 mm.) comp.
11 7/8 x 9 1/4 in. (301 x 234 mm.) sheet

5. Definitive Catalog (Soby 53)

6. Price Paid $ (Parke-Bernet Galleries N.Y., Curt Valentin sale, cat.no.39, Dec.1948) Insurance Value $

7. Signature "Klee" lower right, in pencil

8. Paper Laid, ivory

9. Watermark None

10. Condition Upper edge of margin wrinkled from former hinges

11. Collections No marks

12. References and Reproductions

13. Remarks State: inscribed lower right above signature, "Probedruck des schwarzen Steines / erster Zustand" (Trial proof of the black stone, first state)
Title: "Der Verliebte" center bottom, in pencil

Date and Klee no. "1923 91" on stone lower left

Cataloged By dl Date March 1949 Mat Size I

Figure 52.—Catalogue sheet for individual print.

CATALOGUE SHEET

The form shown in figure 52 is printed on white bond, 8½ x 11 inches. Plain white bond second sheets are used. An identical form on inexpensive stock (pink) is used as a work sheet.

The following are some explanatory notes concerning the catalogue sheets shown in figures 52 and 53.

DATE: a print is considered to have been dated by the artist if the date is either written by hand on the print or worked on the stone, plate, block, etc. If the date appears on the print, it is recorded within quotation marks, exactly as given,

PRINTS: CATALOG DATA

Accession No. 174.46.1-31

Artist PICASSO, P.

Negative No. See list of individual prints

Credit Line Gift of Mrs. John D. Rockefeller, Jr.

~~Accepted 10-26-46~~

1. Title Buffon: Histoire naturelle
   Text by Comte de Buffon (Georges Louis LeClerc, 1707-88)
   Illustrated with 31 aquatints

2. Date and Place Executed (1936.)

3. Medium Aquatints, printed in black and gray

4. Dimensions 14 3/8 x 10 7/8 in. (365 x 275 mm.) sheet size, with variations
   See also list of individual prints

5. Definitive Catalog (Johnson 120)

6. Price Paid $0000 (Bucholz Gallery, N.Y. 1946) Insurance Value $0000

7. Signature Not signed

8. Paper Laid, ivory

9. Watermark "Ambroise Vollard"

10. Condition Some pages slightly soiled at edge from turning of pages

11. Collections No marks

12. References and Reproductions
    Museum of Modern Art Bulletin, Vol XIX, No. 2, Winter 1952, Ostrich (.16) reprod. p. 1

13. Remarks Commissioned by Ambroise Vollard
    Published after Vollard's death by Martin Fabiani, Paris, 1942
    Edition: 226 copies
    No. 1 One copy on papier vergé ancien, with suite on papier ancien bleuté
    Nos. 2 - 6 5 copies on Super-Nacré Japan with suite on China paper

Cataloged By dl Date Dec. 1946 Mat Size Book

Figure 53.—Catalogue sheet for illustrated book.

Picasso
Buffon: Histoire naturelle
174.46.1-31

Remarks (Cont.)

Edition (cont.)
Nos. 7 - 36 30 copies on Imperial Japan with suite on China
37 - 91 55 copies on Montval (Copy No. 53, numbered by letterpress)
92 -226 135 copies on Vidalon

In original buff paper wrapper, with "Buffon" in black letterpress, unbound

Contents: Flyleaf
Half title; colophon
Title page; blank
(pp.1-2) Blank; blank
(3-4) Chapter heading; blank
(5-6) Aquatint .1); blank
(p.7)-134 Text, with 21 aquatints, on separate sheets
Folded sheets with 10 aquatints, without text
Note re printing; blank
Flyleaf

List of Plates. Printed by Lacourière
Composition sizes are given, since in most cases there are no plate marks. Measurements do not include incidental shading in the margins outside the outline; they do include etched lines which extend into the margin.

.1 Horse (Le Cheval) 10 1/2 x 8 3/8 in. (267 x 212 mm) comp.
Leica-1066-D
Studly T53

.2 Ass (L'âne) 10 5/8 x 8 11/16 in. (269 x 221 mm.) comp.
Leica-1067-C
Sunami-7136

etc. etc.

but with any missing part added in parentheses, "(19)'52," and the location and means used are noted as "lower right after signature, in pencil." If the date is known but does not appear on the print, it is recorded in parentheses.

MEDIUM: whether the work is "printed in black" or "printed in color" is specifically noted, although usually in the exhibition catalogues of the Museum of Modern Art a print is understood to be printed in black unless otherwise stated. When black has a decided tone, e.g., brownish black, or grayish black, etc., this fact is indicated.

DIMENSIONS: are given in inches to the nearest 1/16-inch, and also in millimeters, and it is indicated whether they apply to the plate or the composition. Measurements of the plate mark for intaglio prints such as etchings, engravings, aquatints, or drypoints, are taken at the right edge and bottom, and include the outermost mark of the bevelled edge, if any. They are made from a point about ¼-inch in from the corners, particularly if the corners are rounded, so as to record the full size of the plate. If there is no plate mark, the composition is measured. The composition size of planographic and relief prints such as lithographs or woodcuts is measured by lining up two transparent triangles or two strips of plexiglas with the outermost points, top and bottom, of the composition for height, and at its sides for width. The sheet size measured at the right and bottom edges at a point a little in from the corners; if the sheet is quite irregular, this is indicated. The museum uses three mat sizes numbered I (16 x 22 inches), II (22 x 28 inches), and III (25 x 32 inches or oversize). Since the storage cabinets are built in three sizes, the indication of mat size on the catalogue sheet is of assistance in locating a print, as well as in planning exhibition installations.

DEFINITIVE CATALOGUE: if a definitive catalogue of an artist's work has been made, the number and state, preceded by the key letters of the compiler's name, is indicated. If more than one definitive catalogue is listed, the key letters of the catalogue according to which the sheets are filed is underlined (e.g., for Ensor *Music in the rue de Flandre, Ostend:* D.81, only state; C.83 I/II. Delteil describes only one state. Croquez describes two of which this impression is the first). Where a book is in general use as a catalogue, though not actually a definitive catalogue, the compiler's name and the catalogue number are given in parentheses.

SIGNATURE: is cited in quotation marks exactly as given only if written by hand by the artist, otherwise it is noted as "not signed." A signature worked on the plate, stone, or block does not constitute a bona fide signature and such a print is not considered signed unless signed by hand also. A location given as "lower left," "center bottom," or "lower right" indicates that the signature occurs in the usual place on the margin just below the plate mark or composition; otherwise it is necessary to specify, such as "lower left on composition" or "lower left corner of margin." The method of signing is given as, "in pencil," "red crayon," or "blue ink."

PAPER: the general type of paper, laid, wove, China, Japan, etc., is given, together with its color. Shades of white and off-white running into buff are arbitrarily determined by a standard such as the following:

White: lighter than Ivins matboard
Ivory: same as Ivins matboard
Cream: darker than Ivins matboard

Buff: considerably darker than Ivins matboard

WATERMARK: may be a word or words, or monogram; these are recorded within quotation marks, as "Vollard," "(Ar)ches," the parentheses denoting that part of the watermark which is cut off. It may also be a design involving a description, or a sketch. "None" is specified where no watermark appears.

CONDITION: holes, tears, creases, wrinkles, spots, stains, foxing, rippling, etc., are described and located as in composition or printed area, or in margin. "One ⅛-inch hole center left side one inch from edge" might be either in margin or in composition, unless specified. Information regarding later damages and repairs is added as necessary.

COLLECTIONS: former collections are indicated, and whether their stamps appear on the print, and where. If no information or marks are found, the notation is "no marks."

REFERENCES and REPRODUCTIONS: only those which refer to or illustrate the museum's impression are listed.

REMARKS: all information not included above is given under this heading. Other handwritten inscriptions are noted, such as impression number, title, artist's proof, trial proof, dedication, etc. Inscriptions on plate, block, or stone, such as title, signature, etc., may also be mentioned here. For illustrated books or portfolios, the entry should include the publisher, date, and place of publication; size of edition; a description of the portfolio, case, or binding; contents; and a list of plates.

Catalogue sheets are filed in lock-post binders alphabetically by artist, then by definitive catalogue number if a definitive catalogue exists, otherwise chronologically.

ARTIST'S SHEET

Preceding the catalogue sheets of each artist's prints is an artist's sheet on colored paper stock, containing the artist's full name, biographical information, and a listing of definitive catalogues indicating abbreviations of the compiler's name or initials used on the catalogue sheets. The biographical information is stated in the form which would be used in an exhibition catalogue or on a label (legal nationality, country of birth if not that of which the artist is a citizen, years of birth and death, and also any country in which the artist may have done a considerable amount of work—e.g., "French, born Lithuania 1891. In USA since 1941"; or "Swiss, 1879-1940. Worked in Germany"). More detailed information may also be given, such as town of birth, dates of residence in foreign countries, or date of naturalization.

MAT LABEL

Where the print collection is handled by the public, a mat label on white bond, is important. It is pasted with library paste on the lower right corner of the inner matboard, below the print. On the label is included the following: name of artist; biographical information; title (foreign title also given, if desired); date; medium; definitive catalogue number; portfolio or book in which published, if any; credit lite; accession number; and name of institution. (See sample below.)

```
VUILLARD, Edouard                              French, 1868-1940

  The Game of Checkers (La Partie de dames).   (1899.)
  Lithograph, printed in color, R.M.32 III/III
  Plate I from portfolio Paysages et intérieurs, Paris,
        Ambroise Vollard, 1899.
  Gift of Mrs. John D. Rockefeller,Jr.           599.40.2

  Museum of Modern Art, New York
```

CATALOGUE CARD

For the use of the public, a catalogue card is prepared on 4 x 6 inch white all rag stock. It is not printed, except for lines marking off space for a 35-mm. photograph, and it is punched at the bottom. The following information, some of it confidential, is omitted from the public catalogue: negative number, name of anonymous donor, sheet size, price paid, insurance, condition, and name of cataloguer and date of cataloguing. Included on the catalogue card is a 35-mm. photograph that does not appear on the catalogue sheet. Some portfolios and illustrated books require more than one photograph, and these are placed on separate cards. Because of the expense only a selection of plates from a profusely illustrated book or large portfolio is photographed unless the importance of the book or portfolio warrants complete coverage.

The date is placed after the title, without quotation marks, as it would appear in a printed catalogue. If a date is given on the print, its location is indicated under Remarks. On the catalogue sheet this is found under Date, since there is space for it there.

ARTIST'S CARD

This serves as a guide card with tab and contains the same information as the artist's sheet.

DONOR CARD

A card giving the name and address of the donor and listing his gifts is prepared on 4- x 6-inch white all rag stock. A similar card is also made for each purchase fund and is filed alphabetically with the donor cards. In case of cancellations, red lines are drawn through the entries concerned.

CARD
CATALOGUE

The One in Love. 1923. (Soby 33)
(Der Verliebte)

35 mm.
photograph
pasted here

Lithograph, printed in black
10 3/8 x 7 1/2 in.

Signature: "Klee" lower right, in pencil
Paper: Laid, ivory
Watermark: None
Collections: No marks

Remarks: State inscribed lower right above signature, "Probedruck des schwarzen Steines / erster Zustand" (Trial proof of the black stone, first state)

Title "Der Verliebte" center bottom, in pencil
Date and Klee no. "1923 91" lower left, in pencil; also on stone lower left

Klee, P. 133.49
Purchase Fund

ARTIST
CARD

KIRCHNER, E.L.

Kirchner, Ernst Ludwig German, 1880-1938

Born May 6, 1880, Aschaffenburg, Germany
Died June 15, 1938, Davos, Switzerland

Sch.: Schiefler, G., Die Graphik Ernst Ludwig Kirchners. Berlin, Euphorion, 1925 (Vol.I); 1926 (Vol.II)

DONOR
CARD

RIESENFELD, Victor S.
888 Park Avenue
New York 21, N.Y.

303.48	Adam	The Cage	Engraving
310.48	Beckmann	Street Scene, No.2	Drypoint
315.48	Bonnard	The Laundry Girl	Color litho.

CHARGE-OUT FILE

A charge-out file of 3- x 5-inch cards, white for prints charged to exhibitions within the museum and buff for prints charged to borrowers outside the museum, is kept as a supplementary file to record prints charged out and reserved. It also provides a history of each print from the time it enters the collection. Ideally this file might be incorporated with the catalogue card file, but since the latter is for the use of the public, it seems better that it should be as unencumbered as possible.

When loans have been returned and checked in, a red line is drawn above accession number in case of borrower's card, and above "Circ. Ex." or "Borrower" in case of object card, and cards are filed in another drawer for future use.

SUBJECT FILE

Since requests are often received for prints relating to specific subjects, it is useful to have a file covering the most likely requests. A 3- x 5-inch file is used for this purpose. The subject headings are on blue guide cards with ½ cut tabs for the main categories and ⅕ cut tabs for the sub-headings. For example, under "Architecture" are the sub-headings "Bridges," "Buildings," "Interiors," "Monuments," etc. A separate card on white stock is made for each print. This card includes the name of the artist and biographical information, accession number of the print, mat size, title, date, medium, the file heading, and a cross reference to other subject headings under which the print is filed. On the back of each catalogue card is stamped the main subject headings under which the print falls with subheadings, if any, added in pencil.

PHOTOGRAPH ALBUMS AND FILE

Important prints and those needed for reproduction are photographed in 8- x 10-inch size, are labeled with catalogue information and the negative number, and mounted in loose-leaf binders alphabetically by artist.

A card file of photographed prints, giving the negative number, is also kept. It is less unwieldy than the albums and safeguards the photographic records in case a photograph is removed from the albums.

Reference:

ZIGROSSER, Carl and Christa M. Gaehde. A guide to the collecting and care of original prints, sponsored by The Print Council of America. New York, Crown Publishers, Inc., 1966 (Contains a short list of publications on the history, techniques, and appreciation of prints; a glossary of terms relating to prints; and a chapter on the care and conservation of fine prints.)

CHARGE-OUT FILE, EXHIBITIONS OUTSIDE BUILDING—BORROWER'S CARD.

Orozco The Flag, lithograph 1554.40

Circ.Ex.: Rivera, Orozco and Siqueiros
Sept. 1942 - May 1945

Borrower: Ohio State University, Columbus
April 25 - May 27, 1951

CHARGE-OUT FILE, EXHIBITIONS OUTSIDE BUILDING—OBJECT CARD.

Columbus Ohio State University

Ex. Graphic Art of Orozco
April 21 - May 27, 1951

1554.40 Orozco The Flag, lithograph
1556.40 " Indians, "
1630.40 " Marching Women, "

CHARGE-OUT FILE, EXHIBITIONS WITHIN BUILDING—OBJECT CARD.

Reder Clown and Centaur. Color woodcut 195.50

3rd fl. American Prints,1945-50 7/31/51 - 9/13/51
Aud.Gal. Recent Am.Woodcuts 9/10/52 -11/16/52
2nd fl. Museum Collection 10/11/53 -

SUBJECT FILE—SAMPLE CARD.

FEININGER, Lyonel (American, b.1871) 151.45 II

Railroad Bridge. 1919. Woodcut

Architecture - bridges
See also: Transportation

Article 7

A CLASSIFICATION SYSTEM FOR ART OBJECTS

WINIFRED KENNEDY

Registrar
Walters Art Gallery, Baltimore

A situation occasionally presents itself in which a director or registrar is faced with the problem of recording a collection already formed. The records available may be so inadequate that long and patient research is required to ascertain the data usually prerequisite to registration. The usual method of procedure by acquisition date may then prove impractical.

The Walters Art Gallery, housing a collection of over twenty thousand objects bequeathed to the City of Baltimore by Henry Walters in 1931, presented such a situation. The system instituted here for the accessioning of this large and diversified collection may be of interest to registrars whose collections offer similar problems. It is not, of course, recommended in instances where the established practice of accessioning by acquisition date and running numbers is applicable.

The Walters Art Gallery based its system of accessioning objects of art on a system for classifying and cataloguing photographs of works of art initiated by the Metropolitan Museum of Art.[1] This system divides the arts by classes and further subdivides them geographically. The Metropolitan Museum system has been used with certain modifications by many other museums for the classification and cataloguing of photographs. In the case of the Walters Art Gallery, the system usually applied to cataloguing photographs was revised and worked out as a system for accessioning and classifying the actual collections. Our revision of the system for works of art, as set forth below, employs two numbers to denote the class within which an object falls and differs from the system of accession by date, solely in that the class number is substituted for the year of acquisition. Running numbers (21.1, 21.2, 21.3, etc.) are used to identify the individual items.

[1] *Classification Systems for Photographs and Books,* Ethel A. Pennell and Luise E. Wallace, Metropolitan Museum of Art, New York, 1912. (Now out of print.)

In addition to making it possible to proceed with the work of registration without first establishing acquisition dates for all objects, this method was found to have other advantages. It permitted us to retain as accession numbers the catalogue numbers long associated with our paintings through the publications of Bernard Berenson. It automatically classified objects and records in a logical sequence that facilitated the task of marking and cataloguing—a task which as a result could be handled by several people without the risk of duplicating numbers—and made it easier to trace numbers that had become rubbed or obliterated in handling. The cards, furthermore, during the early stages of cataloguing, could be easily located for reference or for the addition of such new information as further bibliographical material, comments of visiting scholars, notes concerning restoration and location changes. This method further enabled us to keep the registration numbers for many classes of objects down to five, or at most six, digits. Very small objects will not permit the use of more than three or four digits. The first two, being the same for all objects within a class, could if necessary be left off. A small gem, for example, need carry only its serial number, the 42 indicating its class being omitted.

As set up at the Walters Art Gallery, the system calls for a minimum of three 4 x 6 inch catalogue cards, with photographs printed on the backs, for each object—one for the numerical index, another for the location chart, and the third for the classified index—and an accessions book (a Ty-Po-Fax loose-leaf book, which can be permanently locked when all entries have been completed) in which the entries are listed in the same order as in the numerical index, the number being placed at the left of the page. This book constitutes a permanent record of the collection as it existed at the time of Mr. Walters' death. A second accessions book, in which to record objects acquired since the collection was taken over by the city in 1934, has also been set up. In this book additions to the collection are entered by acquisition date and the classification number is placed at the right of the page.

CLASSIFICATION FOR ART OBJECTS

10. MANUSCRIPTS (except as below)
    15. Holograph manuscripts (letters, deeds, documents, etc.)

20. SCULPTURE
    21. Ancient Near East (Asia)
    22. Ancient Egypt
    23. Classical (Ancient in Europe)
    24. Near East (Muhammadan)
    25. Oriental (China, Japan, etc.)
    26. Africa and Oceania
    27. Post-classical in Europe
    28. America
    29. American Indian (includes pre-Columbian, South America, etc.)

30. PAINTING AND DRAWING
    31. Ancient Near East (Asia)
    32. Ancient Egypt
    33. Classical (Ancient in Europe)
    34. Near East (Muhammadan)
    35. Oriental (China, Japan, etc.)
    36.
    37. Europe and America
    38. Miniatures
    39.

40. WORK IN MINERAL STUFFS
    41. Stone (includes alabaster, rock crystal, marble when not under *20*)
    42. Gems (includes Oriental jades, Egyptian scarabs, seals, stamps, etc.)
    43. Mosaics and cosmati
    44. Enamels (includes metalwork when decorated with enamel)
    45. Niello
    46. Glass (stained and painted)
    47. Glass (cut and other)
    48. Ceramics (all ceramics except as under *49*)
    49. Oriental ceramics

CLASSIFICATION FOR ART OBJECTS

50. WORK IN METALS

- 51. Arms and armor
- 52. Iron and steel
- 53. Brass and copper
- 54. Bronze (includes ormolu)
- 55. Pewter and lead
- 56. Other metals
- 57. Gold- and silversmith's work (includes snuff-boxes, jewelry, etc.)
- 58. Timepieces (clocks and watches)
- 59. Coins and medals

60. WORK IN WOOD

- 61. Woodcarving (statuettes, altarpieces, etc.)
- 62. Painted wood (mummy cases, coffins, etc.)
- 63. Church furniture
- 64. Wood, decorative (carved panels, ceilings, doors, etc.)
- 65. Domestic furniture
- 66. Vehicles
- 67. Lacquer, inlay, boulle, marquetry, etc. (except when furniture)
- 68. Gourds
- 69. Baskets and wicker-work

70. WORK IN IVORY, LEATHER, ETC.

- 71. Ivory and bone
- 72. Tortoise-shell, mother-of-pearl, horn, etc.
- 73. Leather
- 74. Amber
- 75. Wax
- 76. Composition
- 77. Pápier mâché and paper manufactures
- 78. Stucco
- 79. Mummies

CLASSIFICATION FOR ART OBJECTS

80. TEXTILES AND LACES
    81. Carpets and rugs
    82. Tapestry
    83. Textiles
    84. Lace
    85.
    86. Costumes and accessories
    87.
    88.
    89.

90. PRINTS
    91. Incunabula
    92. Printed books after 1500
    93. Prints
    94.
    95. Japanese prints
    96.
    97.
    98.
    99.

Article 8

ACCESSIONING, MARKING, AND STORING SCIENTIFIC COLLECTIONS

WILLIAM A. BURNS

Director
Witte Memorial Museum, San Antonio, Texas
Formerly Assistant to the Director
American Museum of Natural History, New York

In the American Museum of Natural History each scientific department records and numbers its own specimens and maintains its own files. A report of accessions, however, is made on a form (figure 54) provided for that purpose and forwarded to the Office Services Department for recording and filing in the museum's central accessions file. A central accession record number is assigned by the accessions clerk and entered in a ledger with a description of the accession and how it was acquired, the name of the department receiving it, etc. This number differs from the accession or file numbers used in the various scientific departments. The accession record sheets are kept in the central file by department, donor, or other source of acquisition. If requested by scientific departments, the central accession record numbers are sent to them.

Each scientific department has developed a method of marking and storing based on methods fairly standard for all museums of natural history but modified to meet the needs of this institution and the requirements of each individual department. In this report, the departments of geology and paleontology, mammals, birds, insects and spiders, amphibians and reptiles, and anthropology are used as examples. All these methods are subject to local modification, depending upon the needs and the resources of each institution. Air conditioning and humidity control are desirable but expensive, and neither is absolutely essential for the climate in which the American Museum is located.

DEPARTMENT
File or Accession Number..................... Accession Number.....................

THE AMERICAN MUSEUM OF NATURAL HISTORY

ACCESSION RECORD

New York 24, N. Y...
DATE OF RECEIPT OF SPECIMEN

Received from ....

Address ....

Description of Material ....

....

....

....

....

Locality .... No. of Specimens..........................

Collector .... Estimated Value $..........................

How Acquired:
- *GIFT ☐ ....
- *PURCHASE ☐ PRICE $..
- *EXPEDITION ☐ ....
- EXCHANGE ☐ ....
- TRANSFER ☐ ....

Condition:
- GOOD ☐
- FAIR ☐
- POOR ☐

Loans received for:
- EXAMINATION ☐
- DEPOSIT ☐
- STUDY ☐
- IDENTIFICATION ☐
- VIEW TO PURCHASE ☐
- EXHIBITION ☐
- USE IN LECTURE ☐

Department Catalog No. ....

Number and nature of specimens given in exchange, or other information..........................

....

....

....

Signed ....

SEND TO ACCESSIONS FILE—OFFICE SERVICES

*INSERT NAME OF EXPEDITION OR FUND

Dept. of ....

FORM OS-48 1/14/54 2M

Figure 54.—Accession record sheet, filled in by curators and sent to central accessions file, American Museum of Natural History (size 8½ x 11 inches).

GEOLOGY AND PALEONTOLOGY

Vertebrate fossils are numbered and accessioned as they come in and are reported on the museum accession record form which is forwarded to the accessions file office. The accession number there assigned is not used by this department but a file of these numbers is kept for reference.

Specimens are catalogued individually. Two cards of all-rag stock are made for each specimen. The larger cards, 3⅜ x 6¼ inches, are always handwritten in India ink and are filed numerically; the smaller cards, 3 x 5 inches, are frequently typed and are filed systematically by genus and species. Samples of these are shown below.

12011 Gen. et Sp. Notharctus matthewi Hor. Bridger
Locality Grizzly Buttes, Bridger Basin, Wyo. Type Figd. Publication
Description Lower jaws & upper teeth
Case
Collector A.M. Expd. 1904 Field No. 506
03- REMINGTON RAND NC.-13 BP. 12662

12011		NOTHARCTUS MATTHEWI
	Figd. Type	Bridger Grizzly Buttes, Bridger Basin, Wyo. A.M. Expd. 1904 Lower jaws & upper teeth *Notharctus matthewi
Granger & Gregory	1917	Bull.A.M.N.H., XXXVII, 847, pl.103, fig.1

If the number of a specimen is known, data concerning it can be found immediately in the numerical catalog. If the department wishes to know how many specimens of a particular kind are in the collection, the information is quickly available in the systematic catalogue.

The number on vertebrate fossils, including fossil fishes, amphibians, reptiles, and mammals is marked directly on the specimen with India ink. On black or very dark specimens, a dab of white paint is applied and the number marked on it when the white pigment has dried. When the marking is dry, the number is covered with a coating of shellac for permanence.

Markings are made on any part of the specimen which is smooth enough to permit the use of pen and ink. A steel nib is used so that an inconspicuous but clear number will result. No markings are made on any location that will interfere with the use of the specimen for study.

Vertebrate fossils, if small, are stored in cardboard or wooden trays, in cases with glass doors, or in storage cans. Storage cans are sealed with felt strips to keep out dust, not because the dust might affect the specimen, but for cleanliness in handling. Large specimens are stored on shelves or on open racks.

Invertebrate fossils classed as megascopic, or visible to the naked eye, are marked with numbered paper labels with glue backing. These are pasted on the specimen on any surface smooth and flat enough to hold, but not in any spot likely to interfere with its study. Small specimens are placed in vials or capsules with a label enclosed. The labels are prepared in the museum's print shop.

Specimens are placed in small cardboard trays, in wooden drawers, or in steel storage cans sealed with felt strips to keep out dust so that handling will be a clean operation. Large specimens are kept on shelves or on wooden racks.

Invertebrate fossils, including groups classed as microscopic, and thin sections of megascopic invertebrates are marked with India ink on their cardboard or glass mounts. A space is provided on the lower margin of the mount for the descriptive material and specimen number.

Microscopic specimens are stored in cardboard slides with a central depression covered by a glass slide. Thin sections are covered by glass cover slips that protect the specimens.

All storage rooms should be well lighted for quick reference and study.

MAMMALS

In the department of mammals, specimens or shipments of collections are counted, given accession numbers which are also catalogue numbers, and entered by number in a ledger or accessions book. Catalogue cards, a sample of which is shown opposite, are also made.

On the accession record form (see figure 54) are noted the nature, locality where collected, number, condition of the specimens, catalogue

Museum No.-	**Original No.-**	**Sex-**
Name-		
Locality-		
Date-	**Collector-**	
Total length-	**Length tail vert.-**	**Length hindfoot-**
Skin, skull, skeleton	**Wgt.-**	**Ear-**
		Forearm-

numbers, and date of receipt; likewise the name of the collector and donor, whether the accession is a gift, purchase or exchange, and the estimated value. In instances where the specimen or specimens are sent in as a loan, catalogue numbers are not given, and the specimen or specimens are marked "on loan."

The accession record form is made in triplicate, one copy for department files, one for the accessions file office and one, if the accession is a gift, for the secretary's office where a formal acknowledgment is prepared and sent to the donor.

The department has six collection classifications for marking and storage: small and large mammal skins, small and large skulls, skeletons, and mammals in spirits.

Small mammal skins are marked with India ink on a label attached to the left hind foot of the specimen. As in marking most specimens, a fine steel nib is employed. Small skins are stored in trays and kept in slide-tight, mothproof cases. The storage areas must be relatively dry and be fumigated twice a year with paradichlorobenzene.

Large mammal skins are marked with perforations made with a three-cornered awl in the middle of the lower back. The skins are stored in a dry area and are hung by the head.

Both small and large skulls are marked with India ink on the cranium and mandible. Small skulls are kept in glass vials or in pasteboard boxes, usually with their skins. Large skulls are kept in boxes or in trays and are stored in slide-tight cases. Skulls should be de-greased. Large mammal skulls with antlers are hung from metal racks on the wall. A relative humidity of 55% is desirable, as is air-conditioning, and stored materials should receive moderate light and air circulation.

Skeletons are kept in boxes or in trays, with the markings on the shaft of each bone. Again, the air-conditioned storeroom is desirable, with moderate light and good air circulation.

Mammals preserved in spirits are marked by attaching a paper or parchment label, written in India ink or soft pencil, to the left hind foot of the specimen. A sized cloth label should not be used.

BIRDS

Material in the department of birds is recorded by number in a ledger kept in the department, and reported in triplicate on the accession record form, two copies going to the accession file office for its files. The third copy is filed in the department, by donor. All pertinent information, including a list of material and departmental catalogue numbers, is recorded on the accession form.

Temporary accessions such as loan materials are recorded by the department and reported in duplicate on the accession record form, both copies going to the accession file office, where the loan is registered and one copy immediately returned to the department to be filed under "open loans." When the loan is returned, the department copy is marked "returned," dated, signed by a staff member, and then sent to the accession file office so that the loan may be closed in its files. The accession file office retains this signed copy and returns its office copy to the department, where it is filed in the "closed loan file."

Bird skins are marked by using waterproof ink on a label cut from heavy, strong paper. The label is tied to the feet of the specimen with good linen or nylon thread. The study skins are stored in special metal cabinets with plastic-bottomed trays. Cases with rubber strips exclude dust. In this climate, no special humidity or temperature arrangements are absolutely essential. Insect repellents are introduced into the cases as a precautionary measure. Mounted birds receive the same treatment.

Whole bird specimens, preserved in fluid, are marked by putting a label, written in ink or crayon, into the jar or crock with the specimen. A second label may be pasted to the outside of the container. The problem in storing jars with formalin or alcohol is to prevent breakage.

Bird skeletons have their catalogue numbers written in ink on the larger bones. A label is also pasted on the box in which the specimen is kept. Skeletons in boxes need little attention and may be stored in any convenient dust-free area.

A label may be tied to the feet of mounted specimens. If this is objectionable or if the bird is to be displayed, the label may be pasted to the bottom of the stand or perch.

INSECTS

In the department of insects, the accession is recorded on the accession record form and sent to the accession file office. All the information on specimens of this department is contained on the label which accompanies the specimen. This includes the date of collection, the collector's name, and the exact locality where found, and any other information that would help in the study of the specimen. There is no accession or catalogue number and no need for a card catalogue file as the specimens are stored in easily accessible drawers by orders and families.

Insects on pins are marked by writing the information with India ink on small labels on good quality paper. The label is then put on the pin directly below the specimen. Its position on the pin is kept uniform by the use of a pinning block. Pinned insects are kept in glass-topped insect drawers in insect-proof, fireproof cabinets. A low percentage of humidity is desirable, light is excluded as far as is possible, and constant protection is given by fumigation.

Arachnids, myriapods, or insects in a liquid preservative are marked by inserting India ink or soft-pencilled labels in the jar or vial. Labels written with an alcohol-proof typewriter ribbon are also suitable. Specimens are stored in ethyl alcohol in vials or jars of various standard sizes. The jars or vials are kept in standard metal cabinets and are periodically inspected to make sure that the alcohol has not evaporated.

AMPHIBIANS AND REPTILES

When an accession is received in the department of amphibians and reptiles, it is tagged and catalogued under reptile or amphibian. Three copies of the accession record form are then prepared, two are sent to the accession file office and one copy is filed in the department under "gifts," "purchases," or "loans." The catalogue numbers are also noted on these copies.

Preserved specimens are marked with a metal tag corresponding to the data entry in the catalogue. In some instances, an alcohol-resistant fiber tag is also used. Tags are tied with carpet thread to the hind leg of a limbed specimen or to the neck region of legless forms. The alcohol-filled jars are arranged taxonomically in wooden trays that fit movable shelves in metal cases. Both trays and cases have labels indicating their contents. The storage area is ventilated by blowers and the specimens are protected from heat and from light.

Skeletal specimens are marked with metal and fiber tags attached to the larger parts. They are stored in boxes with typed labels permanently affixed. Boxes are stored in trays inside metal cases. Again, heat and light are excluded and blowers circulate the air.

ANTHROPOLOGY

In the department of anthropology collections fall into three categories: ethnology, archeology, and physical anthropology.

When a collection is received, an abbreviated notebook record is made giving the name of the donor (or vendor, collector, or expedition, depending upon the circumstances), the type of collection, provenience, number of objects, and estimated value or actual cost. Each acquisition in this department's system is numbered sequentially for each calendar year (1956-1, 1956-2, 1956-3, etc.). All correspondence, photographs, final catalogue numbers, and notes concerning a given accession are kept in an envelope filed in an annual file under the appropriate number. A donor or purchase file giving name, accession number, locality, and catalogue numbers of the collection furnishes easy access to these original data. The cataloguing system, although a relatively old one dating from the organization of the department, is very practical. A card catalogue is not used but the system is adaptable to one.

Since the collections fall into the three major categories noted above, a series of area or subject catalogues, each with an index number, is maintained. For example, North American ethnology bears the index number 50, which becomes the numerator for the sequence number of a specific object, so that a specimen catalogued in 50 would bear a number like 50-6742 (which may also be written $\frac{50}{6742}$ or 50/6742). When 50-9999 is reached, the numerator for North American ethnology changes to 50.1, and so on.

Other designations in this system of subject or area catalogues are: Middle American Archeology, 30, 30.1, 30.2, etc.; African Ethnology, 90, 90.1, 90.2, etc.; Physical Anthropology, 99, 99.1, etc.; Pacific Island Ethnology, 80, 80.1, etc.; North American Archaeology (exclusive of Mexico), 20, 20.1, 20.2, etc. The numerator designations are, of course, arbitrary. The actual catalogue records are in manuscript volumes designated as above. Triplicate typed copies of these are bound in loose-leaf binders for laboratory and office use.

Archeological specimens—stone, bone, shell, clay, or wood—are marked according to the color of the specimen. Chinese red mixed with varnish on dark-colored specimens and black drawing ink on light ones. They are usually marked on the reverse side or on the base (e.g., pottery). Brush or pen is used and the marking is shellacked when dry.

Ethnological specimens, which represent a great variety of materials, are marked as are archeological specimens, according to color. Where possible, the catalogue number is also written on a metal-rim tag attached with copper wire to the specimen. Location of the marking is in an inconspicuous place, such as the sole of a moccasin or the outer base of a basket.

Archeological specimens composed principally of shell, bone, wood, ceramic material, or horn are kept mainly in wooden or metal trays in wooden or metal storage cabinets and in storage areas below exhibition cases.

Ethnological non-perishable materials are kept on open racks with metal-mesh shelving. Costumes are stored on hangers suspended from metal pipe racks. Fur and wool are stored in air-tight metal cans. Large objects of various materials are kept on the open metal-mesh shelves and may also be hung from the ceiling or on walls. Small objects of various materials are kept in wooden trays on open racks. All the above materials, with their containers or racks, are enclosed in room-size storage vaults which are fumigated frequently to prevent damage from insects.

Textiles are marked by sewing a linen tape label to one corner of the fabric. Storage is again in the vaults where fumigation prevents damage.

Skeletal material is marked with India ink on each bone. Crania are stored in cardboard boxes on open shelves. Post-cranial material is kept in wooden trays in wooden cabinets or in metal storage cans.

SUMMARY

Summing up the essentials of efficient accessioning, marking, and storage, in addition to the department files, the museum maintains a central accessions file from reports provided by each department; it marks clearly with permanent inks or pigments on suitable label material on places easy to see but not interfering with the use of the specimen for study; it stores in containers best suited to the nature and size of the specimen, and the storage areas are kept free of dust, vermin, heat, and light where these procedures are indicated.

Article 9

REGISTRATION METHODS IN A MUSEUM OF SCIENCE AND INDUSTRY

STERLING H. RUSTON

Registrar
Museum of Science and Industry, Chicago

The registration of exhibits in the Museum of Science and Industry makes use of a simple system of numerical chronology. Its essential simplicity makes it particularly good for this museum where constant change in the physical condition, content or purpose of a specific exhibit makes it impossible to establish specific categorical identifications.

Unlike other museums, the Museum of Science and Industry contains little in the nature of collections, historical items, or other single exhibit specimens which by virtue of uniqueness, authorship, or intrinsic value come under the general classification of "museum pieces." And while there are broad exhibit categories such as "physics" and "chemistry," any system of identification based on a coded category would be useless. The ¼-horsepower, split-phase induction motor used to activate a demonstration of some law of physics might burn out and be rebuilt, removed, or used to replace a similar motor in the chemical section. Assigning a number to that single piece of equipment is simply a matter of giving it a permanent status in an inventory.

The registration of an exhibit may involve a single item such as a motor or hundreds of items as in a large industrial exhibit like the General Motors' "Story of the Automobile." It begins with the formality of giving and the acknowledgment of acceptance in writing. This correspondence, whether letter of transmission or contractual agreement, is assigned a general file number.

A numbered receipt covering the entire exhibit is issued upon its arrival. This number is part of a consecutive record of such receipts. No. 1, issued when the museum first began, was for a telephone receiver while the last one issued at this writing, No. 3638, covered three watches. This receipt number becomes the file number by which the exhibit may be traced and it is recorded in the file of correspondence which preceded the physical acquisition of the exhibit.

Individual items in this exhibit are then recorded by consecutive accession numbers prefixed by the last two digits of the year of acquisition. The museum's accession number, 29.1, covers the first item it ever acquired, in 1929, and the last one issued at this writing, 55.21, covers the 21st item acquired in 1955.

The accession number and the receipt number are entered with other pertinent information on a Kardex visible record that provides space for complete name identification, value for insurance purposes, dimensions, weights, cost data, date acquired, whether it is a loan or donation or purchase and any qualifications on such status, its location (in an exhibit or in storage), and a brief history and related facts. As any of these data change, additional dated entries are made on this master card, so that the current status of the item, as well as its past history, is known.

In the past, the descriptive account of the item was supplemented by a "record" photograph attached to the acquisition file card. This has now been discontinued, but it would be a recommended procedure for items not readily recognized by name or form.

Exhibits are acquired either through donations, loans, purchases, or by construction in the museum's shops. These groups are distinguished in the Kardex master record by color: white for donations, salmon for loans, blue for purchases, and buff for the shop. The last method is now rare, as museum shops are primarily concerned with maintenance.

Supporting the Kardex record are four 3- x 5-inch card files:

Alphabetical list of all sources of exhibit material
Alphabetical list grouped by the museum's technical subject classifications
Classified list, by divisions, of all material, by name of exhibit
Alphabetical list of exhibits by name

For reference purposes, a chronological index list is maintained in a ring binder, classified into "donations, loans, purchases, and shop jobs." A typed list of exhibits received is maintained, somewhat like a running inventory and another is kept of exhibits returned to owners or otherwise disposed of. Quarterly reports are made to the accounting department of all exhibits acquired and disposed.

Separately typed index lists are kept of material imported under U. S. Customs permanent exhibition bond; of exhibits under the museum's fine arts policy; of temporary loans; of special contracts or agreements; and of Government "return of property" bonds.

Since the museum's opening, more than 10,000 separate acquisitions, ranging in size from a single radio tube to a full-size submarine, have been catalogued by this method.

Article 10

ACCESSION RECORDS IN HISTORICAL MUSEUM

MARGOT P. PEARSALL
Curator, Department of Social History
Detroit Historical Museum

The accessioning procedures of a historical museum will usually differ considerably from those pursued by art or science museums. Unlike the former, for example, where acquisitions may be few during a given year but of high monetary value, the receipts of a historical museum are likely to be many and perhaps of small intrinsic worth individually. And unlike the science museum, there does not exist a universally accepted classification nomenclature for materials in history. The extent of historical collections aggravates the basic problem of record keeping; the personnel and the time to catalogue every button, hatpin, card case, or car are not usually available.

The recording program of the Detroit Historical Museum may be cited as an example of one designed to handle the problems contingent upon large numbers of accessions and limited staff. Since 1945, this institution has been an official department of the City of Detroit. At that time, the Historical Commission was created and the city was authorized to accept from the 23-year-old Detroit Historical Society their extensive collection of artifacts together with a building fund in the neighborhood of $400,000.00.

For almost twenty years, the museum had existed in fact. Beginning with the gift of a piece of water main to the then President of the Historical Society, the collections had grown to thousands of items—from flintlocks to fire engines, from furniture to fans. Thus, while the scope of the museum is limited to local history, with consideration to the State, the Nation, and the world as it relates to Detroit, it is interested in all phases of human activity—in cultural history (industrial, military and marine), social history, and the relationship of the individual citizen to organized community services, since each of these is important as it contributes to the picture of our heritage. The accessioning procedures of the museum were developed, therefore, to meet this diversity together with problems of prior acquisitions.

This pattern of establishing a formalized museum, with record keeping facilities, after years of informal acquisition, is not unique. But it is a pattern that compounds the responsibilities of the registrar. In addition to maintaining satisfactory records of new acquisitions, this individual must establish orderly and adequate records of materials received prior to the creation of the department.

The basic processes involved are three: accessioning, acknowledgment, and cataloguing.

ACCESSIONING

Accessioning new materials is the responsibility of the curatorial staff. The registrar assigns the basic numbers from the master list (to avoid duplications), and supervises the preparation of follow-up records. (The master list is maintained in a bound ledger and in this volume new accessions are listed in order of their receipt; the rule of order is numerical and other information shown includes the name of the donor, number of objects included in the accession, and a highly condensed description.)

Accessioning is done either on a typewriter or with India ink on rag paper, since these sheets become permanent records. At the end of each year, all accession sheets for that period are bound together. The possibility of loss of original records is therefore kept to a minimum. It would be desirable to have all accessions typed but since this is not always expedient, those legibly printed with India ink are accepted.

The accession number is composed of two figures, one indicating the year of receipt and the other the number of the accession within the year. For example, 55.43 indicates that the accession is the 43rd for the year 1955. The accession number is applied to the receipt of a gift from a specific donor at a specific time—and may cover one item or many. When the individual items within an accession are recorded, a decimal point and another number are added to the basic number and the whole becomes the object's catalogue number. For example, a handbag, lady's, c. 1910, etc., might be catalogued as 55.43.13, to indicate that it was the 13th object in that particular accession to be recorded. This number is painted on the object itself or marked on it in some other permanent manner. When and if a catalogue card is prepared, this number remains unchanged.

The basic accession sheet shows the name of the donor (or donors), their address, telephone number if known, and name of interested person through whom the gift was obtained if such a situation applies. It further includes the date of receipt of the gift and has headings to indicate the number of objects making up the accession, the catalogue numbers used, and the completion of such processes as acknowledgment, marking, and preparation of catalogue card. In listing items on the accession sheet, basic pertinent facts such as origin, association, maker, and date are included. The object is named, described, measured, and in some cases a sketch is made. A photograph, ultimately to be affixed to the catalogue card, would be desirable but is often impractical because of the cost.

Notes relating to the history of the donor, his interest in the objects presented, and any other information which might be of future use are likewise made on the accession sheet. The accession number is typed in the lower right hand corner. Information included on the accession sheets is summarized and transferred to a 4- by 6-inch donor card, filed alphabetically, which lists in brief the objects received from a specific donor at a specific time.

An indication is further made on the sheet as to whether one or all of the items included should be listed in the association file. This file consists of 4- x 6-inch cards, arranged alphabetically within certain classifications, such as people, events, or celebrations.

For each of those persons who have figured prominently in the development of the community, and whose possessions or philosophies might be of considerable interest in the preparation of either "object centered" or "idea" exhibits, a card is maintained. The obverse gives pertinent biographical data with notes as to other references where additional information can be obtained. On the reverse are listed in numerical order, the objects owned by the museum which bear a direct relationship to the individual named.

Events or celebrations such as the Michigan State Fair, Detroit International Fair and Exposition, Christmas, or Thanksgiving are also covered in another association file. This series includes references to specific items in the collections having a distinct relationship to Detroit and to the particular event, as well as references to other folders, files, or envelopes which contain additional information.

The association file, it should be emphasized, is primarily a quick reference which indicates whether the museum possesses any material or information pertaining to a specific person, event, or location. In the latter instance a series is being developed, which will be maintained in alphabetical order, of major public buildings, monuments, schools, and business houses. This file has proved to be extremely useful in connection with anniversary celebrations.

De-accessioning takes place when an object is permanently removed from the museum's collections by virtue of deterioration or transfer to another institution; appropriate notes are made, in red ink, on the original accession sheet, the donor card, the association file card, and the accessions record book. The catalogue card is removed from the active file and destroyed. Such action is taken only on the recommendation of the curator and with the official permission of the governing board.

ACKNOWLEDGMENTS

For each new accession a formal printed acknowledgment is sent. It lists the objects received and is signed by the curator in whose department the material falls and by the director of the museum. Items are not described in great detail, rather in a way which serves to identify the objects given and expresses appreciation for the gift. Each acknowledgment also bears the accession number assigned to the gift so that if there is any question, the original records can be readily consulted.

Known, and living, donors are notified when any of their gifts have been placed on exhibit. This is a routine function employing a standard "Gift on Exhibit" form with space provided for indicating what the object is and where it can be found.

When a gift is accepted for the museum, the donor is required to sign a "Certificate of Gift" card waiving all rights of ownership or control of the objects given. This is a printed form authorized by the museum's governing commission and incorporating recommendations of the American Association of Museums in relation to gifts; namely, that policy should forbid the acceptance of a collection under the condition that it be kept intact, of material under condition that it be exhibited permanently, or of a gift under condition that the museum keep it permanently. The accession number is typed on the card and it is filed by the registrar in numerical order. If the form does not accompany the accession sheet when it is given to the registrar for processing, it is sent to the donor for his signature at the time of acknowledgment; should he be unwilling to sign the release, the "gift" is returned.

Additional recognition of donors is made through acknowledgment in the Bulletin of the Detroit Historical Society. In this publication are listed all gifts received by the museum, and those presented by members of the Society are starred (*) in further recognition of their support of the local history movement. A copy of the Bulletin, appropriately marked, is sent to each donor listed.

Two exhibit cases are devoted to displays of recent accessions exclusively. One is located in the exhibit halls of the museum and the other in the members' lounge of the Society. Both are accessible to the public, although the latter case is reserved for members' gifts.

CATALOGUING

Within a framework of five basic divisions, military history, marine, social history, industrial, and metropolitan services, collections of like materials are sorted and stored and appropriate catalogue cards prepared. It has been found expedient to catalogue specific subject groups rather than process individual items indiscriminately because of a great backlog of uncatalogued materials. Subheadings are employed where practical. For example, under Tools, Carpenters, will be found such titles as chisels, planes, and hammers. The use of subject titles has made it possible for the catalogues to be used by persons who could not be expected to be familiar with a complex numerical classification code.

The 4- by 6-inch catalogue card contains all known information pertaining to the object described; i.e., donor, address, association (person or place), in addition to a complete description. When feasible a photograph of the object is stapled to the reverse of the card. When the amount of descriptive information exceeds the space available, additional cards are prepared, marked with the appropriate catalogue number followed by (2), (3), etc. General information is never typed on the reverse of a catalogue card. Information for catalogue cards is supplied by the curatorial staff for processing by the registrar.

LOANS

The general policy of the governing commission is to limit loans to the museum. There are, of course, certain exceptions to the rule. In common with most institutions, exhibitions are sometimes planned requiring infrequently used materials which it would be impractical to obtain and store. When it is necessary to borrow one or more items for a specific exhibit, a standard loan form is prepared. The basic policy is that loans should be for a specific purpose and for a stated time.

The loan form provides space for the name of the lender and his address and telephone number, with a generous space for listing the objects borrowed and their value. The lender and individual accepting the items for the museum sign this form. Provision is also made for signature of the lender verifying the return of the objects. Certain regulations pertaining to the responsibility of the museum in relation to loans are printed on the reverse side of the form; one copy, properly executed, is given to the lender at the time the loan is made. Conditions governing the receipt of items loaned are the customary ones relating to display, insurance, acknowledgment, etc. They also provide that any item left with the museum as a loan for a period of five years without a request having been made for its return shall, in consideration for its storage and safeguarding during this period, be deemed an unrestricted gift to the Detroit Historical Museum and shall thereupon become the property of the museum; in practice, this has meant that the museum has been unable to return the loan.

Loans to the museum are usually initiated by the director, assistant director, or curatorial staff but all original copies of loan forms are retained by the registrar, and loan numbers are assigned by him when the loan is received. These numbers are prefixed by the letter "L" and reverse the order of digits used for accessions. For example, L13.56 indicates that the object thus identified is the 13th loan item in the year 1956. Because loans to the museum are restricted and because not all items received from the same lender are necessarily returned at the same time, a blanket number such as is used in accessioning is not assigned. The loan number consists of two sets of digits only. Each loan is individually recorded in a bound ledger and when returned an appropriate entry is made in red ink. Active loan forms are kept in a current file. At the end of each year, those covering items which have been returned are placed in a manila folder in chronological order according to the original date of the loan. All loans are reviewed at the end of the fiscal year, and are required to be returned to the lender if not in active use.

Article 11

A STANDARD TERMINOLOGY FOR DESCRIBING OBJECTS IN A MUSEUM OF ANTHROPOLOGY

GERALDINE BRUCKNER

Archivist and Editor, University Museum
University of Pennsylvania, Philadelphia

The collections in the University Museum include the archaeology of Europe and the Mediterranean area, Egypt, the Near East, North, Middle and South America; the material culture of the native peoples of Africa, Australia, the islands of the Pacific, southeastern Asia, and the Eskimo and American Indian; a Chinese, an Indian, and an Islamic collection. We do not have examples of Western European civilization after about the Fall of Rome; that is, no European or American painting, sculpture, furniture, ceramics, silver, etc; nor do we have documents and memorabilia, or folk art. We use the same catalogue card for all our collections, and our aim has been to adopt a terminology basically uniform and at the same time flexible enough to include the specialized terms peculiar to any one area or people. Our catalogue card includes the accession number, the name of the object, the locality, the culture or date or people, a physical description of the object, photographic negative number, field number or former owner's number, dimensions, how and when collected and acquired and by whom, and the initials of the cataloguer together with the date of cataloguing. Here, I shall deal only with the description and name of the object.

DESCRIBING AN OBJECT

Correct identification of the materials, and accurate, precise statements of the dimensions, decoration, and condition of an object are essential to its description.

Materials

The same materials are used for such a variety of objects that it seems best to proceed first to the identification of the materials. For this, some knowledge of mineralogy, metals, botany, zoology, ceramics, and textiles is necessary but the registrar can hardly be expected to be an expert in all these fields. If at all possible, one should examine other collections and discuss each type of material with an expert (even if only briefly), perhaps have a small type collection, and always have a good unabridged dictionary. Usually it is relatively easy to determine into what large category the material falls. If the particular material is not recognized, describe its physical properties, as "hard, dark green stone, highly polished," "porous, grey stone," "soft wood," "very hard, close-grained wood." With a little practice, however, one can be much more definite.

Of the igneous rocks, those most frequently found in archaeological collections are basalt, diorite, pumice; of the sedimentary rocks, shale, sandstone, limestone; of the metamorphic, gneiss, schist, quartzite, slate, marble, serpentine. The appearance of some of these varies considerably with the locality; for example, Chinese limestone and Northwest Coast slate differ markedly from the limestone and slate encountered elsewhere. On the other hand, quite different stones sometimes look very much alike and identification must be made by one of the recognized tests—for relative hardness, type of fracture, specific gravity, or chemical content. Hardness is determined according to the Mohs scale where 1 is very soft, 10 the hardest known. Any material can be scratched by a harder material; for example, 6 will scratch 5 but will be scratched by 7. In testing by scratching, care should be taken to distinguish between an actual scratch and a chalk mark which is powder from the softer material. The finger nail will scratch up to a hardness of 2.5; a copper coin up to 3; a knife blade up to 5.5. In the following table, the first material is always that given in the Mohs scale, the others are materials which the museum worker frequently encounters:

1. Talc: steatite (soapstone)
2. Gypsum: alabaster; amber, which is a fossil resin (both 2.5)
3. Calcite: marble, limestone
4. Fluorite: malachite (3.5 to 4), serpentine (2.5 to 4)
5. Apatite: lazurite, usually called lapis lazuli; glass; and obsidian, which is volcanic glass (all 5 to 5.5)
6. Feldspar: turquoise, hematite (5.5 to 6.5)
7. Quartz: agate, amethyst, carnelian, chalcedony, chert, flint, jasper, onyx, rock crystal, jade (5.5 to 7)
8. Topaz
9. Corundum: sapphire, ruby
10. Diamond

It should be noted that the terms flints and flint implements are used even though the substance may really be jasper. Actually, flint is translucent and is usually grey, black, or smoky brown in color; jasper is opaque and is usually red, yellow, or grey; chert has a horn-like appearance, but the name is also used for impure flints and jaspers.

Both jadeite and nephrite are called jade, and the name is also used loosely for the very hard, opaque, white to green stone found in Middle America, and for the hard, usually translucent dark green stone found in Alaska and British Columbia and in New Caledonia and New Zealand, though sometimes this is called greenstone.

Much of what used to be called alabaster in ancient Egypt is really limestone; true alabaster is not found in Egyptian collections but it is found in quantity in Iraq, Iran, and Arabia. There is a very simple chemical test: alabaster and gypsum are calcium sulphates, while limestone, marble, calcite, and chalk are calcium carbonates; the latter will effervesce with any acid, as hydrochloric, while alabaster and gypsum will not.

Hematite, if used as a pencil, will leave a red or reddish brown mark.

In describing stone objects, say how the stone was shaped—by chipping, flaking, grinding—and whether the surface is polished.

Pottery, terra cotta, and brick are basically clay that has been baked. Pottery covers the vast range from the lump of clay pressed into shape and slightly baked to the most exquisite vessels and sculpture. In describing pottery, note the color and texture of the ware (called by ceramists the biscuit); whether there is a slip or a glaze; how it was made, built up with coils of clay or shaped from a lump of clay either by hand or with the potter's wheel; how well it is baked; and whether there is any decoration.

The word terra cotta simply means cooked earth. It is used to describe the material of which architectural adornments such as antefixes are made. It is also used as a general term for any small figure of baked clay, whether god or human, animal or bird, miniature bed or chair; these are known collectively as terra cottas, even though in describing the individual piece it is treated as pottery. Terra cottas are modeled or made in a mold, or occasionally both techniques are used, one for the head, the other for the body of a figure. Other small objects such as spindle whorls or game pieces, if well baked, are usually called terra cotta; if not so well baked, clay.

Brick is really the name of an object, rather than of a material. It is clay that has been formed usually into a comparatively small rectangular slab and dried in the sun or fired in a kiln for use in building. Depending on the degree and method of baking, it is termed sun-dried brick or brick. Either may be inscribed.

The dictionary defines glass as a substance resulting from the fusion of a combination of silica (rarely boric acid) with various bases. It may be built up from coils; or it may be blown. It should be noted that the beautiful iridescence of Roman glass is a break-down of the surface due to the action of minerals in the soil in which it has been buried.

The faience of Egypt and the Near East is completely different from the glazed pottery made in France and Italy and named for Faenza in Italy. Archaeological faience has about the same chemical content as glass but is not so completely fused; it has a very grainy texture, and there is usually a thin glaze which tends to wear off. In other words, it is a glazed frit. The color varies from white through blue and green to a quite heavy turquoise.

Most metals are easily recognizable and should be described by their common names. Bronze is the exception. The formula for bronze is copper with up to ten percent tin added to harden it; but in Old World archaeology, unless there is a specific reason for distinguishing between copper and bronze, this metal is all called bronze and objects made of it are spoken of collectively as bronzes. In American archaeology the practice has generally been reversed; all is called copper unless proven by analysis to be bronze. Why there should have arisen such a difference in terminology is not clear, but there is good reason for using just one name; chemical analysis is required to distinguish between copper and bronze, and in many places a certain amount of tin occurs naturally in copper, so that it may be problematical whether the presence of tin was intentional or accidental. Metal objects may be hammered into shape, modeled from sheet metal, or cast.

Ivory, bone, antler, horn, wood, shell, and coral are all well enough known to need no description, but it may be worth mentioning that ivory is of various kinds. The most common sources of ivory are elephant tusks, walrus tusks, and whale teeth. Ivory is more uniform throughout and therefore heavier than bone, which is porous inside or even hollow; antler is solid and rather like wood in appearance; horn is hollow where it joins the animal's head but solid towards the tip; horn has rather an oily feel and, when cut into a very thin sheet, is translucent, but otherwise can easily be mistaken for wood. Baleen, the material our grandmothers called whalebone, is the horny material that comes from the fringe-like strainer in the mouth of certain whales; by whalebone is meant any bone of the whale. Shell, particularly the shell of the large tridacna clam, sometimes looks like stone; the distinguishing characteristics are that the outer surface is always slightly curved and that both inner surface and cross section show its construction of many curved layers. Shell is very fine-grained and takes a high polish. Pearl shell and mother-of-pearl are usually thought of as light in color, but abalone is a darker iridescent blue to green. Coral, which is the skeleton of a tiny marine animal, contains principally calcium carbonate and is always white to red in color; it has a hardness of 3.5 and will take a high polish.

The identification of the material of which textiles are made is for the expert, but with a very strong magnifying glass one may distinguish wool, cotton, and silk. Wool threads are curly; cotton, almost straight; and silk has an even, fuzzy outline and is lustrous.

Particularly in dealing with an ethnological collection, many different animal and vegetable products are encountered—tusks, teeth, bones, claws, feathers, skins, reeds, gourds, seeds, berries—the precise identification of which, if necessary, is also for the expert.

Dimensions

Dimensions are an important part of the description of an object, and are always maximum unless otherwise noted. They are given in the following order: height, length, width; or length, width, thickness. Diameter may be substituted for length and width. Sometimes the dimension is given for a part of an object, as the mouth diameter of a jar as well as the maximum diameter, or the length and width of the blade as well as the length of the whole knife; this is always done for things composed of several parts, as an arrow or spear. If part of an object is missing, it is noted that the dimension is incomplete, or an estimated complete dimension may also be given.

Decoration

An explanation of the ways of decorating a surface, such as painting and engraving, does not belong here, but it should be noted that by negative painting is meant painting the background rather than the decorative motif itself; that pottery as well as stone can be carved; and that finger impressions, gouging, and punctates (punctured dots) are included among the decorative techniques.

Decorative motifs may be in abstract or natural forms. The former may be rectilinear or curvilinear and may include any combination of straight, angled, curved, or wavy lines, as well as geometric forms such as squares, diamonds, circles, hexagons, or triangles. Some are named: hatching, cross hatching, chevron, ladder, stepped, net, meander, scroll, rosette, star. Natural forms, whether human, animal, or vegeable, may be realistic, stylized, or conventionalized; the conventionalization sometimes being so great that the original form is barely recognizable. There have been some attempts at a uniform nomenclature for design elements, but except for such general terms as those given here, these terms have been limited to single areas.

Condition

Unlike the collections in an art museum, archaeological and ethnological pieces in absolutely perfect condition are relatively rare; so, except for an especially fine piece, minor cracks and chips are not noted. Serious damage and completely missing parts are noted, and a distinction is made, in measuring, between complete and incomplete. Any change in the material such as the corrosion of metal or the charring of wood or ivory is noted. For archaeological bronzes, which are an exception, it is noted if they have been cleaned; but as they always have a green patina it is unnecessary to mention it. Patina is any change in the surface and while most often used in connection with metals, the term can be applied to any material; sometimes it is very beautiful, sometimes destructive. A specimen may have been broken and mended in antiquity or a piece may have been broken and refinished. If so, it is always noted.

TERMINOLOGY

In naming many archaeological and ethnological objects everyday usage is followed, as, for example, in speaking of a hat, dress, shoe; bow and arrow, sword; axe, chisel, knife; basket or box. Frequently in addition to the English name the native name is also known and may either be substituted for or added to the usual name. The blouse worn by the Indian women of Guatemala today is called a huipil; an Eskimo woman's knife is an ulu. The use of these names saves considerable description, as each has a very definite meaning. Care must be taken, however, not to carry such names over into any other area simply because the pieces from the two areas have a superficial resemblance. The use to which a thing is put is quite often indicated by the name, as a sewing basket, a tool chest, a blacksmith's knife. But, again, great care must be taken not to imply a use that is not really known; therefore, figurine is usually a better term than doll or idol, and miniature vessel is better than model or toy. It is even more important not to imply cultural traits which do not exist; a nonagricultural people could not have a hoe or spade; nor a people with no knowledge of textiles a spindle whorl or a loom-weight.

There are many other things which, although they fit into one of the common categories, are peculiar to a certain area and have a particular name. A long, carved wooden box with a handle at each end and an inset lid, made by the Maori of New Zealand, is a feather box because in it are kept the feathers worn by the men. In those parts of the world where betel or coca mixed with lime (which is usually finely powdered shell) is chewed, lime gourds and lime spatulas are used, the latter usually of bone or wood. The piece of rawhide folded and painted and used as a carrying case by the Plains Indians is a parfleche, while the small netted bag carried by the Australian native is a dilly bag. The list could be extended indefinitely. Actually, while these terms, if known, are helpful to use, a simple description will generally suffice for identification.

Categories of Objects

Vessels. An important exception to the complete acceptance of the everyday name of an object is in the names used for vessel forms. As vessels (archaeologically principally of pottery with some stone and metal and ethnologically of a variety of materials) form such a large and important part of the collections in a museum of anthropology, and as there is no consistency in the common usage, it is useful to establish a nomenclature in which the names of the basic shapes are determined by the relation of the mouth diameter to the over-all size of the vessel. These basic shapes are: plate, bowl, pot, jar, bottle, and a high, wide-mouthed vessel for which there is no completely satisfactory name. For certain groups of objects of which extensive studies have been made, as Attic vases and Chinese bronzes, there are particular names; but these should be used only in their original meaning unless the name has been generally accepted in other areas.

The following names are applied to specific vessel shapes:

PLATES:

PLATE: an extremely shallow vessel, the diameter at least eight times the height.
SAUCER: a small plate.
PLATTER: a very large plate, usually longer than wide.

BOWLS:

BOWL: a vessel with open mouth, the height never greater than the diameter and usually much less. If the height is less than one-third the diameter, it is a shallow bowl; if as great as the diameter, a deep bowl. It may have any number of handles, but it should be noted that a bowl with a very long handle is a ladle or scoop.
STRAINER-BOWL or SIEVE: a bowl, usually rather shallow, with many pierced holes in the bottom.
GRATER-BOWL: a bowl, usually rather shallow, the bottom interior deeply striated.
MORTAR: a bowl with extremely thick walls; for use with a pestle.
BOX: a bowl, usually deep, and usually with a cover, more often rectangular than round; nearly always with vertical sides.
CUP: a small bowl, sometimes with one handle. Occasionally used for a vessel with vertical sides and wide mouth but with a height in excess of that proper for one of the bowl category; this vessel probably should be called a tumbler.
GOBLET: a cup on a high foot.
MUG: a deep cup, usually with flat base and straight vertical sides; with one handle.

Pots:

Pot: a vessel with a slightly constricted mouth. The height and the maximum diameter are about the same and the mouth diameter is at least half the maximum diameter. It may have any number of handles.

Cooking Pot: a crude, poorly made pot meant to be used over the fire.

Kohl Pot or Cosmetic Pot: a name used mostly in Egyptian archaeology for a small pot, usually with high shoulder; it has a cover and between the pot and the cover frequently a flat ring.

Jars:

Jar: a vessel whose apparent height is usually but not always greater than its diameter; the mouth is much more constricted than that of a pot; usually with a neck, which may be quite high, but may have only a spout opening directly from the body of the vessel; does not necessarily have handles but may have two or more; (a jar with one handle is a jug).

Storage Jar: any very large jar.

Olla: a term used most often for the archaeological and recent pottery from the southwestern United States. An olla has a very low neck and the body diameter is never less and sometimes considerably more than the height.

Seed Jar: this name is also used in the Southwest; it is a squat globular vessel with small hole-mouth.

Hole-mouth Jar: usually cylindrical in form; top nearly flat, with an opening in its center.

Ginger Jar: a Chinese porcelain shape. It is a jar with a rather high, flat or slightly rounded shoulder and a small hole-mouth with a very slight rim, just pronounced enough to hold the cover, which is a small, inverted, straight-sided cup.

Stirrup Jar: in Mediterranean archaeology, a small vessel, usually spherical, with a closed, flat top, open only at the base of a very small spout; beside the spout and also set on top of the vessel is a strap handle supported in its middle and at both ends. In South American archaeology, a vessel with the neck at the top of a hollow handle which is stirrup-shaped and set on top of the vessel.

Jar with Double Spout: a vessel, usually more or less spherical whose only openings are two spouts set at opposite sides of the top; it may have a strap handle connecting the spouts. This is found archaeologically in South America.

Jar with Spout and Bridge to Head: also found archaeologically in South America. It differs from the jar with double spout in that one of the spouts is replaced by a head or figure (human, bird, animal), and this head or figure is always connected with the spout by a strap handle.

Whistling Jar: two jars, each complete in itself, but with the bodies joined and with a handle connecting the vessels at the top. Occasionally more than two vessels may be so joined.

Jug: a jar with a single handle at one side; sometimes has a pouring lip but this is not essential.

Pitcher: a jug with pouring lip. Not used for archaeological specimens.

Juglet: a small jug with rounded or pointed base, meant to be carried. A term used almost exclusively in Palestinian archaeology.

Ewer: a jug of sophisticated shape with long spout.

BOTTLES:

BOTTLE: a vessel with a very narrow mouth; usually, but not always, with a high, narrow neck.

FLASK: a bottle meant to be carried, usually small, and somewhat flat so the dimensions of the body are width and thickness rather than diameter; small neck and mouth; usually with some provision for the attachment of a carrying strap.

ARYBALLOS: One of the Greek vase forms; as such, it is a globular bottle having a small neck with wide overhanging rim. In South American archaeology the name is used for a jar or bottle with pointed base and two small handles placed very low on the body; such jars were carried on the back, the handles holding the tumpline in place.

HIGH, WIDE-MOUTHED VESSELS:

BEAKER: a vessel with nearly vertical or flaring sides which may be convex near the base and either straight or recurved to the open mouth. The bell beaker of Neolithic Central Europe and the quero of South American archaeology are two variations.

TUMBLER: a small but relatively high vessel with open mouth; usually an inverted cone with small base. But see the note under "cup."

CYLINDER JAR or CYLINDER VASE: a high cylinder with flat base. The name is used particularly for the beautiful painted vessels, sometimes also called picture vases, made by the Maya.

The following names are applied to more than one vessel shape:

FOOTED VESSEL or VESSEL WITH FOOT: any vessel which has a base or foot which is not an integral part of the container itself. It is better to be definite: footed bowl, footed jar, etc., or alternatively, bowl with foot, jar with foot. A vessel with three feet is a tripod; with four, a tetrapod.

EFFIGY VESSEL: a vessel made in human, animal, or plant form. Again, it is better to use effigy bowl, effigy bottle, etc. Such vessels are described as are figures, the position of the vessel mouth and whether or not there is a handle also being noted.

LAMP: in its simplest form a saucer with a lip into which the wick is laid; but lamps are made in a variety of forms, sometimes quite elaborate. The "Roman lamp" is a low, circular or oval pot with a rather small mouth and a horizontally projecting nozzle having a hole for the wick; sometimes a horizontal or vertical handle is on the side opposite the nozzle; sometimes there are several nozzles.

LANTERN: may be of any form, usually has some provision for the attachment of a candle or small lamp to the base interior, must have openings of some kind to allow the air to enter and the light to shine out.

INCENSE BURNER: any vessel designed for the burning of incense.

CENSER: an incense burner to be carried.

MINIATURE VESSEL: any tiny vessel. It is better to be definite: miniature jar, miniature jug.

VASE: in a particular sense, any vessel, usually ornamental rather than useful, which cannot be fitted into a definite category. In a general sense, any group of more or less decorative vessels.

LID or COVER: anything used to cover the mouth of a vessel; it varies from a simple disc or slab to another vessel, inverted.

SHERD: potsherd; a fragment of a vessel, usually of pottery but occasionally of stone. Sherds are described as rim sherd, body sherd, etc., of a particular type of vessel; sometimes it is possible only to name the ware of which the sherd is made, frequently it is possible to determine from it the exact shape and size of the whole vessel.

While the name of a vessel gives a general idea of its shape, further description is necessary. Sometimes the description can be very simple, as hemispherical or truncated conical; frequently it is very detailed. This description should follow a definite order, beginning at either the bottom or the top of the vessel (the former is usually more convenient) and mentioning such added parts as lid, handles, spout, at the end.

The base is described as flat, flattened, rounded, ring; or it may have a foot or feet, which are described as hollow or solid, rattling, ball, slablike, effigy, or a high ring.

The body is described as spherical, hemispherical, squat, i.e., spherical with top and bottom compressed, lentoid in section; or, if no simple term applies, the sides are described as rounded or straight, as expanding to the shoulder, which may be high, wide, flat (on top), convex (on top); or perhaps expanding to the maximum diameter, which is below the middle of the vessel, and then contracting to the mouth or neck. The term carination is used for the more or less sharp angle formed when the sides, which have expanded from the base, contract to the mouth.

The neck is described as wide, narrow (remembering that by definition the widest neck of a bottle is narrower than any jar neck), high, low.

The mouth is the vessel opening; the rim the edge of the mouth. The rim may be wide or narrow, inturned, outturned, flaring, rolled, vertical, overhanging, or with pouring lip, and may have a crenellated or a serrated edge. Spout is sometimes used instead of pouring lip, but is preferably used only for one added to the vessel proper.

Handles may be loop (attached at both ends), and may be set on the shoulder, or vertically as from neck to shoulder or side of body, or horizontally; strap (a flat loop); bail (a loop handle over the top of a vessel, a bucket handle); or ledge (flat and projecting, usually horizontally). A lug is a small projection, sometimes pierced for the insertion of a carrying cord, or for the attachment of a lid.

Implements, Tools, and Weapons. Whether to classify implements, tools, and weapons by form, or by function, or to use a combination of the two, presents a problem. In the classification by form, the flints of the Stone Age, which are made by chipping and flaking, are divided into two large categories: those made from the flint core, as the fist or hand axe and the chopper; and those made from a flake struck from a core, these flake tools being further subdivided into those struck from a prepared core.

For Stone Age material this completely objective approach seems ideal, but there has, in fact, grown up for European flints a whole French terminology with a somewhat different English counterpart, and for American stone tools a quite different one. For example, the European blade is a long, narrow flake struck from a prepared core; by secondary flaking and chipping it can be made into a knife, scraper, burin, or saw. The American blade is a flint with a cutting edge; it may be of any shape. The French burin (English graver), is a small thin tool with small sharp edge, used for cutting fine lines, i.e., an engraving tool; its working edge has been formed through the removal of an additional small flake by the characteristic burin technique. It is only from recent excavations that scientists have learned that there were burins in America before the coming of Europeans. The term graver has been used in America, but for a flake with one or more projecting points (also an engraving tool), and when there are at least two points, the edge between them is always concave.

Efforts to establish a uniform terminology for European and American Stone Age material have thus far been unsuccessful. Until such a terminology has been worked out, the local custom should be followed. Since the use of later archaeological objects (such as those found in collections from the Near East) is frequently but not always known from representations on sculpture or from written evidence, a compromise in classification leaning toward the functional is most satisfactory. The use of each ethnological specimen is usually known, so classification by function is best.

With the Bronze Age, metal as well as stone began to be used, and ethnologically there is a variety of materials.

The following names of implements, tools, and weapons are used:

Blade: a tool used for cutting; it may be complete in itself, or it may be hafted; if it has a serrated edge, it is a saw.

Scraper: a tool, usually with one flat surface, the edges of which are used for scraping; it has many forms and uses, some of which have specific names, as flesher or hide scraper.

Awl: sometimes called a perforator, a tool for punching holes; it is circular or rectangular in section and tapered to the point, which is the working part.

Drill: an implement similar to the awl, sometimes used with a bow; but it is very thin and of more uniform circumference than an awl, and has a tiny point.

Axe and Adze: the difference between an axe and an adze is in the use, and that depends on the manner of hafting. An axe is used vertically to the surface to be cut, whereas an adze is used horizontally to the surface and working toward the user. The term axe or adze should always be used to refer to the complete tool; without the haft, it is "axe blade" or "adze blade." Sometimes these can be distinguished—an axe blade is bifacial, an adze blade has a sharp bevel on one face to the edge—but the distinction is not always clear and there is the further complication that the Eskimo use the same blade for both, converting it from one to the other by a quarter-turn change in the hafting. In describing an axe or adze blade, give the shape, whether parallel-sided, triangular, oval in section; whether the faces are rounded or beveled to the edge; and whether there is a groove near the butt end for hafting. Celt, although it has been applied quite generally to such a tool, is one of those indefinite terms which it is best not to use; a celt may be but usually is not hafted; if it is hafted it is called a hafted celt.

CHISEL: has one flat face which rests on the surface to be chipped, the end of the upper face being rounded or beveled to the working edge which is away from the user. The term chisel is used whether or not the tool is hafted.

HAMMER or POUNDING STONE: just what the names imply; may be of any shape.

GRINDING STONE: also just what the name implies; it is usually rather flat.

PESTLE: a pounding or grinding stone used in a mortar; it is usually quite long, circular in section, with a small working surface.

KNIFE: may be either a tool or a weapon; it is used for cutting or slashing; it may be hafted, in which case the working part is called a blade. In describing a knife, give the shape of the blade, whether the faces are flat, convex, or concave, and whether they are grooved, the position of the cutting edge, and what provision has been made for hafting. The long, spike-like projection for insertion in the handle is called a tang. The general category of knives includes all the highly specialized forms, as the kris and the barong, as well as the better known sword and dagger.

SWORD: a large, flat-bladed knife, always used as a weapon.

DAGGER: a long narrow knife, always a weapon.

THROWING KNIFE: a knife, frequently with several subsidiary blades, thrown either in hunting or in warfare.

BOW: may be used with an arrow, when it is a weapon; but it may also be used as the driving force for the drill in fire-making and in drilling holes. In describing a bow, indicate whether or not it is composite, i.e., made of one or more materials, and what string is used.

POINT or HEAD: the effective end of an arrow or any similar weapon, it is described as to shape (triangular, long triangular, lanceolate); whether the base is straight, convex or concave, or is tanged; whether there are barbs, and their position.

ARROW: a long, thin weapon meant to be used with a bow; it may be of one piece with a sharpened end; or it may consist of a point, a foreshaft (not always present), and a shaft. It is described as to each part, whether the shaft is feathered and what has been used for the feathering, and how the parts fit together.

SPEAR: a thrusting or throwing weapon; it is much larger and heavier than an arrow and is described in the same way.

SPEARTHROWER, THROWING BOARD, ATLATL: used to give additional leverage and power in throwing a spear. May be long and narrow with a groove in which the spear rests, or may be flat and wider; has a hook at the farther end (from the hand) to engage the spear.

HARPOON: a spear with long detachable head connected to the shaft by a long cord.

DART: a small, very thin, lightweight weapon meant to be thrown; used with blow gun; frequently poisoned.

BLOW GUN: an extremely long narrow tube (perhaps ten feet long, with a diameter of little more than an inch) through which darts are expelled.

CLUB: a weapon of a variety of shapes, whose efficacy depends on the force of the blow. The shape is described; but it is to be noted that in some areas the names of clubs are as carefully differentiated as are knives in other areas.

MISSILE CLUB or THROWING CLUB: any club meant to be thrown.

BOOMERANG: a long, thin, curved throwing club. In spite of the name, few are returning; those that do return (ones having a very sharp curve, sometimes an angle) must be noted.

BOLA: a throwing weapon composed of several balls, each attached to a thong.

MACE: originally a club with ball head. Frequently used as a symbol of authority.

Sculpture. For architectural sculpture the accepted architectural terms are used—column, capital, lintel, antefix, etc. The description includes the material, the shape, and the type of decoration and what it represents.

STELA: a term peculiar to archaeology, a free-standing upright slab of stone (rarely of pottery), decorated on at least one face, sometimes on both faces and both edges, and of any size from a few inches to many feet. A stela may be set on a pedestal or base, as also may a statue.

PEDESTAL: may be of any shape and size and may be elaborately decorated; the essential characteristic is that it is a support for something else.

PLAQUE: a slab, not free-standing, either with one decorated face or used as a background for a figure.

FIGURE and STATUE: the distinction between the two is in the material, a statue being made of stone or metal, a figure of wood or clay, though occasionally a large important figure is called a statue and a small piece meant to be hung from necklace or belt is a pendant figurine, no matter what the material.

FIGURINE and STATUETTE: the distinction between figure and figurine, statue and statuette is one of size; using the human figure as a guide, a representation less than approximately one-fourth life size is a figurine or statuette. For all these, note who or what is represented, the position (standing, seated), and how dressed; any attributes or attendant figures; and state whether the figure is in full round or forms part of a stela or plaque.

Ceremonial Objects. The very large category of ceremonial objects includes everything to do with a religion or a cult: dance paraphernalia (costumes, masks, musical instruments, wands); totemic objects; votive objects; amulets; fetishes, and the tools of the medicine man. Each of these should be given its own proper name and described just as if it had no religious significance, simply noting its use. The use of the term ceremonial object as the designation for an individual piece is permissible only in the rare case of an object for which there is no better identification. Following are some of the types of ceremonial objects:

AMULET or CHARM: any object, usually small, which either because of its form (as the figure of a god or of a sacred object), or because of its association, or because of some formula of blessing or cursing said over it, is thought to have power to protect or destroy.

SCARAB: an Egyptian amulet in the form of a beetle. The base is frequently inscribed with the owner's name or cartouche and the scarab may then be used as a seal.

FETISH: an object also thought to have protective or destructive power; applied particularly to the African figures with a cavity in the head or the abdomen to contain "medicine" which really imparts the power.

TOTEM: an object peculiar to a group or an individual; frequently in the form of an animal which is associated with their history or character. An elaborated form is the totem pole of Alaska and British Columbia. The conical headdress with totemic bird or animal on top, worn by the Tlingit Indians of Alaska, is called a crest.

CHURINGA: an Australian totemic object, a slab of stone or wood, usually long and narrow but occasionally nearly round, inscribed with totemic symbols.

BULLROARER: a wooden churinga pierced at one end for the insertion of a string by which it is twirled rapidly to make a loud, whirring noise.

KACHINA: a painted wooden figurine made by the Pueblo Indians of New Mexico and Arizona, representing the gods and other personages associated with the corn-growing and other ceremonies.

SHAWABTI: a figurine, usually of faience but may be of stone or wood, in mummy form, placed in an Egyptian tomb.

Miscellaneous. Among the miscellaneous objects not fitting into the other categories are the following:

PAPYRUS: actually the older form of paper made from the papyrus plant, but the term is used for any document written on papyrus.

CUNEIFORM TABLET: a Babylonian document in the form of a rather thick, rectangular (occasionally circular) piece of clay, inscribed with a triangular stylus, and baked; it may have an envelope, also of clay and inscribed.

BULLA: a clay or metal ball with inscription or seal impression; used as a tag.

SEAL: there are two forms, stamp and cylinder, the impression of the latter being made by rolling the seal over the surface to be marked. The designs on seals are the contemporary record of physical type and material culture as well as of myths and beliefs and worship. They must, therefore, be described in detail. Cylinder seals are particularly plentiful in Near Eastern archaeological collections.

SEAL IMPRESSION or JAR SEALING: a lump of clay which has been placed over the mouth of a jar (usually over a cloth or reed cover) and stamped, usually many times, with the owner's seal. These are peculiar to Near Eastern archaeology.

QUIPU: a mnemonic device used archaeologically in Peru for recording information; it consists of cords of various lengths and colors, knotted.

CAT'S CRADLES: string figures made on the fingers in recognized patterns.

BARK CLOTH: frequently called by its Samoan name, tapa, is cloth made by pounding the inner bark of certain trees, most frequently the paper mulberry, the breadfruit, and the fig. Frequently painted and sometimes waterproofed.

BEADS: the most common shapes are: ring, short tubular, tubular, disc, ball, barrel-shaped, cylindrical (i.e., long narrow, slightly tapering to the ends), biconical, and irregular. Most of them can be faceted or fluted. The term string of beads is used rather than necklace unless it is definitely known that the beads were worn about the neck.

PENDANTS: when spoken of in connection with beads, are beads with the suspension hole at the top rather than through the middle.

GORGET: a pendant, usually flat, worn on the breast.

BANNERSTONE: an object found archaeologically in the eastern United States. It is rather flat, more or less rectangular with a greater width than height, the center section vertically pierced and flanked by two wings, and was almost certainly used as an atlatl weight.

BIRD STONE: also found archaeologically in the eastern United States and also almost certainly an atlatl weight. It is long and narrow with flat base and somewhat resembles a resting bird.

References:

CHURCHILL, WILLIAM. Club types of Nuclear Polynesia. Washington, 1917.

CLARK, J. G. D. The Mesolithic settlement of Northern Europe. Cambridge, England, 1936.

COLTON, HAROLD S. Potsherds. Flagstaff, Arizona, 1953.

EDGE-PARTINGTON, JAMES. An album of the weapons, tools, ornaments, articles of dress of the natives of the Pacific Islands. Manchester, England, First-third series, 1890-1898.

FOSTER, KENNETH E. A handbook of ancient Chinese bronzes. Claremont, California, 1949.

FRANKFORT, H. Cylinder seals. London, 1939.

GARDNER, HELEN. Art through the ages. New York, 1948.

GRIFFIN, JAMES B., editor. Archaeology of eastern United States. Chicago, 1952.

HODGE, FREDERICK W., editor. Handbook of American Indians north of Mexico. Washington, D. C., Smithsonian Institution, Bureau of American Ethnology Bull. 30, 1907-1910.

Illustrated catalogue of the International Exhibition of Chinese Art, 1935-36 (at Burlington House). London.

KIDDER, A. V. The artifacts of Pecos. New Haven, Phillips Academy, Andover, Mass., Dept. of Archaeology, Papers of Southwestern Expedition No. 6, 1932.

———. The artifacts of Uaxactun. Washington, D. C., Carnegie Institution, Publ. 576, 1947.

KROEBER, A. L. Handbook of the Indians of California. Washington, D. C., Smithsonian Institution, Bureau of American Ethnology Bull. 78, 1925.

LUCAS, ALFRED. Ancient Egyptian materials and industries. London, 1948.

———. Antiques, their restoration and preservation. London, 1932.

LYFORD, CARRIE A. Quill and Beadwork of the Western Sioux. Lawrence, Kansas, U. S. Office of Indian Affairs, Indian Handcrafts No. 1, 1940.

MARCH, BENJAMIN. Standards of pottery description. Ann Arbor, Michigan, 1934.

MCGREGOR, JOHN C. Southwestern archaeology. London, 1941.

NEWBERRY, PERCY E. Scarabs. London, 1906.

Paul, Frances. Spruce root basketry of the Alaska Tlingit. Haskell Institute, Lawrence, Kansas, U. S. Office of Indian Affairs, Indian Handcrafts No. 8, 1944.

Richter, Gisela. Attic red-figured vases, a survey. New Haven, 1946.

Richter, Gisela, and Milne, Marjorie J. Shapes and names of Athenian vases. New York, 1935.

Schofield, J. F. Primitive pottery. Handbook Series No. III. The South African Archaeological Series, Capetown, 1948.

Seltman, Charles T. Attic vase-painting. Cambridge, Massachusetts, 1933.

Schweinfurth, Georg. Artes Africanae. Leipzig, 1875 (German English translation).

Shorter, Alan W. The Egyptian gods. London, 1937.

Steward, Julian H., editor. Handbook of South American Indians. Washington, D. C., Smithsonian Institution, Bureau of American Ethnology Bull. 143, 1946-.

Stone, George Cameron. A glossary of the construction, decoration and use of arms and armor. Portland, Maine, 1934.

Underhill, Ruth. Indians of the Pacific Northwest. Riverside, California, U. S. Office of Indian Affairs, Indian Life and Customs No. 5, 1945.

———. Pueblo crafts. Phoenix, Arizona, U. S. Office of Indian Affairs, Indian Handcrafts No. 7, 1944.

Wormington, H. M. Ancient man in North America. Denver, Denver Museum of Natural History, Popular Series No. 4, 1949.

Article 12

PREPARING ART EXHIBITIONS FOR TRAVEL

VIRGINIA PEARSON

Circulation Manager, Department of Circulating Exhibitions Museum of Modern Art, New York (1944-1962; d. 1964)

In the preparation of any exhibition to be handled by many people, some of whom may not be experienced in handling works of art or other museum material, it is of prime importance that the objects themselves be made as safe as possible and that all instructions that accompany the material be concise and clear. The originating institution, it is assumed, has prepared the material in such a way as to assure its safety in transit and has prepared instructions to insure the same care and handling by the borrowers.

It is therefore essential that the receiving institution read and carefully follow all instructions that accompany an exhibition. The procedures outlined below are based on the experience of the Museum of Modern Art in New York and have worked satisfactorily in the preparing and packing for travel both of single works of art and of entire exhibitions.

PREPARATION FOR TRAVEL

Paintings

The frames of all paintings that are to travel should be simple moldings made of wood. The frame should project out on all sides from the face of the canvas or panel a half inch beyond the greatest thickness of the painted surface. Carved plaster frames should never travel, as they are too easily broken and may cause damage to the canvas if pieces become loosened in transit. It is definitely advisable to make special traveling frames to replace all fragile or plaster moldings.

On the back of the painting metal straps should be used to fasten the frame to the stretcher on all four sides, care being taken that the screws do not go through either frame or stretcher. Stretcher keys should be checked to be sure all are in place and tight. Then a heavy cardboard (not corrugated) backing should be screwed to the back of the stretcher.

Tacks should not be used, as they may loosen and become a hazard to the painting. Any projecting nameplates or screw eyes for hanging should be removed. If it is necessary to provide a hanging device for the painting, a flat metal plate provided with a hole for the wire may be screwed to the frame. (See figure 55.)

Figure 55.—Protective backing on a painting and metal plates fastening stretcher to frame, Museum of Modern Art.

It is essential that glass on paintings be protected with masking tape. It is recommended that strips of 3-inch masking tape be laid on the glass not more than ¼-inch apart across the longest measurement of the painting (see figure 56). Never use a water soluble tape as serious damage may be caused to the painting by water running to the edge of the glass and penetrating beneath. If the painting is larger than 25 x 30 inches it is advisable to replace the glass with a plastic such as plexiglas or lumarith. If this is too costly to be practicable, the glass should be removed, covered with masking tape, and packed between corrugated cardboard in a separate compartment in the box.

An identification sticker should be attached to the backing board of the painting identifying it by the name of the exhibition, museum number, artist, title, date, medium, and lender. The box number should be indicated on the sticker if the painting is part of a large shipment. This facilitates handling in installation as well as repacking.

Figure 56.—Masking tape applied to glass on a drawing, Museum of Modern Art.

A condition record should be made before any work of art is to travel, carefully noting in diagram form the location of all marks, damages, and spots as they appear at the time shipment is made. This record should also note separately the condition of the frame. It is suggested that for a traveling exhibition separate condition sheets for each item accompany the shipment, so that each exhibitor will be able to check the original condition against the condition in which it is received. Any change should be noted and sent to the originating institution so that insurance records may be kept accurately and up to date. The condition of a single painting for a single loan should be checked upon its receipt, and a report sent to the lending institution.

Watercolors, Drawings, Prints

Frames of all watercolors and other work on paper should be simple narrow wood moldings.

The backs of these works should be checked to be sure that brads are driven firmly in the wood of the frame and that tape is used to cover the brads and edge of the frame rather than a sheet of paper to cover the backing board. By using tape there is less danger of the brads loosening and causing damage by working between the frame and glass. Screw eyes for hanging should be removed and flat metal plate hangers screwed into the frame.

The glass with which this type of material is usually covered should be protected in the same manner as are glass-covered paintings.

Identification stickers and condition records are required, as for paintings.

Sculpture

Each piece of sculpture must be treated as a special case depending upon its size, weight, and fragility. In general, the shipping of fragile pieces should be avoided, particularly plaster pieces and those with thin projecting portions in the composition.

Ceramics and Small Fragile Objects

These objects must always be carefully prepared for packing by completely wrapping them with tissue or a soft cloth. If there are projecting parts, these must be carefully wrapped independently of the body of the piece. The entire object should then be wrapped so it is a large soft package and thus fully protected against shock. The wrapped package should be floated in excelsior in a corrugated cardboard box. If the object is to be shipped locally, this is all the packing that will be necessary. However, if it is to be shipped any distance, the corrugated cardboard box should be "floated" in excelsior in an outer wooden box and packed firmly so it will not shift position in transit. The *Manual of Traveling Exhibitions* by Elodie Courter Osborn,[1] is recommended for further information on this type of packing.

[1] Museums and Monuments, Publication 5, United Nations Educational, Scientific, and Cultural Organization.

PACKING FOR TRAVEL

Boxes should be made of seasoned wood such as no. 2 pine shelving three quarters of an inch to an inch thick and free of knots and cross grain; crates should never be used. All boxes should be lined with waterproof paper. Boxes should be nailed with coated nails, as they have greater resistance to withdrawal, and the lids should be bolted in place if the box is to be used for more than one trip. If the box is to be used for shipment to one place and return, the lid should be screwed in place, never nailed. When any box is unpacked it is important to save all packing materials for use in repacking. Any worn packing materials should be replaced with new material of the same kind and same size.

Figure 57.—Painting with pads fitted around corners of frame before packing, Museum of Modern Art.

Paintings

In packing a single painting, individually fitted corner pads made of excelsior wrapped in heavy wrapping paper should be fitted diagonally across the corners, as shown in figure 57, and stapled (never tacked) to the back of the frame. This will provide a cushion within the box to lessen shocks in transit. The open ends of the pads must be folded back before stapling so the excelsior will not leak into the box. The painting should be placed face down in the box, which must be at least 2¼ inches larger in each dimension than the painting. The box should be padded at the corners with a cushion material such as foam rubber. If this type of padding is not possible, long rolled excelsior pads may be fitted between the outside edge of the frame and the inside of the box to prevent movement within the box, to absorb shocks in transit, and to protect the frame. A sheet of corrugated cardboard should be placed on top of the painting. If there is space between the cover and the painting, a wood batten cleated at the ends should be gently forced into contact with the corrugated board and nailed from the inside of the box. To make the removal of the battens easier when the box is unpacked, the cleat nails should not be driven in all the way. The box lid should be screwed in place. (See chapter 7, figure 38.)

A more elaborate method for packing a single painting, and one particularly recommended for paintings traveling long distances or going into an overseas shipment, is to pack in a box padded with foam rubber. For this method, foam rubber strips about 5 inches wide, covered with muslin or canton flannel, should be attached vertically at the corners of the box and diagonally across the bottom corners to connect with the two vertical strips. If the painting is large, additional pads should be firmly attached along the sides and bottom of the box. The painting should then be placed face down in the box. Battens padded with foam rubber and cleated at the ends should be placed across the narrow dimension of the box, with the pads resting across the back of the painting, as described above, to hold the painting firmly in place. By this method, illustrated in figure 58, the painting is completely "floated" in foam rubber and no extra pads need be attached to the frame or loose pads added to the packing.

Two or more paintings of similar size can be packed in one box by following this method for packing a single painting. However, it is absolutely necessary to place a separation sheet of corrugated cardboard or Upson board between each painting. The size of the paintings should determine the number to be packed together, but it is not advisable to pack more than four or five paintings in one box at any time. (See chapter 7, figure 38.)

The tray packing method is sometimes used for packing two or more paintings of varying sizes in a single box. The paintings are prepared

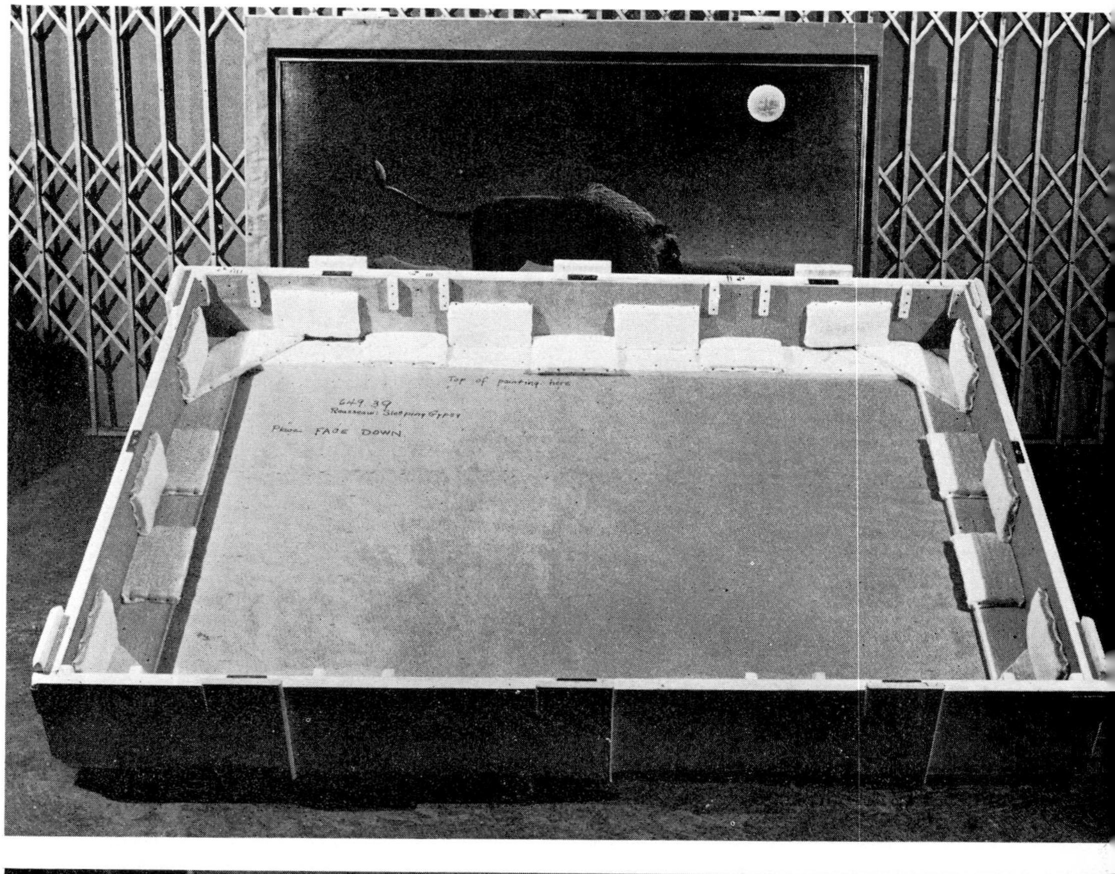

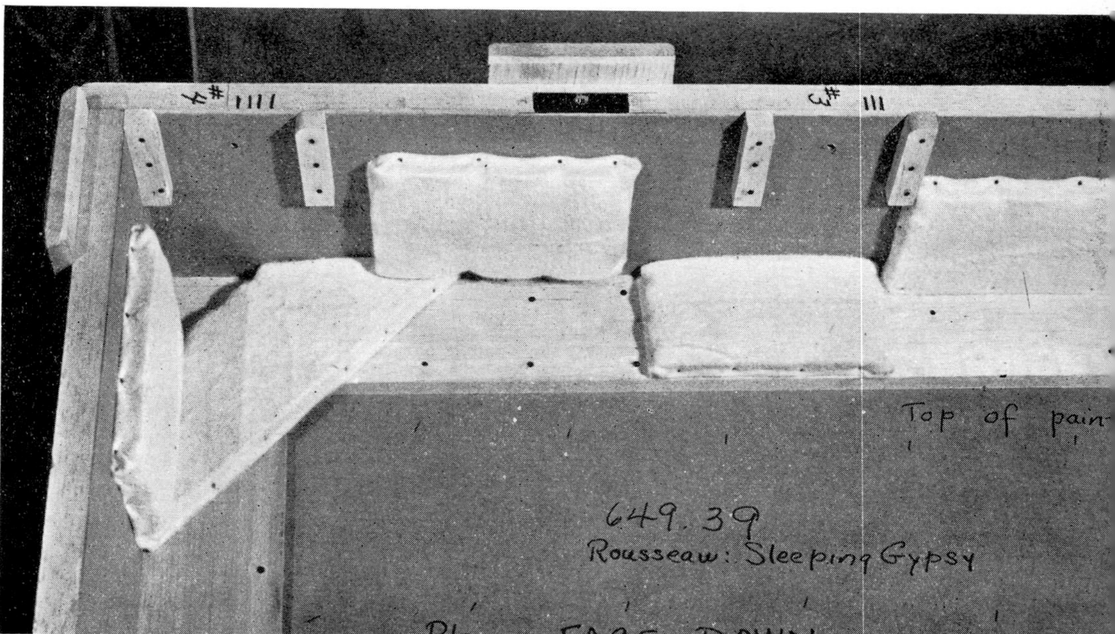

Figure 58.—Foam rubber padded box for packing a single painting, and detail of foam rubber padded box, Museum of Modern Art.

in the same manner as for a single painting in a box. The largest painting should be packed in the bottom of the box. The tray unit is attached to supporting battens which are cut to fit the inside of the box. The painting is then packed in the tray in the same manner as described above. It is important to place a sheet of corrugated cardboard on top of each painting before the tray is nailed in place at the batten cleats.

The groove packing method is by far the most highly recommended and most satisfactory for packing several paintings in one box. Unfortunately this type of box is the most expensive but it requires the least amount of handling and gives the greatest amount of protection to the paintings. Individual felt-padded wood grooves fitted to each painting are firmly attached to the top and bottom of the box so that the painting will slide into its own compartment, which is clearly marked at the end of the groove which remains open (see figure 59). The closed end of the groove should be padded with foam rubber. The lid of the box should have strips of foam rubber padding so attached that the pads touch the outside edges of *all* the frames in the box. The paintings are thus completely cushioned against all transit jarring. Even in this type of packing, not more than six or seven paintings should be packed together. The number to be packed in one box is again determined solely by the size of the paintings.

Watercolors, Drawings, Prints

The groove method for packing paintings is also applied to packing watercolors, drawings, and prints. This is the most recommended method (see figure 60). Another method for preparing watercolors, drawings, or prints for packing is to place them in individual slip cases. Strip sponge rubber pads should be placed across the bottom and sides of the box to protect the pictures against shock in transit. A liner of composition board, preferably masonite, placed over the pads at the bottom and sides will make it possible for a group of cardboard-cased pictures to ride on one surface thus distributing the weight evenly. If pictures of various sizes are packed in one case, all empty spaces at the sides and top of the box should be filled with excelsior or sponge rubber pads, as shown in figure 61, so that the pictures are held firmly in place.

If cardboard cases are not used, a sheet of corrugated cardboard should be placed between each picture. It is advisable to wrap about five pictures of like size in heavy paper and to seal the package with tape. These packages should then be placed in the box with an Upson board or homasote separation board between each package.

Sculpture

Each piece of sculpture presents its own problem. Certain general

Figure 59.—Groove packing for several paintings of varying sizes, Museum of Modern Art.

methods of packing may be used, however.

Small solid pieces can be wrapped in a soft cloth and tied, then the piece can be nested or "floated" in thick layers of excelsior, as shown in figure 62. Cut paper, which soon loses its resiliency, is not recommended.

Small fragile pieces may be wrapped in cloth and nested in excelsior or cellulose padding in a small wooden box which in turn is nested in excelsior in a large outer packing box. This method is recommended for packing ceramics and other small fragile objects.

Large pieces, such as stone, bronzes, and those of breakable materials should stand on their bases in the box and then have padded braces fitted to the shape of the sculpture to hold it firmly in place, as in figure

Figure 60.—Groove method for packing watercolors, drawings and prints, Museum of Modern Art.

63. The simplest way to hold braces is to construct tracks on the sides of the boxes into which the braces slide. Braces and tracks should extend to the front of the box where braces are held in position by the attached lid. (See figure 63.) It is important that large pieces of sculpture ride in the position in which they would stand while being exhibited. Boxes should be stenciled THIS SIDE UP.

BOX MARKINGS

All boxes should be marked (stenciled preferably) with the name and address of the originating shipper and of the consignee. In addition the following outside markings are suggested and should be stenciled as appropriate on the box: "fragile," "works of art," "glass," "paintings,"

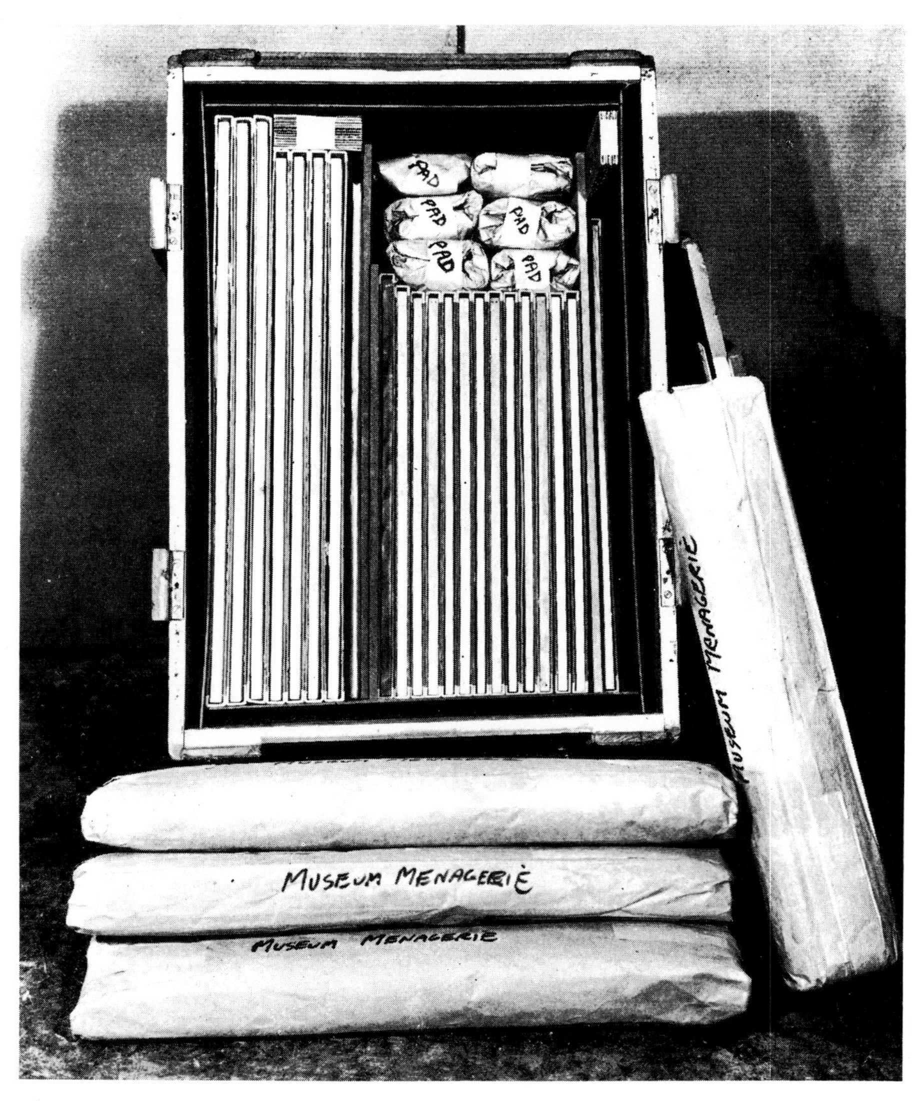

Figure 61.—Watercolors, drawings and prints packed in box lined with sponge rubber strips, Museum of Modern Art.

"sculpture," "open here," "this side up."

Instructions for repacking should be clearly marked on the inside of the box. Where the box contains a single painting, the museum number of the painting should be marked in the bottom, noting whether or not the painting is to be placed in the box face up or face down. Paintings are generally placed face down but there are enough exceptions, usually because of the frame, to warrant such an indication.

If the box contains two or more paintings, it is advisable to mark each

Figure 62.—Several solid pieces of sculpture packed in box with partitions, Museum of Modern Art.

loose piece of packing material with the museum number of the painting to which it applies, and to affix whatever simple instructions may be necessary for replacing the braces, separation boards, excelsior pads, etc.

Groove packing is usually used for traveling shows. Each groove should be marked at its open end with the museum number of the painting it contains, as well as an indication of the direction in the box the painting should face. For all shows that will be packed and unpacked

Figure 63.—Sculpture braced in box, Department of Circulating Exhibitions, Museum of Modern Art.

many times, instructions for unpacking and packing should be attached to the lids of the boxes and these should include any special directions regarding glass- and plexiglas-covered pictures.

Sculpture should have each brace marked with the box number and museum number of the pieces, as well as an indication such as parallel lines I, II, III, IIII, etc., running across the end of the brace and the edge of the box, to show where and how the brace is fitted into the box. It is often helpful to outline with a marking pencil the position of the brace against the side of the box. Any bolts that must be loosened on the outside of the box or attached through the box should be so indicated.

When sculpture is contained in a box packed inside another box, the lid of the inner container should indicate contents and any special instructions regarding the piece.

FORMS

For each traveling show, a checklist, unpacking and packing instructions, special instructions regarding glass, condition records, and special information regarding installation should be prepared. Some of these instructions are also required for single works of art.

Checklists

Checklists should be prepared for all shipments containing several works of art. The minimum information such a checklist should contain is artist, title, date, and medium; but it would be helpful to add the museum number, lender, and box number, particularly if the exhibition is being sent to a number of institutions. A checklist that has proven its worth with Museum of Modern Art circulating exhibitions includes the installation number, museum number, artist, title, date, medium, framed size (for paintings), height and weight (for sculpture), box number.

Some museums allow space on these lists for the receiving institution to indicate the condition of each individual piece upon its receipt or a brief description of condition is sometimes noted on the checklist prepared by the institution originating the exhibition. In the Museum of Modern Art, condition records for original works of art are prepared—a separate sheet for each piece—giving the condition when it left the museum. These sheets travel with the exhibition and each exhibitor is requested to check the condition upon arrival against the original condition and note it on the sheet. The exhibitor then reports any changes to the museum. This running record keeps the information up to date and greatly facilitates the processing of insurance claims should any damages occur. Whether or not a checklist includes space for this information, it is important that obvious changes in condition should be reported to the originating museum immediately.

If the material is available for sale, this information and the method of handling the sales can be added on a separate sheet and attached to the checklist.

Unpacking and Packing Instructions

If the shipment is comparatively small, most of the instructions may be incorporated in the markings inside the box. However, for larger or unusual or complicated packing, instructions should be prepared for each box and attached to the lid of each. These instructions should include as separate items information regarding glass and the use of masking tape.

Article 13

THE IDEAL CONTAINER AND THE TRAVEL OF WORKS OF ART

NATHAN STOLOW, B.Sc., M.A., Ph.D.

Scientific Consultant, National Gallery of Canada
Ottawa, Canada

The effect of variations of external temperatures and relative humidities upon internal conditions in a sealed case containing humidity-sensitive works of art has been recently studied (see references). If a work of art is acclimatized to a fixed relative humidity and temperature in a museum and is then shipped to another museum—it is important to maintain the same environmental conditions for reasons of preservation. The transit stage for a work of art may often be lengthy, as in international exhibitions, and cases of works may be exposed to unusual weather conditions and unsatisfactory warehousing. Fortunately, there are now means and methods for maintaining constant conditions in transit. The specifications described below are for the transport of the most valuable collections of works of art, where cost is secondary to maximum preservation. In more ordinary situations, some of the more rigorous conditions may be modified for reasons of economy. Here the use of silica gel, recording instruments, and accompanying personnel may be omitted. (Items Nos. 6, 8, part of 11 concerning escort, and Nos. 15 and 17).

Specifications and Procedures:

1. Records should be available indicating environmental conditions (relative humidity, and temperatures) to which the works of art have been initially exposed in the museum. The same conditions should be specified for exhibition in the borrowing institution. The system of packing and the mode of transportation must be adjusted to maintain the specified temperatures and relative humidities (R.H.) in transit.
2. All container materials must be pre-conditioned (seasoned) to the same level of R.H. and temperature as for the works of art to be transported. Thus if the R.H. and temperatures are 50% and 20°C (68°F) respectively, then the wood,

plywood, insulating boards, papers—should likewise be kept in such an environment for two to three weeks or longer prior to use. (See figure 65.)

3. The case should be constructed of plywood (water-impervious adhesives) of ¼" to ½" thickness, reinforced on the exterior with sufficient pine wood battens to offer rigidity. The lid should close down firmly against rubber gaskets by means of screws, bolts, or other positive locking devices. The case should be made as air-tight as possible. The exterior should be painted with a waterproof paint, and labels stencilled on rather than fixed with staples.
4. The shape of the case should be as "cubical" as possible to conform to desirable temperature retaining properties, i.e., to have a minimum external surface for a given total weight.[1]

[1] The assessment of thermal properties may be obtained from the relationship $t_{0.5} = \frac{0.69\ Hl}{KA}$

where K = thermal conductivity of case in calories metres/hr. m.^{2} °C,
H = thermal (heat) capacity of case and contents in Kg. calories/°C,
A = average surface area of case in square metres,
l = thickness of case walls in metres,
$t_{0.5}$ = time in hours for the case to reach half of the total temperature change.

Therefore, to increase the half-time factor ($t_{0.5}$) as much as possible one must strive for low values of K, low surface areas, and thick case walls. Some typical data are given below (Tables I and II).

TABLE I

THERMAL CONDUCTIVITY, SPECIFIC HEATS, AND DENSITIES OF TYPICAL PACKAGING MATERIALS USED FOR WORKS OF ART (UNDER STANDARD CONDITIONS).

Material	Density	Thermal Conductivity K †		Specific Heat Φ	
	gm/cm^3	B.T.U. in / hr. ft.^{2} °F	Kg. Cal. m. / hr. m.^{2} °C	B.T.U. / lb. °F	Kg. Cal. / Kg. °C
White Pine (across grain)	0.45	0.78	0.097	0.33	0.33
Plywood (Douglas Fir)	0.57	0.80	0.099	0.35	0.40
Oak (& hardwoods)	0.51	1.02	0.127	0.57	0.57
Corkboard (no binder)	0.10	0.26	0.031	0.43	0.43
Ten-Test (Aspen Fibres)	0.28	0.35	0.043	0.25	0.35
Cellotex (Veg. Fibres) ‡	0.28	0.33	0.041	0.25	0.25
Homosote (Paper Pulp) *	0.43	0.40	0.050	—	—
Masonite (Dense Wood Fibres) **	1.02	0.33	0.041	0.34	0.34
Styrolite (Expanded Polystyrene)	0.019	0.25	0.031	0.27	0.27
Klegecell (Expanded Polyvinyl Chloride) ‡‡	0.040	0.21	0.026	—	—
Silica Gel	1.69	0.59	0.073	0.19	0.19

NOTES:

‡ Cellotex, a fibreboard product marketed in U.S.A. In sheets 4 feet x 8 feet x 0.5 inch and composed essentially of matted vegetable fibres, and quite similar to ten-test.

* Homosote, a compressed pulp-board product marketed in U.S.A. In sheet form of sizes 4 feet x 8 feet and larger, and of thicknesses 0.5 inch and greater.

** Masonite, a compressed fibre-board of high density composed of "exploded" wood fibres.

‡‡ Klegecell, a type of expanded Polyvinylchloride foam of French manufacture.

† 1 B.T.U. in/hr. ft.^{2} °F = 0.124 Kg. Cal. m./hr. m.^{2} °C.

The values of K and Φ have been obtained from various sources including Severns, W. H. & Fellows, J. R. "Air Conditioning and Refrigeration," WILEY, N.Y., 1958; and Miner, B. F. & Seastone, J. B. "Handbook of Engineering Materials," WILEY, N.Y., 1955.
The "Standard conditions" referred to are generally 65% R.H. and 20° C.
The specific heat for plywood is estimated at 0.35, and that for silica gel at 0.19.

TABLE II

CALCULATION OF EFFECTIVE THERMAL CONDUCTIVITY K AT HALF-TIME FOR COOLING CYCLES 21°C TO 4°C.

Description	A m.^{2}	l m.	H* Kg. Cal./°C	$t_{0.5}$ hrs.	K Kg. Cal. m. hr. m.^{2} °C
(a) Plywood case (empty)	2.8	0.015	9.7	0.5	0.072
(b) Plywood case with 2 layers ten-test (2.5 cm)	2.6	0.04	15.6	2.0	0.082
(c) Plywood case with 2 layers ten-test (2.5 cm) with 2 Silica gel panels	2.5	0.05	21.0	3.5	0.075
(d) Plywood case with 5.1 cm Styrolite with 2 Silica gel panels	2.4	0.075	15.6	4.0	0.084
(e) Pine case with 2 layers ten-test (2.5 cm)	1.8	0.05	11.8	3.0	0.075

* Included in each experiment is the thermal capacity of the FUESS recorder calculated to be approximately 0.3 KCal./°C.

5. The immediate inside surfaces of the case should be lined with heavy gauge polyethylene film to act as a water and vapour barrier. Any seams should be either heat-sealed or taped—but not stapled.
6. *Silica Gel System:* The inside of the case should be lined with an expanded foamed plastic e.g., polystyrene foam (or polyvinylchloride foam) of at least 2 inches (5 cm.) thickness on all six interior faces. By careful cutting of these boards of plastic they will hold snugly in position. Two screened silica gel panels should be mounted on the two largest vertical interior surfaces, next to the foamed plastic. The amount of silica gel should be as large as possible to buffer the humidity changes which may occur.[2] (See figure 64.)
   Trays and packing devices should be placed inside the .case as to permit continuous free circulation of air between the exposed silica gel surfaces and the supported works of art. The latter should *not* be wrapped in polyethylene, wax-paper or other moisture-impeding films.
   Prior to packing the works, the silica gel, trays, packing devices (if they are of wood) should be pre-conditioned for, say, three weeks to the desired level of R.H. and temperature (e.g., 50% R.H., 20°C(68°F)). The conditioning of the silica gel is most important, at 50% R.H., it should contain 30% by weight of moisture (dry weight basis).

[2] The amounts required for a compactly packed case may be roughly gauged from this equation:

$$R_2 = R_1 + \frac{0.063[T_2 - T_1]}{0.18W + 0.6S}$$

where R_1, T_1 are initial case relative humidity and temperature (°C) respectively. W is weight (dry basis) of wood (canvas, etc.), gms.

S is weight of silica gel (dry basis), gms.
T_2 is the external temperature to which the case is subjected,
and R_2 is the final internal R.H. after time taken for equalization of case and contents (usually after many hours).

Therefore, to minimize the difference between R_2 and R_1, i.e., to stabilize the R.H., it is necessary to have appreciable quantities of silica gel. For a case of 255 litres volume approximately 6 kilograms of pre-conditioned silica gel are required.

7. *Fibre-board System:* If it is desired to use pre-conditioned fibre-board (cellotex, ten-test, homosote, etc.) to line the cases instead of foamed plastic, the silica gel may be omitted. The fibre-board acts as a humidity buffer itself. To be effective as a thermal barrier (heat insulator) it should be at least double thickness, 2.5 cm. or greater. The application of silica gel panels as in 6) above does give better humidity control.
8. Provision should be made for installing within the case a recording hygrometer with a 7 or 8 day movement (or longer) and which has been recently calibrated to read R.H. and temperatures accurately. It may be feasible to introduce small strips of cobalt salt indicator papers to indicate R.H.—although they do not give a time record of the events within the case.
9. The paintings(s) or other objects should be packed in the case at the level of R.H. and temperature previously decided upon for conditioning.
10. The case(s) so packed should be handled by experienced, trusted personnel.
11. The external temperatures at all points (truck, train, railroad station, aeroplane, ship, etc.) should be specified and maintained at 20°C ± 5° (68 ± 3°F). It may prove useful to escort the shipment and to monitor the external conditions with a portable hygrothermograph.
12. In the event of air travel, the cabin must be *pressurized* as well as temperature controlled. Ambient R.H.'s in aircraft are often dangerously low, and this may cause replacement of air within the case when the external pressures change.
13. Excessive vibration and shocks should be avoided. If necessary blankets, foam rubber pads, corrugated cardboard may be placed around or near the cases.
14. If through misadventure the case(s) have suffered a change in temperature on arrival beyond the range of 20°C ± 5°, then it should be specified that the cases remain unopened for at least 24 hours at the destination (where the R.H. is also 50% and the temperature 20°C). If this is not done then condensation, thermal or humidity "shock" may be experienced. In any event, it is prudent to specify that the cases remain unopened for 24 hours on arrival at the destination of the exhibiting centre, to allow for temperature equilibrium.
15. The opened cases, packing materials, etc., should be stored under the same conditions, 50% R.H. and 20°C (68°F) and not removed to a totally different environment (e.g., warehouse, basement). The silica gel panels should be taken out of their cases and directly exposed to the environment so that their moisture content may be restored if necessary.
16. The return shipment should be followed through in the same manner as above.
17. The R.H. records for the transit should be incorporated with the condition reports and other documentation pertaining to the travelling exhibition.
18. Loan contracts and agreements should clearly specify methods of packing, control and transportation. Provision should be made for consultation regarding alternative methods of packing, transportation, and care in transit.

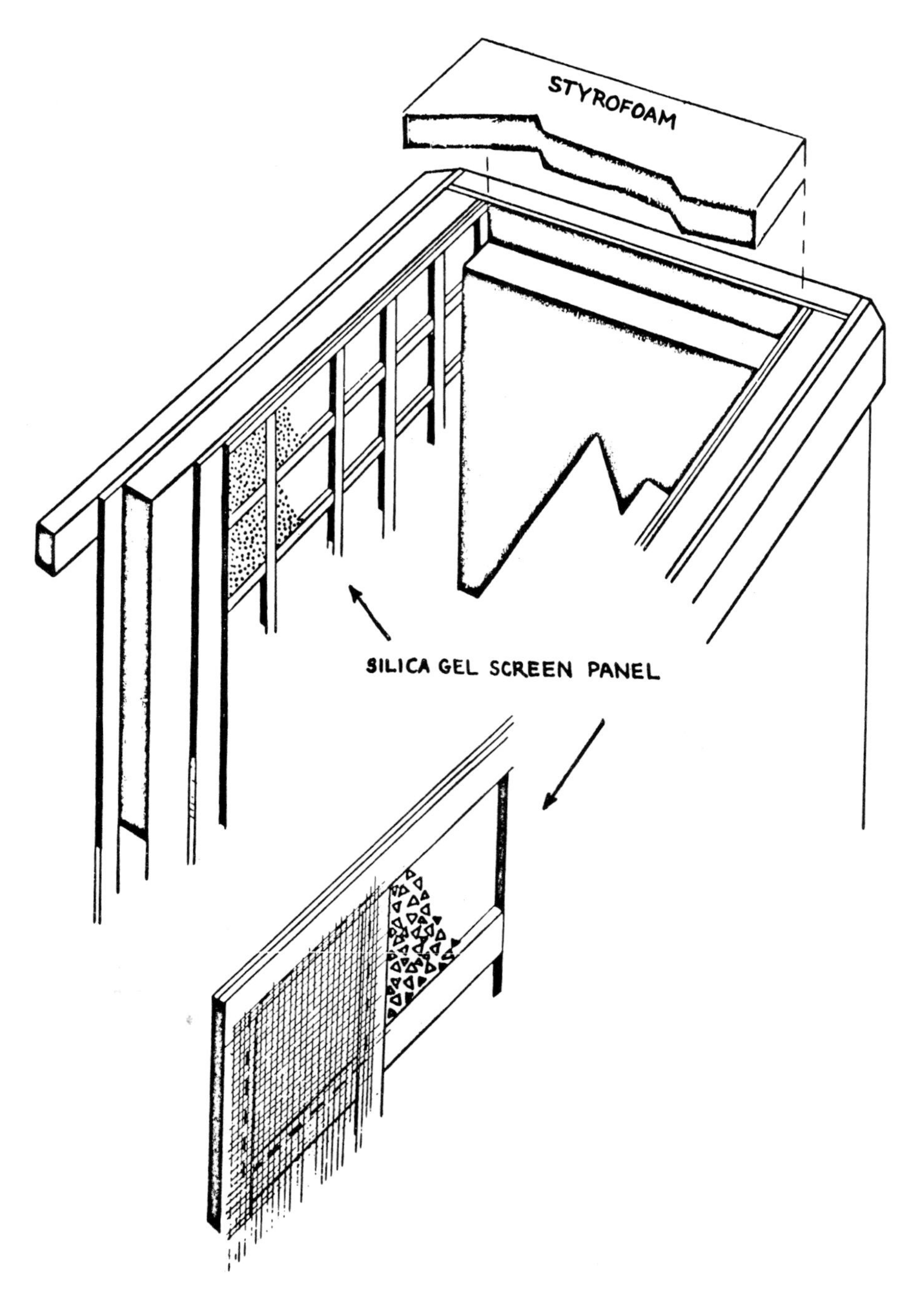

Figure 64.—Schematic drawing of plywood case containing styrofoam insulators and screened silica gel panels. These panels are made of ¼ inch plywood and covered with polyethylene sheeting prior to fixing the ¼ inch plywood dividers. The chambers (also ¼ inch deep) are filled with pre-conditioned silica gel. Aluminum or fibre-glass screening is then stapled over to retain the gel in position.

The silica gel, 3 to 8 mesh size—grade 308, may be obtained from: Eagle Chemical Co., P. O. Box 107, Mobile, Alabama.

The gel is initially dry and must then be exposed for approximately two weeks in shallow pans to the required environment, e.g., 20°C (68°F) and 50% R.H., when it will gain approximately 30% by weight. This will then be the pre-conditioned silica gel.

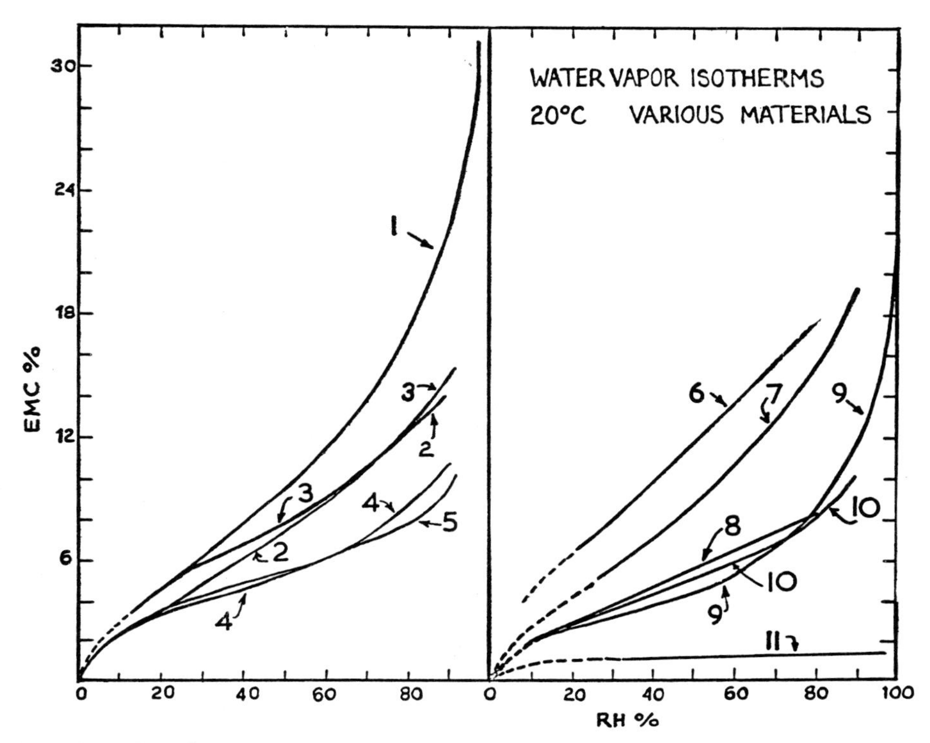

Figure 65.—Effect of R.H. on moisture content (E.M.C., equilibrium moisture content) of typical packing materials. Legend: 1—Wood; 2—Tentest (compressed fibre-board of soft wood fibres, no binders 0.5 inch thick, density 0.28 gm/c.c. manufactured by Canadian International Paper Company, Canada); 3—kraft paper; 4—newsprint paper; 5—two-ply kraft paper with bitumen sandwich, thickness 0.018 cm, density 0.75 gm/c.c.; 6—British Columbia fir plywood, 3 ply, synthetic glue binder; 7—Homosote board, compressed paper fibres, 0.5 inch thick, density 0.43 gm/c.c.; 8—Masonite board; 9—cotton; 10—linen; 11—Styrolite, an expanded polystyrene insulating board of thickness 2 inch, density 0.02 gm/c.c. (Data for curves 2,5,6,7,8,9,10,11 from author's laboratory.)

References:

TOISHI, K. Humidity control in a closed package, Studies in Conservation, IV, 1959. pp. 81-87.

STOLOW, N. Controlled environment for works of art in transit. Butterworths, London (joint publication with Rome Center for Study of the Conservation of Cultural Property and the International Institute for Conservation of Historic and Artistic Works), 1966, 46 pp. + 20 fig.

THOMSON, G. Relative humidity—variation with temperature in a case containing wood, Studies in Conservation, IV, 1964. pp. 153-169.

STOLOW, N. Some studies on the protection of works of art during travel, in Recent Advances in Conservation (Rome Conference IIC, 1961.) Butterworths, 1963. pp. 9-12.

STOLOW, N. Fundamental case design for humidity sensitive museum collections, Museum News, Feb. 1966. Technical Supplement, No. 11, pp. XX-XX.

BROWN, K. Package design engineering. New York, Wiley and Son, 1959. 263 pp.

Article 14

COMPETITIVE EXHIBITIONS

IRMA BEZOLD WILKINSON

Formerly Registrar
Metropolitan Museum of Art, New York

The competitive exhibition "American Water Colors, Drawings and Prints" of 1952 was chosen for discussion here because it presented special problems in the handling of material as well as in the keeping of records.

For this nation-wide exhibition the Metropolitan Museum established regional centers in San Francisco, Chicago, Atlanta, and New York. In order that the various sections of the country might be better represented and more fairly judged, two juries, one conservative the other modern, were set up in each center. By this means, too, the Metropolitan was relieved of much handling of entries.

SPACE PLANNING

In planning a competitive exhibition on a national scale, the sponsoring museum must keep in mind the volume of material likely to be involved and the facilities within the museum itself for handling it. Because the material for an exhibition of this sort is received concurrently with the normal load of museum business, additional space must be assigned for receiving and unpacking entries brought in by hand and by truck, preferably near both an entrance to the building and to the galleries allotted for the exhibition. There must be wall space for sorting and stacking framed material and floor space for tables on which matted material may be piled.

The procedures worked out for the exhibition by the Metropolitan enabled it to handle 4,455 entries, of which 4,093 were rejected. The same procedures were used for the regional centers: Atlanta received 496 entries and rejected 454; Chicago received 1,350 entries, rejected 1,264; San Francisco received 808 entries, rejected 739. Of a total of 7,109 entries submitted to the exhibition, 6,550 were rejected and thus had to be returned as quickly and efficiently as possible.

INSTRUCTION FOR ENTRANTS

A prospectus, sent out several months in advance, outlines the scope of the show and establishes the procedure.

The prospectus put out by the Metropolitan included an entry blank and record forms; a statement of requirements for eligibility and for acceptance and removal of entries; a list of the juries of selection and award; and regulations and information concerning reproduction of exhibits, liability, sales, and awards.

Of these categories, the registrar is responsible for the arrival and return of entries, unpacking and packing, and the establishment of a system whereby entries and the information concerning them are handled accurately and efficiently.

For this last purpose the Metropolitan supplied contributors with both a preliminary entry blank and a record form, made up of four cards, to be attached to the back of each entry. These are illustrated in figure 66. Each card required the same information: name and address of the artist; title, medium, and size of the work; the artist's jury preference; and the address to which the entry should be returned. One card remained attached to the back of the entry for identification. The second, filed alphabetically by the name of the artist, was used by the regional juries for identification. The third card was filed alphabetically according to the method of delivery, i.e., by hand, by truck, or by Railway Express. The fourth card was used as a depositor's receipt if the entry was brought in by hand, as the artist's receipt if delivered by truck, or was held in a numerical file by shipment number if the entry had been shipped.

ENTRIES DELIVERED BY HAND

For maximum protection and efficiency in handling and judging the entries delivered by hand, it is best that matted and framed material be treated separately.

In setting up, from the third card of each set, the alphabetical name file of all entries delivered in person, the Metropolitan grouped all the contributions of each artist together. The matted material was numbered consecutively, the letter "M" preceding the number, and framed material was given another number sequence preceded by the letter "F"; these numbers were entered on the third set of cards. In organizing the rejected entries for return, the two series were stacked separately in numerical order. When the artist presented his receipt (the fourth card), the rejected entry could be quickly located through the corresponding card in the alphabetical file. These two cards, dated and signed, were then filed in an alphabetical "returned" file.

THE METROPOLITAN MUSEUM OF ART
FIFTH AVENUE AT 82ND STREET
NEW YORK 28, N. Y.

AMERICAN WATER COLORS, DRAWINGS, AND PRINTS 1952

ENTRY BLANK

Fill in this entry blank completely and return it promptly to Roland McKinney, Department of American Art, The Metropolitan Museum of Art, New York 28, New York.

Typewrite or print all answers, except in item 8, where your signature is required. Fill in all items. The biographical information in item 5 is required for publicity in connection with the exhibition.

This entry blank must be received by the Museum not later than August 15, 1952.

1. (MR.) (MISS) (MRS.) ______

2. ADDRESS ______ CITY ______ STATE ______

3. RETURN ADDRESS (if other than above) ______

4. DEALER'S NAME ______

ADDRESS ______ CITY ______ STATE ______

(OVER)

5. Give biographical information here.

YEAR OF BIRTH ______ BIRTHPLACE ______

Summarize briefly the following: your art training; places where your work has been exhibited; awards you have won, naming the dates and places of the awards; and other pertinent information. (Use an additional page, if necessary.)

______

______

______

6. I intend to submit the following entry or entries to the Jury:
(NOTE. Not more than three entries may be submitted, *one each* from two or three of the four media to be judged – water color, pastel, drawing, and prints.)

TITLE ______ TITLE ______

SIZE ______ MEDIUM ______ SIZE ______ MEDIUM ______

INSURANCE VALUE $ ______ SALES PRICE $ ______ INSURANCE VALUE $ ______ SALES PRICE $ ______

TITLE ______

SIZE ______ MEDIUM ______

INSURANCE VALUE $ ______ SALES PRICE $ ______

7. My choice of jury is A ☐ B ☐ (Check one.)

8. I agree to comply with all the conditions set forth in the accompanying prospectus.

______
SIGNATURE

RECORD FORM

Fill in a record form for each entry. Fill in all sections legibly and affix this part of the form, at the upper right-hand corner, on the back of the entries. Do not separate or paste down the other sections.

RECORD CARD

NAME ______

ADDRESS ______

______

TITLE ______

RETURN ADDRESS ______

______

MY CHOICE OF JURY IS A ☐ B ☐ (CHECK ONE)

AMERICAN WATER COLORS, DRAWINGS, AND PRINTS 1952

THE METROPOLITAN MUSEUM OF ART
NEW YORK 28, NEW YORK

- - - - - - - - - - - - - - - - - - - -

REGISTRAR'S RECORD

NAME ______

ADDRESS ______

______

TITLE ______

SIZE ______ MEDIUM ______

RETURN ADDRESS ______

ON RETURN OF ENTRY,
SIGN HERE: RECEIVED BY ______

DATE ______

AMERICAN WATER COLORS, DRAWINGS, AND PRINTS 1952

THE METROPOLITAN MUSEUM OF ART
NEW YORK 28, NEW YORK

- - - - - - - - - - - - - - - - - - - -

REGIONAL JURY RECORD

NAME ______

ADDRESS ______

______

TITLE ______

MEDIUM ______

RETURN ADDRESS ______

ON RETURN OF PAINTING,
SIGN HERE: RECEIVED BY ______

DATE ______

AMERICAN WATER COLORS, DRAWINGS, AND PRINTS 1952

THE METROPOLITAN MUSEUM OF ART
NEW YORK 28, NEW YORK

- - - - - - - - - - - - - - - - - - - -

ARTIST'S RECEIPT

NAME ______

ADDRESS ______

______

TITLE ______

MEDIUM ______

RETURN ADDRESS ______

IMPORTANT NOTICE. This receipt will be given to the artist or his agent when an entry is delivered personally to the Regional Center. The receipt must be presented when an entry is called for. A Railway Express receipt will serve as a substitute for this card for an out-of-town shipment.

AMERICAN WATER COLORS, DRAWINGS, AND PRINTS 1952

THE METROPOLITAN MUSEUM OF ART
NEW YORK 28, NEW YORK

Figure 66.—Entry blank and strip of record cards accompanying the prospectus for the national competitive exhibition, "American Water Colors, Drawings, and Prints."

ENTRIES DELIVERED BY MOTOR VAN

In registering these entries, the Metropolitan marked all the cards for each van-delivered entry with an easily identifiable "T," so that immediately after the judging these cards could be quickly sorted out. The cards were likewise marked with the name of the moving company and the number of entries per artist, and the third card was filed in a separate alphabetical name file arranged by trucking concern. The fourth card, the artist's receipt, was given to the trucker for return to the artist. Rejected entries were returned on presentation of this receipt which, together with the third card, was filed in the "returned" file.

For material delivered by REA Express, a method must be set up whereby rejected entries can be returned in their original boxes.

In registering over 200 boxes, the Metropolitan found that errors were most easily avoided by assigning a number to each box and marking the box, its contents, and accompanying cards with that number. The third card of each set thus marked was placed in a separate file arranged alphabetically by the artist's name. The fourth card was filed numerically according to box number. As a further check, the number of entries included in each box was also recorded both on the box and on the cards. Thus, when the time came for rejected entries to be returned, their boxes could be found accurately and quickly. The date when the boxes were sent off was noted on the third and fourth cards and filed.

ENTRIES ACCEPTED FOR EXHIBITION

The method of registering accepted entries shipped to the sponsoring museum from the regional centers can be the same as that used for regular REA Express shipments.

In handling shipments from regional centers, the Metropolitan numbered each box and also marked it with the name of the regional center from which it was sent. The cards were similarly marked, and the third and fourth cards set up in two files, one numerical and the other alphabetical by region.

The procedure for returning accepted entries after the exhibition, whether by REA Express, by van, or by hand, follows the same plan as has already been described. The third and fourth cards for these entries are filed in the "returned" file, which now becomes the complete alphabetical name file of all contributors. The jury files made up of the second card from each set, one an alphabetical name file or rejected entries, the other a similar file of accepted entries, are merged when the judging is concluded. This file thus becomes a duplicate of the "returned" file, and can be used as a double and final check on the disposition of all entries submitted to the exhibition.

Article 15

RECEIVING CENTERS FOR COMPETITIVE EXHIBITIONS

PAUL MILLS

Curator, Oakland Municipal Art Museum
Oakland, California

A receiving center (or collection center or depot) is set up as an encouragement to artists who send to competitive exhibitions. Artists who bring their exhibit entries to the center enjoy a sometimes considerable saving through share-the-cost packing and shipping. The centers divide into two types, according to the kind of transportation involved.

For an exhibition by artists from a large metropolitan area, to which artists in nearby sections and suburbs are being encouraged to send entries, local receiving depots are set up, and at the end of the announced receiving period, a museum truck, or one hired by the museum at its own expense, picks up the paintings and delivers them to the museum. At the close of the exhibition, works are returned by the same means.

For a regional or national exhibition, the same general procedure is followed, except that the artists pay the expenses, making a deposit at the time of entry toward the estimated cost of packing and shipping. The group of entries is packed, either by the center or by a commercial firm, and sent by railway or motor express to the exhibiting museum.

It has been found that museums within a local area will generally consent to act as a center on an exchange basis, and many museums are willing to undertake the task for regional and national shows. Artists Equity Association chapters and other artists' groups are available as centers. Commercial galleries and art supply stores or framers are also possibilities.

The artists are informed of the center primarily by the entry blank, on which is listed the name of center, its location, receiving days and hours, and return days (the center should be well supplied with entry blanks). Notices should also be sent to the newspapers and other media of public information.

Certain records should be kept. The receiving center should record the artist's name, address, entries, deposit paid (if any) in triplicate—one copy for the center, one for the express company or trucker, one for the exhibiting museum. The exhibiting museum should provide similar records on return shipment.

Where packing and shipping costs are involved, it is desirable to have the artists pay all costs when the entries are brought to the center. Since it is hard to establish an exact cost in advance, it is advisable to obtain from the packers and the express company an estimate of cost, which can be prorated and collected in advance from each artist. The balance can be collected, or refunded, when he picks up his returned entries.

Returns are sent prepaid or collect—or free, in the case of a local center—according to the exhibiting museum's policy. To save answering many queries, this information and the approximate date the return shipment will reach the receiving center should be noted on the original entry blank.

Insurance on the entries, from the time they arrive at the center until they are picked up by the artists, may be arranged with local companies and the costs added to the charges. For museums which do not insure entries in competitive exhibitions, as is generally the case, an optional insurance plan, in which the artist pays, may be arranged. The Oakland Art Museum, through the Western Association of Art Museum Directors, has arranged a policy whereby the artists can state on the entry card the amount of coverage desired and send in the fee with his entry. The museum, in turn, forwards a list of insured items and the fees to the association office. Information about this policy can be obtained from the Western Association of Art Museum Directors, 1807 38th Street North, Seattle, Washington.

Article 16

PLANNING AHEAD—THE REGISTRAR'S ROLE IN A BUILDING PROGRAM

DAVID VANCE

Associate Registrar
Museum of Modern Art, New York

Buildings are used differently than in the past. Suddenly (within the last few decades) we are faced with hordes of visitors, fabulous insurance values, temporary installations, traveling shows, and now, a vogue for museum burgling. Today's buildings, like factories, must provide for safe, efficient *movement* of goods. They needn't be any less beautiful for that.

This is in a book on registration methods because in many museums the registrar, together with the building superintendent, the security chief, conservators and curators, has to understand the real, physical operation of the plant. There is no way for him to be of greater service to his museum than by making his, frequently unwelcome, contribution before and during a building program. That is the only time for neat, lasting solution of handling and security problems. (As used here, "building program" includes even the most trifling alteration.)

The registrar has a special stake in the design of new facilities since they will become the physical framework of his operations and determine how well he and his successors will be able to do their job.

For the sake of convenience this is written as if all handling of exhibition material were the registrar's responsibility. In most museums this is not the case, the headaches being shared with other departments. So this article is really addressed "to whom it may concern." It could not have been written without the benefit of years of informal discussion with many different conservators, curators, engineers, architects, building managers, and even registrars, all of whom have been generous with their time and knowledge.

THE FIRST STEPS

Unless he insists and keeps insisting, the registrar may never be consulted about such vitals as loading docks, air handling systems and elevators. As the program gets under way he should learn the chains of command: who are the architects, the contractors, sub- and sub-subcontractors, who is responsible for what, who takes orders from whom and who knows what? It may prove very difficult to find out. Make the acquaintance of key personnel in each organization. Obtain plans of the whole project and keep them up to date, never taking it for granted that drawings are current just because nobody has mentioned that they aren't. For areas of particular interest get hold of shop drawings and learn to read them. This, incidentally, is one of the best ways to cultivate the technicians, who appreciate intelligent interest in their special fields. The respect and confidence of these men is important. Furthermore, a rudimentary grasp of their methods will show that there are usually (not always) compelling reasons for the seemingly nonsensical arrangements that will be found in every set of plans.

Merely keeping abreast of the plans isn't enough. If it is at all possible, you have to keep an eye on the job itself. The organizational web on even a simple project is so intricate that changes often appear without the knowledge of interested parties. Mistakes happen too. Sometimes one has to take the responsibility for ordering a gang to stop work until the boss can be located. It's a great help if the foremen and supervisors know you and respect your judgement.

The rest of this article is written with special reference to a registrar's needs in a large art museum, but the fundamentals apply as well to smaller institutions and to museums of other kinds.

STORAGE DURING A BUILDING PROGRAM

To go or to stay? That is one of the worst of many tough choices facing a museum when it remodels. There are risks in moving a museum collection and dangers in leaving it under the same roof with construction work. Special factors in each case determine which is the more to be dreaded. The registrar's recommendations may tip the balance.

Other things being equal, it is probably wiser to move: The hazards in that are well known while those of staying put are easy to underestimate and may come as a rude surprise to an inexperienced staff.

Permanent Storerooms

If only part of the museum is affected by reconstruction, it may be safe to leave some collections in their regular storage places, somehow crowding in the material that would ordinarily be on exhibition. Often this is the answer. The trouble is that it looks safer than it is. The greatest dangers are fire and unauthorized entry, either of which may precipitate the other. Construction crews cannot be screened by the museum. Theft and vandalism on their part are common enough to bar any attitude save total mistrust by the museum staff. Then too, the building trades take people into unlikely places—hollow walls, ceiling spaces and air ducts—in pursuit of pipes and conduits. Breaking through a wall to reach some fixture is commonplace and usually innocent behavior. But the other side may be your storeroom. *Always keep at least two fireproof barriers between any storeroom and the nearest demolition or construction.* And inspect the storeroom often.

Local flooding from broken pipes is fairly common during construction, so it is even more important than usual to keep everything well off the floor. The dirt problem too is aggravated, and plaster dust is an especially vicious kind. Tape the cracks around doors, put cheesecloth over ventilators, and keep things covered.

Safety and security depend upon electric light, alarm systems, telephones, heating and cooling devices, etc. All these things are likely to fail in a building under construction.

Temporary Storerooms

Every temporary storeroom raises problems of its own, but some standard precautions will always be necessary. In the first place, locks must be changed and security established. Windows and doors should be tightly sealed against dust and opened as seldom as possible. If the room receives direct sunlight, fluctuations in temperature can be minimized by hanging fiberglass insulation material against the window glass. Some degree of humidity control can be achieved with portable humidifiers or dehumidifiers or both with hygrostatic switches. Depending upon the local humidity situation, it may be advisable to keep the temporary storeroom below the usual temperature or not to heat it at all. All the dangers cited above under "Permanent Storerooms" exist to at least the same degree in temporary ones.

Evacuation

One objection to moving is that it takes a lot of time. Since most of the work may have to be done while the museum is closed but not actually under construction, evacuation tends to lengthen the closed interval.

Usually storage space at least as safe as the collection's old quarters can be found in a warehouse—at considerable expense. Rooms under consideration should be examined personally by competent staff members and by representatives of the underwriters.

In fact the whole move should be worked out in cooperation with the insurers. Plans will be complicated by the need for prudent dispersal. Avoid huge concentrations of value (economic, historical or esthetic) in one place or vehicle: don't put all the capital works of one master on one truck even if the total insured value is within your limit.

When a storeroom is emptied, it's important to remove any equipment that will be needed again. This includes lifts, dollies, ladders, tables and chairs and the storage units themselves. Anything left behind must be written off.

Reopening is usually timed to take advantage of a busy season or to coincide with some event that can't be postponed. There is a deadline. But building usually takes longer than anyone would have thought possible. Time pressure mounts and so does sentiment for moving in before the place is quite ready. The registrar and others concerned with safety may have all they can do, first to delay the return until conditions are tolerable, and then to accomplish it quickly and safely in a semi-hostile environment.

In unfinished spaces all the usual hazards are intensified. Security is shaky because construction crews are used to going where they please and resent interference, while the guard force may be under strength and under trained, especially if the museum has been closed for a long time or has been greatly enlarged. Once exhibition material enters a room, that room is off limits to *all* outsiders unless they are accompanied by a competent staff member.

Elementary registration procedure, on a grand scale, accomplishes miracles on moving day. Lists are the essence of it, precise lists of objects or of sealed containers for each space. Take one area at a time according to a working schedule; deliver all the material on the list and check it off; inspect each unpackaged item for condition; protect it against dust; seal the room and move on to the next. You will have not only moved the collection but also made a complete inventory and condition check, all in a relatively short time.

Of course, the ideal thing would be to move at leisure into a finished and furnished museum, where the airconditioning has been running for at least six months to get the kinks out.

PLACING YOUR EQUIPMENT

Other chapters discuss various types of storage equipment. These units and such heavy equipment as examining tables and supply cabinets must be selected or designed for specific locations. Open spaces have to be reserved for handling, box stacking, and parking trucks and dollies. None of this can be worked out until you have an exact idea of the space available.

To form such an idea you need the following: 1) final architectural drawings, 2) reflected ceiling plans of suspended plumbing, and 3) reflected ceiling plans showing duct work, air vents and humidifiers in and around the ducts. (Reflected plans are drawn as the room might be seen from above looking down through a transparent floor. They should indicate the clearance under each pipe, duct or other feature.) What you must *not* have at this stage is the wiring and lighting plan. That has to be set up after the equipment has been decided upon.

You know the functions the rooms must serve and the desired capacity. The puzzle is to fit in all the necessary objects without infringing the fire or building code; interfering with planned circulation of air; allowing any vulnerable object to come under a humidifier, cold pipe or air vent or within range of any other source of dirt, water or wind; inviting congestion; or blocking anything that has to be serviced.

Special attention must be paid to local fire regulations. Otherwise the museum may be denied a certificate of occupancy. Some of these rules are very tricky and may prohibit an otherwise suitable room from being used as planned.

If circumstances force your museum to use storage space under a lot of pipes and ducts, give each unit a little roof of its own. One simple method is to place a sheet of cardboard or hardboard on top of the storage unit so that it projects a little from every side. Cover this with a *single* sheet of plastic large enough to hang slightly over the edges. Examining tables should never be placed under anything that could leak.

Liquids other than water may fall. Machinery will drip oil. In a new building the "cutting compound" may ooze from joints in the plumbing. The transformers of fluorescent light fixtures have been known to lose their "ballast," a corrosive substance, which looks like tar. Of course we don't use fluorescents in our well designed museum, but just in case . . . .

When there just isn't enough room for everything to have its own place, some storage units, tables or other heavy equipment may have to be put on casters—with brakes. This can greatly increase the usefulness of space. It also has an intangible advantage in that moveable equipment doesn't show on plans and therefore doesn't count under building and fire regulations. In fact, there is a great temptation to recommend that *all* museum equipment be mounted on casters and designed to go through doorways even though all spaces appear to be perfectly adequate. One drawback to such mobility is the risk that someone someday may park something with a work of art on it under some leak—just for a second.

THE ZONE OF SAFETY

The normal path of an object entering a museum leads through the loading dock, receiving room, examining room, photography studio, storeroom and exhibition hall in that order. (See figure 67.) There may be side trips to the conservation laboratory, the frame shop and curatorial offices. If the object is a temporary loan, it retraces the same path on the way out, probably skipping photography but making an excursion to the carpenter shop for packing. Each location is separated from the last by a door, often a corridor and sometimes an elevator. (If there are steps, it's not a well planned museum.) All these areas, together with the connecting passages, comprise what I call the "zone of safety." An object anywhere in this territory is entitled to protection against all the dangers described in the next section of this article.

If the first consideration within this zone is preservation, a close second, at least in an active museum, is efficiency. Material *moves* along this path. Any obstacle is a double menace: its very existence increases the risk of handling damage; but it also wastes time and leads to dangerous haste.

The design of this part of the building must take account of techniques for handling exhibition material. One major consideration is that it moves almost entirely on wheeled vehicles. Another is that art handling can never be rushed. No matter how pressing the deadline the handlers must not be allowed to sense the slightest urgency. Nevertheless, it is inadvisable to supplement the labor force with untrained help; and overtime, even if permitted by the budget, must be used sparingly to avoid accidents resulting from fatigue.

Vertical Communication

Elevators are the curse of the museum profession, but even they are preferable to stairs or ramps. As plots grow smaller, museums taller, and the population denser we shall need more and more of them. Attention to the following principles will save a lot of trouble:

1) Have the fewest possible levels in the museum building and group consecutive processes on the same level. Vertical transportation is far more dangerous and time-consuming than movement on a level.
2) If you must have elevators, have plenty right from the start. They are expensive in new construction but enormously more so as an afterthought.
3) Don't mix passengers with freight or either with art.
4) Make the one big enough (especially long enough) to handle the largest works you will ever want to take upstairs. And pay particular attention to the approaches on all floors: a sharp corner or low header there can waste the size of the car.

5) Freight elevators usually open on two sides. Three open sides may be possible, but four are out of the question because of the counterweights (except just possibly on a hydraulic lift). In a two-door elevator opposite openings are better than adjacent ones, which may force one to negotiate a turn inside the elevator.
6) The whole side of a freight elevator should open. Its capacity for volume is reduced if the door is smaller.

The Loading Dock

Loading and unloading out of doors is risky. It subjects museum objects to wind and rain, heat and humidity, traffic, children and pigeons. The loading dock should be large enough for any truck that may come, and it must absolutely not be preempted by office supplies, books, groceries, lumber or trash. If possible have separate facilities for these things. Otherwise deliveries may have to be scheduled in advance, and that's hard.

How big? The width of highway vehicles is standard, but remember that trucks have to get in and out. The narrower the street and the deeper your dock the more width must be allowed for maneuvering. Trucks' length is limited by law in most places. Find out the local maximum and plan to get one at least that long all the way in. Height is hardest to anticipate. Trucks seem to get taller every year. At present a dock with less than 14′ clearance is next to useless.

The platform, if any, should allow for end loading and side loading, at least on the right. No matter what height you opt for, it will usually be wrong. Better too low than too high. Some docks have no raised platform at all but rely on moveable ramps and hydraulic lifts, moveable or built-in, for lowering heavy weights to the floor. An overhead crane running on an "I" beam will be a tremendous help on relatively rare occasions.

Modern "container" ships, 747 transport planes, railroad cars etc. are being designed to handle large shipments in standard containers measuring 8 by 8 by 10, 20 or 40 feet. In other words, the height and width will be fixed, but the length will vary in multiples of ten. Such containers may present a nearly ideal solution to the problem of moving "packaged" exhibitions, provided there is no excessive concentration of value. The single case with inner containers can provide maximum protection against damage, while the compact shape is ideal for insulation against climatic change. With such packing pilferage will be difficult and scattering of an exhibition en route impossible. If and when international door-to-door delivery can be effected, the problem of dock-side Customs examination may disappear. The only catch is that almost no existing museum building can accommodate containers of this size. It would be wonderful if all large and middle-sized art museums built from now on were designed to receive and ship exhibitions in the standard containers.

HAZARDS TO BE AVOIDED

Constricted Spaces

Registrars spend a major portion of their working lives, tape in hand, looking for an ingenious way to get some large object in or out. Too often the solution involves dismantling either the work of art or some part of the museum. What makes it absurd is that you wouldn't want to bring the thing in if it were too large to display gracefully in the galleries. It's not. It just won't come through the door.

Bottle-necks take many forms—low doorways or headers, sharp turns, pipes, ducts, conduits and lighting fixtures hung below the slab, small or slow or weak elevators, and narrow doors. You may be told that it is impossible to take into account all possible works of art, past and future; and, in a sense, that is true and obvious: But the size and shape of exhibition galleries impose certain restrictions upon the dimensions of works *to be displayed in that particular museum;* and it is a simple matter to tailor the entrance and preparation areas to works on the same scale.

The possibility of rolling or folding paintings or tilting sculpture should never be relied upon. These are dangerous, destructive procedures, measures of desperation.

Always design or select picture trucks, dollies, lifts, skids, etc. before building plans solidify. Once the wheelbase and turning circle of each conveyance is known, it should be easy to make sure it will go wherever needed.

Nothing is more dangerous than congestion. Because of the variety of materials to be exhibited no ideal ratio of "staging" to exhibition space can be given. However, if the total staging area (receiving and unpacking plus recording and temporary storage) equals the largest single space devoted to one exhibition and if only one exhibition is changed at a time, there will always be enough room for safe handling. If that ratio is halved, the staging area will almost certainly jam up. In institutions where the exhibition program is leisurely and installations simple some of the staging can be done right in the galleries.

The importance of regularly shaped rooms cannot be exaggerated. *Regularity is equivalent to extra space.* This rule applies to overhead clearance as well as to floor plan.

There are very definite reasons why sub-grade (i.e. cellar) spaces are especially congested and irregular. They are often utilized as staging areas but cannot really be recommended for it. Practical objections, other than difficulty of access and the risk of flooding, stem from the fact that water, steam, electricity, telephone lines, gas and sometimes even air enter a modern building under ground. The main air-handling machinery is usually in a sub-basement. Thus the basement becomes a snarl of branching connections. Spaces that seem large, high and clear on the architect's early plans later shrink and fill with bulky, hot, dangerous apparatus. Rooms assume odd shapes and headroom disappears. Lighting is a joke, and chances for leakage multiply. Security is threatened by the need to service equipment.

The "legal" objections to underground space stem from building and fire codes. The latter often require wasteful subdivision of large spaces to allow for fire stairs and passages. The size and placement of storage units may be restricted to facilitate fire fighting. Security is often impaired by required fire exits. If none of these specific objections applies to your museum, there is nothing against basement space as such. Some older museums, built on a grand scale, have good basement staging areas.

Obstructions

Anything projecting into work or storage space is a menace. Pipes, ducts, conduits and fixtures are mentioned elsewhere. Nails partly sunk into walls are very treacherous. Even thermostats may be troublesome on a stacking wall. Worst of all are moving objects—mainly hinged doors and especially self-closing doors. A door with a will of its own poses a real threat when one man has to get through with a truckload of paintings. Sliding doors are harmless if they move inside the wall. Even when hung against the wall they are safer than hinged doors.

Irregular Footing

Irregularities under foot include steps and ramps as well as thresholds, edges of carpets and other surfacing, gaps at the entrance to elevators, etc. Minor irregularities are more dangerous than those which are bound to be noticed. Anything that can jar a moving picture truck or dolly is a hazard. Some kinds of flooring have a relief pattern to increase traction. Such a pattern sets up vibration in a vehicle moving over it.

The softer the floor surface the harder you have to push anything on wheels, and the harder you push the greater the risk of accident. So thick carpets should be avoided. The surface must provide good traction even when wet. Very hard materials tend to maximize breakage when there is an accident. Also it is possible for dollies to roll *too* easily: many floors have an unplanned, imperceptible slope. The best compromise for any given space depends upon the work to be done there and the kinds of material to be handled. At the soft end of the "spectrum" a heavy-duty cork linoleum is good. Where heavier loads are contemplated, ordinary vinyl-asbestos tile will do very well. It may become permanently indented if a large weight remains for long in one place, but this is a minor problem. Tiles that won't take dents are very expensive. For very rugged use there is no substitute for concrete with a heavy-duty surface film.

Darkness

Good illumination is very important in preventing accidents. Plan lighting throughout the zone of safety after the layout of bins and other equipment is known, taking account of suspended pipes and ducts and making sure that intersecting shadows will not develop into blind spots. Floor, ceiling, walls and furniture should be white or as light as possible to promote even distribution of light. (If it shows dirt, so much the better, you'll know when and where to clean.) Pitch darkness is less hazardous than the slight gloom of areas that seem well lighted but aren't. Never settle for less than 20 foot candles of illumination anywhere. Automatic battery-powered emergency lights are essential in any windowless space where works of art will be handled. Flashlights should always be handy.

Light

The choice of a light source is unimportant in passageways where exposure is brief; but where works of art are to be kept for any length of time sources rich in ultraviolet are bad. In practice this means that only incandescent light may be used. If fluorescents cannot be eliminated, they should be shielded; but the shields are only partially effective and tend to deteriorate in use. Daylight is the most destructive of all.

Dirt

There is a tendency to think of dirt as merely unsightly, damaging to museum objects because it affects their appearance or indirectly damaging because of the risks that must be taken in removing it. This is the least of it. Real damage is caused by corrosive and hygroscopic substances, which either attack materials directly or else attract moisture to the surface. A dirty surface or material in which dirt has become ingrained may, in effect, be much wetter than the ambient atmosphere. Excess moisture promotes chemical, photo-chemical and biological deterioration.

Cleaning itself is damaging to a work of art, so the trick is to keep dirt out in the first place. It is usual to combine more than one kind of filter in a high-efficiency system. Mechanical filters are strainers designed to stop particles above a given size. Curtains of water may be used to absorb gaseous pollutants, or activated charcoal may serve the same purpose. (Charcoal also absorbs some of the stench that goes with modern civilization. The building wears a gas mask.) Electronic precipitators remove very fine particles by attracting them to charged elements. This method is little used in museums because it is thought to generate intolerable concentrations of ozone. Water washes, too, seem unpopular at present, but the National Gallery in London has reported excellent results with such a system. The best available combination now seems to consist of coarse mechanical filters followed by very fine ones followed by charcoal. The last is the most expensive to maintain, but must be recommended at least in areas where the atmosphere contains sulphur compounds. Re-circulating air should pass through the filters every time around, as it picks up dirt right in the museum.

Many objects can be kept reasonably clean simply by covering them. There are differences of opinion as to whether circulating air is necessary to keep organic materials in good condition. It used to be said that they must "breathe." Some conservators feel now that, except in special cases, air circulation is unnecessary or slightly harmful. However, in the absence of circulation the temperature must be kept fairly constant because a drop in temperature means a rise in relative humidity in any enclosed air space. In extreme cases water will actually condense on the inside of plastic wrapping or other vapor seal. Another reservation has to do with permanent sources of heat or moisture—a radiator, a sunny window, a moist wall or the like. Pockets of moisture or dryness may build up under such influences unless the air is kept in motion.

The wooden cabinets frequently used to store prints, drawings or photographs keep dirt out and stabilize interior conditions without setting up an impenetrable moisture barrier. Paper or cardboard coverings serve the same purpose but should not come into direct contact with the materials to be preserved since all but the purest papers contain traces of the acids used in their manufacture.

Fluctuations of Temperature and Relative Humidity

It is often argued that, since borrowed objects spend most of their time in uncontrolled atmospheres and since they may be subjected to extremes while in transit, it is absurd to keep them under controlled conditions for their few weeks in the museum. The contention is valid enough but misses the main point—the permanent collection. Most objects of a very high order reach public collections in the end. By the time they do, a great deal of deterioration may have taken place. It has to be arrested, and that is impossible unless the relative humidity, at least, is constant.

Atmospheric shocks received in transit from one institution to another are being reduced (very gradually), and there is increasing reluctance to lend where a controlled environment cannot be guaranteed. Excellent work is being done, especially in Canada, on insulated boxes in which works of art can travel great distances in heavy weather without much deviation from the ideal conditions under which they were packed. (See article 13.)

A lot has been written about the most desirable conditions for preserving museum collections. It can only be summarized here: relative humidity is far more important than temperature; it should never exceed 60% or fall short of 45%; within these limits it should fluctuate as little as possible, preferably within a total annual range of 5% or less. Temperature should be held as constant as possible and the lower the better. Conditions throughout the zone of safety should be uniform. For further information see Chapter Five.

It would be out of place here to describe the machinery needed to make the air safe for art. The important things when a new building is planned are that the exact *conditions* to be provided be set forth in a way that will be legally binding on all concerned and that the museum not accept any equipment until its own independent observations show that the conditions specified are being maintained. Buy performance, not hardware.

Independent measurements can be made easily with a sling psychrometer, but to be sure an area is getting twenty-four hour protection you need a rather costly instrument known as a hygro-thermograph, in which pens trace a continuous record of temperature and relative humidity on a moving chart. These machines, driven by clockwork, are independent of the central system and its controls and may be used anywhere. The important thing is that they be managed by someone primarily concerned with preserving the collections. A conflict of interests arises when those responsible for running the air-handling system also have to monitor its performance. Surveillance goes on forever, not just during the months or years it may take to "balance out" a new system.

Water

Condensation of moisture on windows and other cold surfaces gets to be a problem in cold weather if the relative humidity is kept as high as it should be. Mist on the windowpanes is a minor housekeeping problem; but when water runs down a glass wall and spreads over the floor, a real hazard exists. There are several solutions—double and triple thermopanes, drafts of hot air sweeping the inner surface, or gutters along the base of the window. Not having glass is the simplest.

Cold pipes are less obviously dangerous. Drains and soil pipes as well as cold water lines may get cold enough to condense moisture. The possibility can be headed off by covering such pipes with insulation just as steam pipes are covered.

Condensation is a minor matter compared to leakage. Modern buildings are not immune to leaking roofs, seepage in the cellar, backed up drains and burst pipes. Broken mains outside the building have caused serious flooding. Minor floods, perhaps from a toilet or kitchen overhead, can find their way into a storeroom or gallery, sometimes penetrating several concrete floors along the way.

If water damage is to be avoided, spaces directly under roofs or terraces should not be used for storage. The registrar must always know exactly what is over the storerooms in his care, the recording room etc. and prepare for the worst if there is any possible source of water.

Fire

It has been traditional in the museum profession to rule automatic sprinklers entirely out on the grounds that they do more harm than a fire. Anyone who has been through a museum fire will doubt this. A painting protected in front by varnish or glass and behind by cardboard has some defense against water. If soaked it will be damaged and require immediate conservation, but the substance is there and can be solidified. If fire gets to the same painting, there will be nothing left to fix. And each one that goes up may spread the flames to the next. Sprinklers, on the other hand, tend to limit the disaster area. A sprinkler's discharge of twenty gallons per minute is very gentle treatment compared to tons of water under high pressure from a fire hose.

The chief worry with sprinklers is accidental discharge, where resulting damage cannot be balanced against the probability of much greater fire loss. Such discharge is very rare; but as an additional safeguard, museums should use only pre-action sprinkler systems. The pipes leading to such sprinklers remain dry until an electronic smoke detector is activated. There can be no discharge until this has happened *and* the air temperature has reached the usual 165°F. needed to activate any sprinkler head.

If sprinklers are the last line of defense against fire, isolation in fireproof surroundings is the first. There should be two fire barriers between works of art and works of construction, destruction or house painting.

CO_2 fire extinguishers are recommended, but they may not be as completely harmless as is often supposed. The expanding gas becomes so cold that it may condense moisture and cause water damage. Extinguishers, like any other apparatus, are useless unless personnel are trained and practiced in their operation.

There is debate as to whether metal or wooden cabinets provide better fire protection. Metal cannot possibly feed the flames, but it transmits heat rapidly and may collapse in less time than it would take a standard 5/8″ board to burn through. (See Chapter Five.)

If plastic coverings are used, choose a material that is non-flammable or self-extinguishing. Try to burn a sample before putting any in the storerooms.

Machinery and transformers should be separated from the art collections by a fire-and-*smoke*-proof barrier. A smoky fire elsewhere in the building may force a museum to clean its entire painting collection since even an invisible smoke deposit will cause corrosion of the surface.

People

The greatest threat of all, people, has been saved for last because the subject is immense—the whole field of museum security.

SECURITY

The registrar makes his main contribution to security through his records, periodic inventories and control of entry and exit. However, we are concerned here with physical defenses; and these are built around the lock on the storeroom door.

This is no place to economize. For about twice the price of a good lock one can buy an excellent one machined to such fine tolerances that only the manufacturer can make a duplicate key. He will do so only on written request with two authorized signatures.

This leads to the question of key policy, where security and convenience are in direct opposition to one another. It would be ideally convenient (assuming that doors be locked at all) to have one key for the lot and let each staff member carry one. On the other hand, maximum security requires that every lock be unique, recognizing one key only (no master), that no more than two copies of the key exist, and that each be signed out from and returned to the security office whenever it is used. Each museum must work out its own compromise.

Whatever key policy a museum settles upon, it is obvious that a record should be kept of every key and its possessor and that all affected locks should be changed whenever a key is missed. It is customary to change all locks in a building that has been under construction as a precaution against keys having been stolen or copied. Some museums employ a staff locksmith so that no outsider will ever have access to keys or locks.

Devices as primitive as bars and throw bolts have a place in the storerooms of a modern museum building, especially on doors that are meant for emergency exit only.

Doors must be strong, fire-proof and opaque: a thief's job is simplified if he can see where his objective is—or isn't. Walls, of course, have to be at least as tough as the doors and so do ceilings and floors. Anyone with simple tools can get through a light partition (studs and sheetrock, for example) quickly and easily. A man who knows how can penetrate a "block wall" just as fast, though not without making a racket. Wire mesh makes a flimsy, transparent barrier.

Pay attention to the various "access panels," so familiar in modern buildings that we never see them. They lead to large ducts, hollow walls and spaces above hung ceilings, where equipment may need to be serviced. Most are dead ends, but each should be checked carefully. Insofar as possible fuse boxes and anything else requiring attention by service personnel should be eliminated from security areas.

A good many electrical monitors are on the market. Some museums use closed-circuit television to cover entrances to the building and other sensitive areas. The difficulty is that the screens have to be monitored by a person, and it's a soporific show at best. Other systems may be roughly classified as peripheral protection or space protection. The former consist of contact point alarms and electric eyes covering every conceivable access to the area. Space protection is based upon sonic, ultra-sonic or infra-red sensing devices detecting respectively, noise within the protected area, movement within the area, or a heat source such as the human body. A sonic system, by listening only to overtones, is able to distinguish between sounds originating within the protected space and those from the outside. It can also be rigged to disregard the creaking of the building, functioning of the air-conditioning, ticking of a clock, or any other inevitable sound. All electrical systems go into a state of alarm when tampered with.

Two reservations must always be borne in mind. First, any kind of automatic system is worse than useless unless it functions.

The second and even more important reservation is that all security rests ultimately on man power. The function of doors, walls and locks is to delay the enemy until the troops arrive. Automatic alarms can only call for help.

In general it is inadvisable for a watchman to enter the art storerooms, but there may be exceptions. Sometimes a special hazard exists, something that may leak or overheat; and it has to be watched. Such situations are temporary since either the danger or the art will have to be removed.

Vandalism and carelessness on the part of the general public afflict the exhibition halls as a rule, not the regions behind the scenes, where the registrar is concerned. Exceptions occur where public and staging areas interpenetrate as when people and pictures ride the same elevators, when storerooms have no entrance except through exhibition halls, and when works of art are carried in or out via the public entrance. There is no excuse for such nonsense in a modern building.

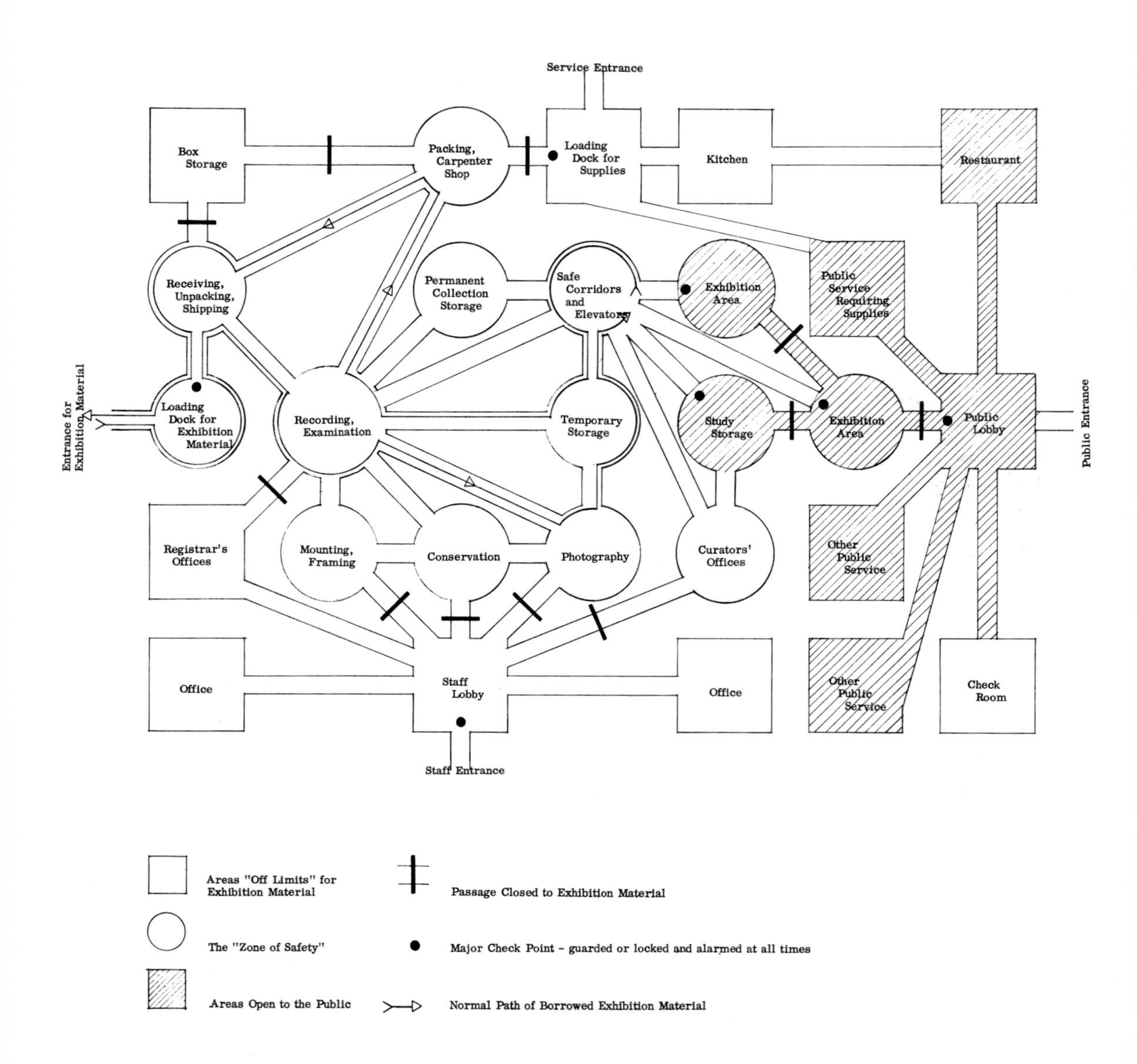

Figure 67.—Zone of Safety.

Recommended proximity and connection of areas in a large museum, with special reference to facilities for the preparation of exhibitions. Connections shown do not necessarily represent doorways but only the possibility of going from one area to another without passing through a third. For example, the Recording and Examination room has nine connections, but one door might do for all. The absence of a connection on the chart means there should be no direct communication. For example, nothing should move from Permanent Collection Storage to the Carpenter Shop without being examined in the Recording Room. Separate connections to each Exhibition Area show that each can be installed or dismantled without moving material through the other. Exhibition material and the public meet only in the galleries and Study Storage.

Article 17

COMPUTERS AND REGISTRATION

DAVID VANCE

Associate Registrar
Museum of Modern Art, New York

INTRODUCTION

Electronic computers' astonishing development from almost nothing in a little more than a decade suggests that in another ten years or less some kind of computing equipment will be as essential to any undertaking as the typewriter and telephone are today. Fortunately progress in cost reduction has been especially rapid.

Computers are tools designed to take the drudgery out of clerical work. The proportion of such drudgery in museum registration and cataloging makes these tasks particularly suitable for computerization.

HARDWARE

The word "hardware" means tangible equipment. A computer installation consists of a cluster of interconnected machines. The main component is the computer itself, called the "central processing unit" or "C. P. U." Attached to it, either adjacent or remote, are input devices, storage units, and output devices. Most installations are designed so that devices can be added or replaced as the need grows for new or expanded services. Input and output terminals may be in any place, however distant, served by telephone lines.

Machines do not yet read handwriting or ordinary type; so other machines (and personnel) are needed to prepare information in machine-readable form such as punched cards, punched or magnetic tape or a machine-readable typeface. The punched card is now the most commonly used input medium.

Input

An input device or "reader" is any machine designed to bring new information (data) or instructions (program) into the system. It usually does so by scanning tape, cards, or pages of machine-readable type, which pass through the machine physically. However, the most direct method employs a "typewriter terminal" with a more or less standard keyboard on which messages may be typed directly into the system by the operator. The typewriter terminal will also type out messages from the system to the operator.

Input devices transform a coded pattern, such as that of holes punched in a card or tape, into a series of electrical impulses, which in turn leave traces of themselves as negatively or positively magnetized patches on the surface of a storage tape, disk, drum or data cell or in core storage.

Storage

The important differences among storage units are in cost and speed of access—the faster the dearer. Core storage is fastest but expensive and comparatively bulky so that it is used only for basic programs (See Software) and data referred to so often that any delay whatsoever would impede operations. Programs and data that ordinarily reside in other storage units may be transferred temporarily to core storage during the actual running of an operation for which they are needed. Drum storage too is fast and costly and more often used for programs than for data. Large masses of information for occasional reference may best be stored on the slower disks or data cells, with a maximum access time to any given item of 180 and 600 thousandths of a second respectively. The maximum storage capacity of a single I.B.M. 2321 Data Cell, occupying about one cubic foot of space, is 400,000,000 characters.

The above are "random access" or "direct access" storage devices. This means that any item of information in them can be found at once without scanning the file from its beginning. Magnetic tape storage costs less but imposes sequential search instead of direct access. It is good for a "back up" or copy file to preserve information that might be lost if another storage device were damaged or inadvertently "erased."

Output

An output device is any machine designed to pass information from the computing system to its human users. This may be done by displaying characters on a screen, by typing, by printing, or by producing punched cards or tape. The device best suited for producing catalog listings is the "high-speed printer." The typewriter terminal is used for output as well as input.

C. P. U.

The central processing unit consists of a vast but very compact network of electronic switches through which electrical impulses representing numbers, letters and other characters flow. Data which these characters embody may move unaltered from input to storage or from storage to output or they may be "processed," i. e. rearranged, by the opening or closing of switches in combinations controlled by the program. This is where the "data processing" or "computing" comes in.

SOFTWARE

As indicated above, input to the machine is of two distinct kinds—data and programs. Both kinds enter the system in the same ways and both are transformed by the input device into the same kind of electrical impulses. But every batch of input must be preceded by a coded signal, showing that what follows is a program of instructions to be stored as such and presently acted upon, or else by a different signal, indicating that what follows is data to be stored, processed or both. Every batch of input is followed by another code indicating the end of program or data. Data may be in plain English (or French or any language for which the characters are available) or in any code or notation the user finds convenient. Programs must be in a rigorously formal program language.

Programming may seem deceptively simple to the casual user, who can communicate with the machine in a language superficially resembling English. But in order for him to do so an elaborate program must have been stored in the system. These instructions must anticipate the kind of questions that will be asked and the way data will be stored and tell the machine what to do and how to retrieve data from storage and translate it back into people-readable form. Programmed instructions, stored permanently in the system or held available on tape or cards, are collectively known as "software." The development of appropriate software goes hand in hand with that of hardware and accounts for a major portion of the total cost. In the same way, specialized software for use at a particular installation may account for a large part of the price of that installation. Museums will need some new software.

Machine Oriented Language

The most basic programming is done in "machine language," which isn't really a language at all but just the technique for introducing the first program into a machine where none exists. Actually *all* programs have to be in machine language before the machine can act upon their instructions. Programs in other languages are translated by the computer itself into machine language, and this translation requires a very complex program (in machine language) known as "a translator."

Above the level of machine language is "assembly language," a little easier to use and a true language in that one instruction may cause the machine to execute a *series* of related steps. Machine oriented languages are the exclusive province of computer specialists.

User Oriented Language

At a still higher level are the "compiler languages," oriented not to the machine but to the human user. The words of these languages are drawn from the ordinary usage of business, science and mathematics; and brief commands cause the machine to perform enormously complex sequences of routines and sub-routines. There are many of these languages in use, mostly designed for some special purpose. Best known are Cobol, with a business orientation, and Fortran, oriented to physical science and mathematics. The newest and most versatile is called PL/I (for "Program Language 1.") The first programs for museum use are being worked out in this language.

Compiler languages, including PL/I, are simple enough to be learned by a determined layman. In fact, it is quite easy to pick up the rudiments, though becoming a professional programmer is another matter. All this is somewhat irrelevant since the future user of museum computing systems will be able to retrieve information without even using PL/I.

OPERATION

Since intriguing possibilities in the areas of insurance reports, up to the minute location records and the planning of preparation schedules and itineraries for exhibitions remain to be explored, this discussion will be confined to the one area that is being investigated actively—the storage and retrieval of catalog information.

There is almost no limit to the amount of information that may be put into one "data bank" and held there indefinitely. Not only descriptions of works of art and other collected material but records of exhibitions, bibliographies and references may be included and cross referenced. New items may be inserted at any point in such a file and old ones changed at will.

There are several ways in which such a file might be organized. I will describe only one (in simplified form) and illustrate its use. In this method, stored information is divided into several parallel files of which the most important are the Item File and the Descriptor File, corresponding respectively to a main catalog and to all the various auxiliary files by donor, subject, number, etc. Before items are fed into the data bank certain key words from each one are formally designated as "descriptors." Generally the descriptors are the same words under which items are filed in our manual files—artists' names, names of countries, types of object, important materials, names of former owners, donors, vendors, and subjects represented. More classes of descriptor can be handled than it would be feasible to use in card files. Every descriptor in the file is associated with the serial numbers of entries in the Item File to which it applies. The Item File is simply the series of all descriptive items, each identified by a unique serial number.

Obviously no new principle is involved. Manual files might be set up in the same way. The only advantage in using a computer is the enormous speed with which very large files can be searched and lists compiled, collated and printed.

A fairly routine inquiry might be a request for all French or British paintings, not including watercolors and pastels, dated from 1910 to 1917 or Twentieth Century and undated, and acquired by purchase since 1950, the response to be a printout in alphabetical order by artist and title giving for each entry the artist, title, date, size, accession number, photo source and inscriptions, in that order and in a specified format.

If this information is in file, it will be printed out as requested but not right away. Even a computer needs some time for all this work. How much will depend upon the length and organization of the file, the choice of equipment and how many people are trying to use it at once. Ordinarily easy questions are given priority and those that promise to tie up the system for more than a few minutes put aside to be run during the night. Any question involving a sequential search of a large file would fall into this category.

When the machine receives the above request it will turn first to the Descriptor file and compile a coherent list of all serial numbers associated with the descriptors, FRANCE, GREAT BRITAIN, PAINTING, PASTEL, WATERCOLOR, TWENTIETH CENTURY, 1910, 1911, 1912, 1913, 1914, 1915, 1916, 1917, and nul date. At the same time it will check its built-in synonym table and find that with the above it should also search for (among others): FRENCH, BRITISH, UNITED KINGDOM, SCOTLAND, SCOTCH, SCOTTISH, ENGLAND, ENGLISH, WALES, WELCH, XX CENTURY, OIL, CHALK, CASEIN, WATERCOLOUR, and GOUACHE. From the item numbers associated with all these it will compile a coherent, non-repeating list including all required nationalities and excluding pastels, water media, and works not of the specified dates. Each of the items corresponding to these numbers will then be scanned to eliminate those with accession numbers showing they were acquired before 1950 or with credit lines containing such words as GIFT, GIVEN, or BEQUEST, since we asked only for purchases. Note how much more efficient this is than scanning the whole file for items matching the request.

At this point the computer would probably be programmed to count the number of items found and give the operator a chance to modify his request if the list would be too long or too short to be useful. It might also give a cost estimate for the whole job. If told to procede it would print the information in the order and format required. The printing would probably be done on a high-speed printer, but the request and interim communications would go through a typewriter terminal.

ECONOMICS

The costs of hardware, software and computer time are in line with the computer's capabilities—on the order of a few millions to set up a major installation. Yet for ordinary, simple questions it may be very much less efficient than a manual card file. In fact it is a general rule that the more sophisticated and costly the equipment the less economical it is for simple work and the more it favors complex research. Another rule is that the larger the file the more economical it becomes to use computers. The usefulness of a data bank will probably increase geometrically with its size.

Time Sharing

Although a computer can actually work on only one problem at a time, its speed is so great that in effect it can serve several masters simultaneously. The high cost forces small users to share facilities and the speed makes this practicable.

It can be done in a number of ways. There are commercial service bureaus supplying the use of computers to enterprises too small to own or rent one. Computing centers established at universities present an opportunity for cooperation, especially to university museums. Tax supported institutions may share facilities owned by the units of government to which the are attached; but these installations, like those of service bureaus, are likely to be oriented toward business and useful mainly in the business side of museum operations.

None of these solutions is ideal for computerizing museum catalog records for two reasons: 1) The staffs, equipment and available software at service bureaus, university research centers and government agencies are necessarily geared to needs very different from those of museum registrars; and 2) probably no one museum has collections large enough to justify a computerized data bank for its catalog.

The obvious thing is for museums, at least those in the same field, to share facilities among themselves. A center largely or entirely devoted to the service of museums could make the effort necessary to develop special techniques. More important, it could combine collection, library and exhibition data from many museums in a single data bank massive enough to become a powerful tool for research. The distance separating one museum from another is no obstacle.

The Consortium

A group of fifteen museums in New York City has recently formed a consortium, with headquarters at The Museum of Modern Art, to study the possibility of sharing facilities. The idea is to purchase one large computer (out of funds to be raised for that specific purpose) to be operated by New York University's Institute for Computer Research in the Humanities and used by the university and the museums on a time sharing basis. It would eventually contain a catalog of the combined holdings of all the participating museums and be connected via telephone lines to five or six satellite computers serving major museums or local groups of museums. These satellites could be large enough to handle the local museum's bookkeeping, inventory and membership routines and have the capacity to store the host museum's collection records, at least on tape. They would be able to call upon the main data bank and the central computer's logical capacities whenever necessary.

It is hoped that the value of housekeeping services to the individual museums will offset their labor in putting records into machine-readable form. Incidentally, no rigid format for records need be imposed. Each institution can put in whatever records it has with only slight editing, consisting mainly of the addition of codes to facilitate retrieval.

Image storage and dissemination is excluded for the time being. Ideally students in the participating institutions, in schools, and in libraries anywhere should be able to query the data bank via a remote terminal and receive not only catalog data but a picture on a screen. Perhaps even a "hard copy" image—in color. The equipment is still too crude and too expensive. Images can only be stored on chips of microfilm. It would be possible to locate and extract individual chips mechanically, under the direction of the computer, and transmit televised black and white images to remote viewing screens, but the quality of the output would be very poor and the expense enormous. Of course, this won't always be true.

If the first regional data bank should be successful there is no reason why it should not be followed by others and linked with them to form a network of unlimited extent.

CONCLUSION

In the present state of the art the computer is certainly not going to eliminate the registrar's catalog cards. It won't even replace the auxiliary files though it may take over their production and upkeep. What it will do is to provide special and general purpose check lists of existing collections and sources. No check lists are in print for most museum collections. Those that do exist are usually incomplete even at the time of publication. The computer, drawing upon a well tended data bank, can print to order a custom designed catalog of any selection from the collections of several or many museums—with all data current! Such listings will be invaluable either to the independent scholar or to the curator preparing an exhibition or publication. Users will be spared the drudgery of assembling a basic listing, arranging it in the desired order and, last but not least, typing.

Index